Rudyard Kipling

SOMETHING OF MYSELF

FOR MY FRIENDS KNOWN AND UNKNOWN

EDITED
BY ROBERT HAMPSON
WITH AN INTRODUCTION
BY RICHARD HOLMES

PENGUIN BOOKS

PENGUIN BOOKS

Published by the Penguin Group
Penguin Books Ltd, 27 Wrights Lane, London W8 5TZ, England
Penguin Books USA Inc., 375 Hudson Street, New York, New York 10014, USA
Penguin Books Australia Ltd, Ringwood, Victoria, Australia
Penguin Books Canada Ltd, 10 Alcorn Avenue, Toronto, Ontario, Canada M4V 3B2
Penguin Books (NZ) Ltd, 182–190 Wairau Road, Auckland 10, New Zealand

Penguin Books Ltd, Registered Offices: Harmondsworth, Middlesex, England

First published in 1936
Published in Penguin Books 1977
Reprinted in Penguin Classics 1987
Reprinted in Penguin Books 1992
3 5 7 9 10 8 6 4 2

Notes copyright © Robert Hampson 1987
Introduction copyright © Richard Holmes 1987

The editor and publisher acknowledge
with thanks the verse quoted on page 196,
from Kipling's *Horace* (Methuen, 1978).

Printed in England by Clays Ltd, St Ives plc
Filmset in Monophoto Ehrhardt

PENGUIN CLASSICS

SOMETHING OF MYSELF

Rudyard Joseph Kipling was born in Bombay in 1865. His father, John Lockwood Kipling, was the author and illustrator of *Beast and Man in India* and his mother, Alice, was the sister of Lady Burne-Jones. In 1871 Kipling was brought home from India and spent five unhappy years with a foster family in Southsea, an experience he later drew on in *The Light That Failed* (1890). The years he spent at the United Services College, a school for officers' children, are depicted in *Stalky and Co.* (1899) and the character of Beetle is something of a self-portrait. It was during his time at the college that he began writing poetry and *Schoolboy Lyrics* was published privately in 1881. In the following year he started work as a journalist in India, and while there produced a body of work, stories, sketches and poems – notably *Plain Tales from the Hills* (1888) – which made him an instant literary celebrity when he returned to England in 1889. *Barrack-Room Ballads* (1892) contains some of his most popular pieces, including 'Mandalay', 'Gunga Din' and 'Danny Deever'. In this collection Kipling experimented with form and dialect, notably the cockney accent of the soldier poems, but the influence of hymns, music-hall songs, ballads and public poetry can be found throughout his verse.

In 1892 he married an American, Caroline Balestier, and from 1892 to 1896 they lived in Vermont where Kipling wrote *The Jungle Book*, published in 1894. In 1901 came *Kim* and in 1902 the *Just So Stories*. Tales of every kind – including historical and science fiction – continued to flow from his pen, but *Kim* is generally thought to be his greatest long work, putting him high among the chroniclers of British expansion.

From 1902 Kipling made his home in Sussex, but he continued to travel widely and caught his first glimpse of warfare in South Africa, where he wrote some excellent reportage on the Boer War. However, many of the views he expressed were rejected by anti-imperialists who accused him of jingoism and love of violence. Though rich and successful, he never again enjoyed the literary esteem of his early years. With the onset of the Great War his work became a great deal more sombre. The stories he subsequently wrote, *A Diversity of Creatures* (1917), *Debits and Credits* (1926) and *Limits and Renewals* (1932) are now thought by many to contain some of his finest writing. The death of his only son in 1915 also contributed to a new inwardness of vision.

Kipling refused to accept the role of Poet Laureate and other civil honours, but he was the first English writer to be awarded the Nobel Prize, in 1907. He died in 1936 and his autobiographical fragment *Something of Myself* was published the following year.

Roger Hampson is a Senior Lecturer in English at Royal Holloway, University of London. He is the author of *Joseph Conrad: Betrayal and Identity* (1992) and edits the journal, *The Conradian* for the Joseph Conrad Society (UK). For Penguin he has also edited Conrad's *Victory* and *Heart of Darkness* and co-edited *Lord Jim*.

Richard Holmes is a Fellow of the Royal Society of Literature, educated at Churchill College, Cambridge. In 1974 he published his first book, *Shelley: The Pursuit*, which won the Somerset Maugham Award. Richard Holmes has since translated a selection of Théophile Gautier's supernatural stories, *My Fantoms*, and in 1985 he published *Footsteps* (Penguin 1990). His most recent work is *Coleridge: Early Visions* (Penguin 1990), the first volume of a two-volume biography, which won the 1989 Whitbread Book of the Year Prize.

Contents

SOMETHING OF MYSELF

Introduction

This is the last book that Kipling wrote, but in many ways the most youthful and surprising. It is the only time in his entire career that he wrote directly about himself, without the mask of fiction.

Something of Myself recalls his childhood in India, his schooldays, and his early career as a writer up to the time when he was awarded the Nobel Prize for Literature at the astonishingly early age of forty-two. It is unfinished beyond that date, but perhaps deliberately so. The figure who emerges is fascinating and unexpected. The familiar Kipling – the Imperialist, the Jingoist, the Man of Black and White – is strangely absent. A new face begins to appear behind the bristling privacy of that renowned moustache. If you thought you knew Kipling – and even more, if you thought you disliked him – this is the book to read.

Kipling began writing his memoir in the summer of 1935. He was nearly seventy years old and, though crowned with honours, isolated from the political and literary movements of the new age. His gaze, while retaining all its old clarity and forthrightness, was now turned inward and backwards towards a world already largely lost. Yet his prose is as sharp, compact and glinting as anything he ever produced. He worked in the famous upstairs study of his Jacobean house, 'Bateman's', at Burwash, in a beautiful and still remote fold of the Sussex Downs, surrounded by woods and streams, where he had lived – dug himself in – for more than three decades.

His desk faced east, looking through mullioned stone windows, and was flanked by two large globes, as he describes with characteristic care and affection in chapter 8. He told his wife Carrie that the book would only 'deal with his life from the point of view of his work'; but in fact he filled it with many rich and curious layers of meaning. It is a pastoral and an elegy;

7

but it is also 'something' – the hesitation is vital – of a self-revelation.

As an autobiographer, Kipling adopts a voice that is easy, name-dropping and humorous in the old, Club-Room manner of Victorian days. He was a lucky fellow, he assures us from the outset, to whom Destiny always dealt the right card, and he had 'but to play it as it came'. But Kipling was a master of assumed voices all his life, and nowhere more so than here. In reality the constant element of the book is bustling activity, struggle and implied drama; and the style is taut and vividly abrupt.

Each of the places he describes – India, North America, South Africa, rural Sussex, in a series of dazzlingly realized chapters – had a completely transforming effect on him, and he captures this with extraordinary energy and colour. Single sentences, or brilliantly detailed paragraphs, continuously rise off the page like so many genii released from the bottle of his memory.

His first concern is to show how as a young writer he was always learning and improving his craft: observing, listening, snuffing out the first, heady scent of a possible story. I know of no other modern book that is of such technical interest, in this respect, to someone learning the *métier*, except Hemingway's *A Moveable Feast*, which has several other points of comparison. Recalling his all-night expeditions as a young journalist for the *Civil and Military Gazette* through the stifling, summer back-streets of Lahore, in search of copy for his earliest *Plain Tales*, Kipling both describes and demonstrates the process in the space of one of those single, unforgettable sentences of his. 'One would come home, just as the light broke, in some night-hawk of a hired carriage which stank of hookah fumes, jasmine-flowers, and sandalwood; and if the driver were moved to talk, he told one a good deal' (p. 64). Here we glimpse the nocturnal world so memorably described in perhaps the greatest of his early stories, 'The Man Who Would Be King'.

The whole of *Something of Myself* is packed tight with such glimpses and anecdotes, dashed in like an artist's sketchbook, seedling stories half-formed and just beginning to quiver with life on the writer's work-bench. With some of them, Kipling indicates how they developed fully. We are given the conception and working out of *Stalky & Co.*, *Kim* and *Puck of Pook's Hill* most notably, but there are also tantalizing insights into the mysterious New Zealand tale, 'Mrs Bathurst' (but nothing is given away); the poems, 'If—' (inspired by the South African Empire-builder, Sir Leander Starr Jameson, of the celebrated Jameson Raid into the Transvaal) and 'Recessional'; and the haunting Sussex vision of 'The Way through the Woods'. For those who know something of the later work, there are hints of how he lit upon the trail of those most puzzling and moving investigations into the cruelty and healing powers of love in 'The Wish House' and 'The House Surgeon'.

This celebration of the writer's craft is the primary and, it is sometimes said, the only subject of the memoir. It is certainly the one of which the reader will be most immediately aware, and it is of the greatest interest. Kipling insists that 'it was necessary that every word should tell, carry, weigh, taste and, if need were, smell.' In this one recognizes his kinship with Maupassant and, again, with Hemingway. In the last chapter, 'Working-Tools', Kipling gives a pithy summary of almost everything* he had learned on the matter, laying a special emphasis on the need to refine, polish and, above all, cut back the narrative to its purest and barest form.

It was indeed Kipling and not Hemingway who first expounded the doctrine of deliberately removing material from a

---

*Further hints on his attitude to writing can be found in the little-known essay, 'Some Aspects of Travel' (1914). He compares writing to the experience of explorers, and the logistical pressures of organizing an expedition into unknown territory. There is a wonderful passage on the evocative powers of *smell*, and the way it can conjure up particular places. 'I rank wood-smoke first, since it calls up more, more intimate and varied memories, over a wider geographical range, to a larger number of individuals, than any other agent I know. My powers are limited, but I think I would undertake to transport a quarter of a million Englishmen to any point in South Africa, from the Zambezi to Cape Agulhas, with no more elaborate vehicle than a box of matches, a string or two of rifle cordite, a broken-up biscuit-box, some chips of a creosoted railway sleeper, and a handful of dried cowdung, and to land each man in the precise spot he had in his mind. And that is only a small part of the world that wood-smoke controls . . .' But the whole essay deserves to be read in detail. See *Select Bibliography*.

story. This could be done in such a way as to increase its pressure on the feelings of the reader. 'A tale from which pieces have been raked out is like a fire that has been poked. One does not know that the operation has been performed, but everyone feels the effect' (p. 156). This pressure of the absent, so to speak, is one of the cardinal marks of the modern short story, and Kipling used it to masterly effect in his own later collections. What is less immediately evident, as we shall see, is how Kipling used exactly this elliptical, modernist method in the memoir itself. As a piece of 'implied' narrative, it is perhaps the most brilliant thing he ever wrote.

The emphasis on the craft aspect of fiction has another intriguing element, as Kipling reveals. Critics had often attacked his apparently philistine attitude to art. In the 1890s he was frequently caricatured as a hard-bitten journalist pouring out Imperial propaganda from a hack's desk. Indeed, in his middle period Kipling, who covered the Boer War as a correspondent, probably encouraged this deliberately. Yet his autobiography shows how deeply he was inspired by the very opposite camp to the philistines: by none other than the Pre-Raphaelites.

Kipling's father was an artist and illustrator, who was for many years curator of the museum at Lahore, and a passionate disciple of William Morris's craft movement. His mother's sister was married to Sir Edward Burne-Jones, and young Kipling frequently stayed at his aunt's house during school vacations, and was a lifelong friend of the Burne-Joneses and their circle. One of his most telling vignettes of famous men is the vision of the burly, bearded William Morris, astride a child's rocking-horse in their nursery, surging backwards and forwards while reciting an Icelandic saga like a man possessed.

Morris's belief that craftsmanship, knowledge and skill with tools and materials lay at the basis of all fine arts, was one that Kipling espouses throughout *Something of Myself*. He discusses his own work in terms of his father's trade, painting and engraving – one story is described as worked in 'lacquer and mother o' pearl' and put down 'in three or four overlaid tints' (p. 145);

another as treated 'as an illuminated manuscript'; a third as solved by painting in the background 'as hard as a public-house sign' (p. 157). He also uses terms from joinery, jewellery, house-building, ship-building and every kind of labouring trade.

There is the marvellous description of the three-decker novel he longed, but never managed, to write, envisaged as the work of some ideal shipyard team: '. . . a vessel ballasted on ingots of pure research and knowledge, roomy, fitted with delicate cabinet-work below-decks, painted, carved, gilt and wreathed the length of her, from her blazing stern-galleries outlined by bronzy palm-trunks, to her rampant figure-head – an East Indiaman worthy to lie alongside *The Cloister and the Hearth*' (p. 168). It is interesting to note here that Charles Reade, the journeyman disciple of Dickens, is the final standard of excellence. The passage can also be compared with Kipling's early poem, 'The Three-Decker'.

This admiration for humble craftsmanship runs very deep into the grain and imagery and even the philosophy of the book. When Kipling describes a mechanical task – the fitting up of central heating, the digging of a well, the mounting of a water-powered turbine generator – he is both celebrating the technical achievement itself and insisting on the secret brother-hood between all 'mechanics' and all writers. Many of his stories of the middle period concern such feats, like 'The Bridge Builders', one of his finest fables. This is a clear development of the Pre-Raphaelite doctrine, one which has un-expected links with the modernist beliefs of poets like Ezra Pound and the early Robert Frost.

When Kipling first moved into 'Bateman's', he explains how he won the heart of his notoriously difficult Sussex labourers, by recognizing them, and paying them, as artists in their own particular trade. 'I had sense enough to feel that most of them were artists and craftsmen, either in stone or timber, or wood-cutting, or drain-laying, or – which is a gift – the aesthetic disposition of dirt; persons of contrivance who could conjure with any sort of material' (p. 140). The key word here is 'conjure'; they had a kind of magic, which is of the same root as artistic inspiration.

When Kipling describes how he first began the historical fiction, *Puck of Pook's Hill*, recreating a folklore version of Britain's beginnings, he first carefully gives an account of how two Sussex labourers, 'two dark and mysterious Primitives', managed to sink a brick-built well-shaft, 'true as a rifle-barrel', down through the layers of the tricky Downland chalk. This grudging earth is also, of course, the compacted layers of English history, which the fiction writer has to penetrate with his well-built shaft of words; and the analogy becomes explicit in the final sentence. 'When we stopped, at twenty-five feet, we had found a Jacobean tobacco-pipe, a worn Cromwellian latten spoon, and, at bottom of all, the bronze cheek of a Roman horse-bit' (p. 142). The reader will find many other, and more subtle, correspondences; and will also wish to reflect, perhaps, on the implications of a view of art so exclusively concerned with structure, frame and polished surface.

Kipling also has a good deal to say on the 'magic' of inspiration, which seizes upon the craftsman and sometimes appears to direct his hand. In five places he refers to the awareness of a personal 'Daemon', and how, when in its grip and 'hatching' a story, he was lost to the outside world, 'a brother to dragons and a companion to owls' (p. 142). The vatic phrase comes from the Old Testament, the Book of Isaiah; yet is characteristically used with a touch of Kipling's most attractive self-mockery.

The Daemon, he tells us, commands the primary impulse of the fiction writer, which he first felt at Lahore when writing his strange tale, 'The Phantom Rickshaw'. This impulse is the 'attempt to think in another man's skin'; to which we should perhaps add for the later stories, 'or another woman's'. For, beginning with the dark emotions of 'Mary Postgate' (1915), Kipling frequently expressed himself as a woman – in 'The Wish House' say, or 'The Gardener'. This is in my view one of the ultimate, most delicate, and least recognized developments of his great art.

When the Daemon is in charge, 'do not try to think consciously. Drift, wait, and obey.' He felt the Daemon most clearly in both the *Jungle Books*, *Kim*, and *Puck*, 'and good care I took to walk delicately, lest he should withdraw'. The Daemon also commands when a work is finished, often with abruptness: 'when those books were finished they said so themselves with, almost, the water-hammer click of a tap turned off' (p. 157). The Daemon is touchy, and cannot be exploited for gain: 'One of the clauses in our contract was that I should never follow up "a success", for by this sin fell Napoleon and a few others.' And again, one notes the self-mockery. In fact Kipling did sometimes follow up his successes, returning for example to the *Stalky* characters in later stories – though he is right that they are a pale shadow of the originals.

How seriously are we meant to take Kipling's Daemon? It is difficult to tell, and it is here we begin to approach the more shadowy and enigmatic side of this richly layered autobiography, in which very little is quite what it first seems. The commands of the Daemon are, I think, those which would be recognized by any writer who is concerned with developing his work as an art and a personal discipline – almost, indeed, a spiritual discipline. Yet to some extent they contradict what Kipling so emphatically describes in terms of pure craft, of word-smith labour. The Daemon too, like that lucky 'card' of Destiny, smacks somewhat of a Club-Room explanation. Kipling makes a sort of smoking-room or music-hall use of the classical, Platonic concept of the poet possessed. One cannot quite forget the popular balladeer, whose *envoi* spoke cheerfully of the time, 'when 'Omer smote 'is bloomin' lyre'.

Yet I do think that Kipling's Daemon was a representation of a real force in his life, even if jocularly expressed by the Old Man of 'Bateman's'. The Daemon points towards strange Powers and Dark Places, zones of pain and anguish and struggle in Kipling's soul, that a careful reading of *Something of Myself* will partly – but only partly – reveal. One of its most suggestive aspects is its connection with his childhood sufferings and the 'night-life' of Kipling's imagination: he refers in his early London period to the first time 'the night got into my head' and how, as part of his creative work, 'such night-wakings would be laid upon me through my life' (p. 43).

The Daemon is also connected in some undefined way with

his love for his parents who, far more than his wife Carrie, are associated with all the high moments of his creative impulse. It is just here that we become conscious of one of the deep bio-graphical enigmas of the memoir: the immense importance he attaches to the inspiration and example of his parents, especially his father; and by contrast, the apparently offhand or reluctant way he refers to his own wife and his three children (who are barely mentioned). What other autobiographer would introduce his wife, and his marriage, in a parenthesis which appears to be describing the difficulty of funeral arrangements? '. . . and then to London to be married in January '92 in the thick of an influenza epidemic, when the undertakers had run out of black horses and the dead had to be content with brown ones' (p. 96).

It is his parents who help him make the discovery of his Imperial mission in the early days of his first stories and poems, described in chapter 4: 'As was the custom between us, I asked into the air: "What am I trying to get *at*?" Instantly the Mother, with her quick flutter of the hands: "You're *trying* to say: 'What do they know of England who only England know?'"' The Father confirmed' (p. 86). Again, it is his father who is intimately linked with the inspiration that produced *Kim*, the deep, autobiographic centre of Kipling's entire *oeuvre*. It began to come to him one 'gloomy, windy autumn' as he pensively raked over the sunlit memories of India; and he instinctively turned to his father for help. This crucial moment is described in terms that skilfully mix the bluff comradeship of the smoking-room with the magic alchemy of the opium-den. '. . . I took it to be smoked over with my Father. Under our united tobaccos it grew like the Djinn released from the brass bottle, and the more we explored its possibilities the more opulence of detail did we discover . . .' Here the story is seen not as a solid structure, but as a sinuous, unwreathing vision which only caught 'one-tenth' of the first 'lavish specification'; the rest, like an iceberg, remaining mysteriously 'below the water-line' of the conscious mind (p. 116). The whole description is curiously reminiscent of Coleridge's Preface to 'Kubla Khan'.

Kipling's apparent silence about his own family life as far as it affected his creative work has long been a point of contention among critics and scholars. While he wrote so freely and vividly about his childhood and his parents in *Something of Myself*, he appears to have cut away almost everything about his early loves, his marriage, his own children (the girls are not even named in the book), and his deepest emotional loyalties. For readers who wish to compare autobiography with biography in this respect, the following notable omissions will be found. Chapter 3 contains nothing of his important relationship with the wife of Professor Hill, who became the adolescent's muse in Lahore. Chapter 4 says nothing of his failed love-affair with Flo Garrard (which shaped the writing of *The Light That Failed*), or the death of his great friend, the American Wolcott Balestier, which precipitated his marriage with Carrie, Wolcott's sister. Nor does it mention his quarrel with Beatty Balestier, his brother-in-law, in Vermont, which was probably a deciding factor in his return to England. Chapter 5 is silent about the death of his beloved daughter Josephine (to whom *The Jungle Book* is dedicated) during the disastrous American visit of 1899; the memory of her was responsible for the moving story, 'They', and the beginnings of the major theme of 'healing' in the later work. Kipling's cousin Angela Thirkell remarked: 'Much of the beloved Cousin Ruddy of our childhood died with Josephine and I feel that I have never seen him as a real person since that year.' Finally, in chapter 7, by refusing to discuss the Great War and the collapse of the Imperial dream, and drawing the line at 1907, Kipling omits the greatest crisis of his middle years, the death of his only son, John, at the Battle of Loos in 1915, which was also responsible for some of the most brilliant, inward studies of love and mourning in the post-war stories, such as 'The Woman in His Life', 'The Gardener' and 'A Madonna of the Trenches'.

This reticence, or, as some have seen it, 'repression', has been severely handled even by Kipling's most favourable critics. His biographer, Charles Carrington, remarked that the book was hardly an autobiography at all, 'but a reluctant release of what little he wished his readers to know'. Joyce Tompkins, the best modern critic of the stories, observes – though not without sympathy – that 'to this generation, eager for psychological evidence, often more interested in what is suppressed than in what has been selected for expression, *Something of Myself* appears defiant and uncommunicative enough.' Even Sir Angus Wilson calls it 'his reticent, self-concealing autobiography'; though later he has conceded that the book was 'under-estimated'.

Of course they are right – in part. Kipling never pretended it was anything else. Throughout his life he held to a Victorian code of decent silence on personal matters in public: the same code that Joseph Conrad and Henry James also held, but Frank Harris did not. He had a detestation of what he referred to witheringly as 'the "Higher Cannibalism"' (p. 146), that is, the biographical and psychological interpretation of an author's literary work. He called it a Chief Mortician's trade, specializing in 'the exhumation of scarcely cold notorieties, defenceless females for choice, and tricking them out with sprightly inferences and "sex"-deductions to suit the mood of the market' (p. 146). The gruff anger is heartfelt. He also wrote that famous and touching verse, 'The Appeal', which should be framed on the study walls of all professional biographers, as a *memento mori*.

> If I have given you delight
>   By aught that I have done,
> Let me lie quiet in that night
>   Which shall be yours anon:
>
> And for the little, little, span
>   The dead are borne in mind,
> Seek not to question other than
>   The books I leave behind.

Yet this, too, is something of a mask; and his critics are also wrong, in my view. As in the case of the 'Daemon', Kipling did choose to reveal a good deal of his secret emotional life, but after his own distinctive fashion: he revealed it through the methods of the master story-teller. In this respect *Something of Myself* is a classic demonstration of 'the pressure of the absent'. The key to this technique in his autobiography is the use of what I shall call the 'symbolic anecdote'. I believe that once understood, it will call for a major revaluation of the whole book, which will place it close to the heart of his achievement as a writer.

The entire work is constructed on a modernist principle. It does not tell the life story as a continuous narrative, but as a series of brilliantly worked fragments, a mosaic of carefully interlocked cameo portraits, memories and anecdotes. The fragments gradually, almost musically, come to group and cluster around certain leading themes of his inner life. In this respect the work is less like *A Moveable Feast*, and much more like T. S. Eliot's *The Waste Land*. It is a pastoral, and an elegy, as I have said, but like so many of the late stories, it is also a work of symbolism and self-exploration, with the same emphasis on 'a certain economy of implication', and the elliptical statement of truth. There are many ways of describing these symbolic themes, and the reader will want to investigate them further and follow them out into the fiction. But I shall start by defining them in three ways, which will I hope be immediately recognizable. They are the Dark Place, the Good House, and the Arcadian Dream.

The first appearance of the Dark Place occurs early in chapter 1. The seven-year-old Kipling is brought from India co England and deposited by his parents at Lorne Lodge, Southsea, for close on six years: 'a dark land, and a darker room full of cold' (p. 35). The regime of 'punishments and humiliations' he suffered here, at what he calls 'the House of Desolation', had a profound effect on the formation of his character. It led him to look back at India as a kind of paradise of warmth and light and family intimacy that he would spend a lifetime trying to recover or recreate. Kipling describes his misery in terms that echo the childhood of Dickens's David Copperfield (the incident of the humiliating placard hung on the boy's back appears in both), and says he suffered a kind of nervous breakdown and the first onset of severe eye-trouble, which led him to fear blindness for the rest of his life. The imagery of light and dark, seeing and going blind, becomes a persistent one in the early fiction; and the Dark Place is established both as a physical location and as an inner condition of the troubled and depressed spirit. In a striking phrase, the American poet, Randall Jarrell, called it Kipling's 'concentration camp of the soul'.

The biographical researches of Charles Carrington and the memoirs of Kipling's sister Trixie have confirmed many of the outward details of this childhood trauma. Kipling's story, 'Baa, Baa, Black Sheep' (1892), and the first chapter of *The Light That Failed* (1891), fully explore its inward significance, and the fear and hatred and periods of black depression it aroused. It is perhaps the most explicit personal revelation in *Something of Myself*, and we meet veiled references to it throughout the rest of the book. The critic Edmund Wilson used it as the basis for an entire interpretation of Kipling's adult character and work, which he saw as a kind of psychological 'submission' to bullying and Imperial authority, in a brilliant essay in *The Wound and the Bow*.

But Kipling himself links the depression of the Dark Place with his struggles to find his way as a writer. In complete contradiction to the jolly, Club-Room claim of the lucky 'card', he in fact shows that this grim confrontation with the Dark Place in himself was the only condition under which he could maintain his integrity as an artist. His description, through a whole series of symbolic anecdotes, presents this spiritual struggle with extraordinary psychological insight and conviction.

In chapter 3 he writes of a '"pivot" experience' during the terrible hot season at Lahore, when he first realized the way out of his suicidal sense of depression and meaninglessness was through writing fiction. 'It happened one hot-weather evening, in '86 or thereabouts, when I felt that I had come to the edge of all endurance. As I entered my empty house in the dusk there was no more in me except the horror of a great darkness, that I must have been fighting for some days. I came through that darkness alive, but how I do not know' (p. 71). How he came through was by reading a book by Walter Besant about 'a young man who desired to write', and having the first clear vision of a literary career in London, 'a dream of the future that sustained me'. The sober passion with which Kipling relates this anecdote, together with various stories of contemporaries of his who *did* go off their heads in Lahore, lends further weight and significance to the childhood experience. Walter Besant (now temporarily forgotten, but an inspiring figure who founded the Society of Authors) is given a heroic description in the following chapter. His book, says Kipling bluntly, was 'my salvation'.

Perhaps the most striking symbolic anecdote of the Dark Place occurs in chapter 4, which hovers at the point of balance between an autobiographical self-revelation and the 'objective' fragment of a short story. It is particularly interesting because it demonstrates exactly that power of evocation, through vernacular detail and highly suggestive compression, which marks Kipling's genius as a prose writer. Here we can observe it in the very act of transforming personal material into impersonal narrative.

Kipling had reached London in 1889 to be hailed as the new Dickens. The success of his stories had put nearly all literary London at his feet: he was praised by Hardy and Henry James; commended in a leader in *The Times*; and editors were flocking to the door of his tiny, grubby flat in Villiers Street. (Typically, he had settled not in a 'bohemian' quarter, but in a bustling side-street off the Strand, with the newspapers of Fleet Street on one elbow, the trains of Charing Cross on the other, and the great steamships of Imperial trade plying the Thames below his bedroom window.) It was the most notable case of literary fame achieved overnight since Lord Byron, and by all normal standards he should have been radiantly happy.

But writers are not easily made happy; and Kipling was very largely miserable. Charles Carrington has shown how this was a time of great loneliness and turmoil. Kipling deeply missed India and his parents; he was in despair over the failure of his affair with Flo Garrard; and he was very uncertain about the direction in which his writing should go. He was assailed by bouts of depression, worried about his sight and health, and working obsessively hard on his first full-length novel, *The Light That Failed*, which well describes the true state of affairs at Villiers Street. At times he was clearly unbalanced and suicidal, and indeed the novel itself is dominated by this idea of artistic failure and self-destruction.

Kipling, as one would expect, says nothing directly about any of this in *Something of Myself*. Instead he expresses it all in one single, grim and unforgettable incident, apparently viewed from his window overlooking Villiers Street. It is, in fact, a complete short story in five sentences – a symbolic anecdote – whose title might be simply 'Fog', but whose real subject is Kipling's own inner darkness. This is what he writes:

Once I faced the reflection of my own face in the jet-black mirror of the window-panes for five days. When the fog thinned, I looked out and saw a man standing opposite the pub where the barmaid lived. Of a sudden his breast turned dull red like a robin's, and he crumpled, having cut his throat. In a few minutes – seconds it seemed – a hand-ambulance arrived and took up the body. A pot-boy with a bucket of steaming water sluiced the blood off into the gutter, and what little crowd had collected went its way (p. 84–5).

The details of this story are so coolly and sharply presented that it is only on reflection – why did Kipling place it just here in his own story of success? – that one begins to realize that it is really a 'jet-black mirror' of his own mind. The use of the observer, of the narrative 'frame', are all characteristic of his best fictional work; and for those who savour such things, there is even a curious, Freudian pun in the image of the blood staining the anonymous man's shirt-front like a robin's red breast: Kipling's intimate name in his family was 'Ruddy'. The story is equally about the self-consuming loneliness of the writer and the callousness of the 'little crowd' who pause to admire and then pass on. Even what the artist produces out of his own suffering and blood, Kipling seems to say, will probably be 'sluiced' away by time and forgetfulness.

It may be thought that I am reading too much into such a passage. But the sheer persistence of the theme of the Dark Place in *Something of Myself* seems to make some such interpretation inescapable. The reader will find many other references to the Dark Place – in the farms at Vermont, in South Africa, in the mysteriously mournful house at Torquay. All of them give evidence of the depth and complication of Kipling's struggles with himself (indeed, with the dark side of his

Daemon), and his battle to mark out areas of light and meaning in his fiction. And what else, for instance, can one make of the haunting description of the unlit palace of the dead Swedish king in which Kipling receives the Nobel Prize?

Moreover, it is a theme so powerfully present in the later fiction – for instance, in 'They', 'The House Surgeon', or 'A Madonna of the Trenches' – and so closely linked with the unspoken grief for his dead children, and finally, for all the dead of the Great War, that it becomes, surely, one of the central revelations of the autobiography. A fuller explanation of its psychological significance lies outside the scope of this Introduction, and besides, readers will want to reflect on it for themselves. But its great importance lies, I think, in the new appreciation it gives us of Kipling's depths and inner struggles and uncertainties. It is impossible to go on dismissing him as a superficial artist, or a hard, unfeeling man. Moreover, his aware-ness of the Dark Place and his persistent probing of that darkness suggest one of the most vital lines of critical re-valuation that still needs to be made of his work as a whole: the comparison with Joseph Conrad.

When Edmund Wilson picked on the 'House of Desolation' at Southsea as the key to open up Kipling's imaginative life, he showed a curious blindness as to the existence of another House in Kipling's autobiography. This is the Good House, the House of Consolation. The search for such a house, and the attempts to build it both literally and metaphorically, is the second leading theme of the book.

Six of the eight chapters of *Something of Myself* are built around this search for the Good House, ending with the dis-covery and fitting-out of 'Bateman's' in Sussex in 1902, 'The Very-Own House'. Along the way we are given, with that signifi-cant emphasis on craft already noted, considerable details about the physical structures of the actual buildings and Kipling's personal efforts to improve them. In chapter 3, the House only really exists in the form of the bachelor Punjab Club in Lahore, but already the importance of comradeship, good talk, and the 'square' set defensively against the outside world – all essential values of the Good House – are present. In his letters, Kipling often referred to his closest relations as 'the Family Square', a term adopted from the formation of foot-soldiers in battle. (The almost metaphysical value he attached to military drill is elsewhere explored in an address he gave in 1917, 'The Magic Square'.)

In chapter 4 we meet the house at Villiers Street, scene of his early struggles in the literary world; and in the following chapter the two houses of his honeymoon and early marriage, 'Bliss Cottage' and 'Naulakha', both of them in the remote farmlands of Vermont, on the east coast of America, where Kipling spent five years. Here the identification between the Good House and the successful partnership of his marriage becomes explicit, with all the implied values of domestic loyalty and consolation for the griefs he was soon to suffer. There is also another superb symbolic anecdote of a solitary farmer's wife, living alone on the opposite ridge, for whom the lights of 'Naulakha' have become a vital source of comfort in the long, dark winters. The two paragraphs in which Kipling draws the picture of her solitude, in a land of 'desolation' – again, that resonant word – where 'strange faiths and cruelties, born of solitude to the edge of insanity, flourished like lichen on sick bark', have all the haunting force of a painting by Andrew Wyeth (p. 103). The implied terrors of solitude and abandonment for the artist are evident. It is in this context that much of the criticism of Kipling's own marriage later made by friends, and dwelt on by both Charles Carrington and Angus Wilson, must surely be placed. It was said that Carrie managed him too much – Kipling never kept his own business accounts after the Yokohama bank failure in 1892 – and that she dominated the social arrangements of his life, so that her matron-like presence gradually cut him off from his contemporaries. There may be much truth in this. But the clear evidence of the autobiography is that Kipling, like so many other fiction writers who dwell most intensely in their own imagination and memories, required both the practical and spiritual support of highly organized domesticity. (One thinks, in their different ways, of the 'stern' marriages of Dickens, or Hugo or Conrad himself; or, by contrast, of the domestic and financial chaos of Balzac's non-marriage to Madame Hanska.) One can say that whenever Kipling writes about the Good House he was, indirectly, paying tribute to Carrie herself; so that although she is absent by name from *Something of Myself*, her unseen presence is everywhere felt. Besides, an examination of the Visitors Book still kept at 'Bateman's' will show the amount of entertaining the Kiplings did in fact keep up: in one post-War year, for example, they had no less than 133 house-guests.

The Good House, especially as represented by the beautiful old mansion of 'Bateman's' in chapter 7, is also a symbol of Kipling's writing: what Henry James called 'the House of Fiction'. It is an obvious symbol of the material success of his creative effort, comparable to Walter Scott's Abbotsford, or Stevenson's Vailima, but more subtly, it frames the spiritual conditions under which he wrote, within the Magic Square. It is a symbol of loyalty, continuity and personal integrity. One of Kipling's most important beliefs as an artist was that one should keep faith with the dreams of one's youth. He carved such a sacred injunction on the underside of his roll-top desk in Villiers Street. One must keep faith with the Daemon. It is typical of him that he remembered the wonderful holidays he had, away from the 'House of Desolation', at the Burne-Joneses', home, 'The Grange', and associated that promise of happiness with the iron bell-pull that hung outside it. 'When I had a house of my own . . . I begged for and was given that bell-pull for my entrance, in the hope that other children might also feel happy when they rang it' (p. 39).

Moreover it was in the House of Desolation itself, when confined to 'a mildewy basement room' as a punishment, that he first identifies the healing magic of the imagination, as he acted out scenes from *Robinson Crusoe* in a make-believe square formed by pieces of packing-case and a tin-trunk. (Incidentally, the extraordinary influence of Defoe's fable of house-building on the childhoods of many nineteenth-century writers is almost worthy of a separate study: Théophile Gautier, for example, assigns an archetypal role to the book in his *Histoire du Romantisme*.) This pastime of creating a Magic House is common to many children, whether unhappy or not; but

Kipling, in one of the shrewdest observations on the sources of his own art, saw that this early form of play mimicked the structural strength of his own fiction in adulthood, holding the outer chaos at bay within an ideal creation, 'which kept off any other world'.

For Kipling, the act of creation was essentially an act of constructive defence. 'Thus fenced about, everything inside the fence was quite real, but mixed with the smell of damp cupboards. If the bit of board fell, I had to begin the magic all over again . . . The magic, you see, lies in the ring or fence that you take refuge in' (p. 38). It was the first answer to the Dark Place, and seems to me to suggest most powerfully the reason for all his later adherence to ritual, institution, 'the Law'; whether in the form of Club or regiment, marriage or Free-masonry, the brotherhood of craft or profession, or the 'bul-wark' of Empire itself.

Here we come upon that third and final theme, the dream of Arcadia. In a sense it is the most controversial and radical element in *Something of Myself*, for it contradicts the most universally accepted fact about Kipling: his passionate belief in the enduring reality of the British Empire. For many readers, Kipling is still the 'unofficial Laureate' of that Empire, and the decline of his literary reputation, until very recently, has been rather crudely associated with Imperial decline, which is to say the social history of Britain since 1914. The most striking, and oddly sympathetic, account of Kipling's reputation *avant le déluge*, can be found in the seventeenth chapter of Holbrook Jackson's *The Eighteen Nineties*, a forgotten but nonetheless classic account of 'art and ideas at the close of the nineteenth century', which has the acute historical interest of being published in 1913.

Yet, as already noted, apart from chapter 6 of the autobiography, 'South Africa' (which is largely an account of Kipling's admiration for Cecil Rhodes), the Imperial theme is strangely muted in the book. Kipling jokes about some of his more portentous formulations of Imperial values and duties, noting wryly that schoolboys were always complaining to him about having to learn the poem 'If—' for imposition. He even quotes the notorious phrase about 'lesser breeds without the Law', in terms of his battle with the publishing pirates of his books, who flouted the copyright laws.

In the autobiographic imagination of the old man, what manifestly replaces the outward and dying reality of the Empire is the inward and growing truth of the Arcadia he has created in his fiction. The whole texture of the book is infused with the memory of 'enchanted places' which were the sources of his best fiction – above all India and Sussex – seen no longer as part of history, but in a golden, gleaming, elegiac light. This light – the light that compensates for another kind of blindness – is like the slanting, caressing evening light that he was so proud of getting into *Kim*: 'the low-driving sunlight which makes luminous every detail in the picture of the Grand Trunk Road at eventide' (p. 116).

It is the timeless, perfected Arcadian world he has achieved in *Kim*, in the *Jungle Books*, in *Puck of Pook's Hill*, which he is most willing to celebrate. Speaking of them, and particularly of *Rewards and Fairies*, he describes them as tales 'to be read by children, before people realized that they were meant for grown-ups', and says they were intended as 'a sort of balance to, as well as a seal upon, some aspects of my '"Imperialistic" output in the past' (p. 145). All these works, as well as much of the later fiction, explore a world poised between fantasy and reality, topographically rich and yet curiously dream-like, open to inexplicable visitations of the spirit (the Lama in *Kim*, the ambiguous wise-woman of 'The Wish House'), and projecting in different ways and levels of seriousness what A. E. Housman called 'the land of lost content': Arcadia.

Looking back at this dream of an ideal world, across what is now three generations and one of the great watersheds in our national history, Kipling's cultural place seems to shift. It is impossible to go on limiting him to a literature of Imperialism: comparisons with G. A. Henty, or Rider Haggard, or W. E. Henley or even Somerset Maugham have long ago become ridiculous. Kipling is both more centrally British than that as a figure; and also more European as an artist.

Kipling's Aracadia, unlike the British Empire, was not

doomed. It has become a permanent free-state of the imagination. Its great themes – the getting of wisdom in youth, the discovery of the inner law, the building of friendship and loyalties (rather than love, I think), the stoic, even humorous, acceptance of suffering and death – are perennial. Out of destruction and desolation come dreams and consolations. It is to this realm that Kipling finally gives his allegiance, a kingdom not of this world.

In one way, this places him at the heart of an 'Arcadian movement' which is so typical of late-nineteenth-century English literature, represented in different ways by William Morris, R. L. Stevenson, A. E. Housman, Edward Thomas and even at times Thomas Hardy of Wessex. But in another way, as a craftsman and conscious artist, it places him firmly on a footing with his European peers – with Conrad, with Maupassant, with Chekhov, each in their fashion great masters of the short, fictional form. Is he as great in stature as they? When one discovers his influence on later writers as diverse as Brecht, Hemingway and Borges, the question can only remain open.

Part of the power of this wonderful, compact and problematic little book is that it poses such questions. It also teaches the writer the value of falling silent. It will one day, I am sure, be recognized as one of the provoking masterpieces among modern autobiographies, precisely because it is only 'something' of himself. After all, that is quite sufficient for an Englishman.

Richard Holmes

Select Bibliography

The portrait Rudyard Kipling draws of himself here can be supplemented in many interesting ways. First of all I would recommend a visit to 'Bateman's' itself, now a National Trust property, some two hours' drive from London (the Sussex lanes should be navigated with slow appreciation). The paintings, photographs and cartoons of him repay close attention: an instructive essay could be written on the rise and fall of his moustache.

Next, Kipling published a book of travel essays, *From Sea to Sea* (1890), and two revealing collections of public speeches: *Souvenirs of France* (1933) and *A Book of Words* (1928). This last contains the superb address to the Royal Geographical Society, 'Some Aspects of Travel' (1914), and also 'Values in Life' (1907) and 'The Magic Square' (1917).

Among biographies and critical studies, the best are: Charles Carrington, *Rudyard Kipling: His Life and Work* (1955; 1978); Joyce Tompkins, *The Art of Rudyard Kipling* (1959), particularly good on the later stories; and Angus Wilson, *The Strange Ride of Rudyard Kipling* (1977), a major feat of rediscovery, drawing on Wilson's own Anglo-Indian background and his profound understanding of the fiction writer's crafts and complexes. Illuminating material can also be found in *Kipling: Interviews and Recollections*, edited by Harold Orel, 2 vols., 1983.

Finally, three very different interpretations of Kipling's character can be found in: Kingsley Amis, *Rudyard Kipling and his World* (1975); Edmund Wilson, 'The Kipling that Nobody Reads' in *The Wound and the Bow* (1942) and Randall Jarrell, 'On Preparing to Read Kipling' (1961) in *Kipling, Auden and Co.* (1981). Further titles are listed on p. 171.

Richard Holmes

Note on the Text

Kipling began work on his autobiography on 1 August 1935. According to his wife's diary, he wrote for a fortnight and then revised what he had written. He worked on the manuscript again in September 1935 – see his reference to a newspaper report of 16 September 1935 (p. 106 and note 35, chapter 5) – and revised from 21 October. The final words were written around 20 December 1935. Kipling took ill on 9 January 1936 and died on 18 January.

After Kipling's death his wife permitted the publication of previously unpublished work only if it was completed: she destroyed the drafts of unfinished work. According to Lord Birkenhead (*Rudyard Kipling*, p. 353), *Something of Myself* was edited and given its name by Kipling's surgeon, Sir Alfred Webb-Johnson. Sections from *Something of Myself* were serialized in the *Morning Post* from 25 January to 12 February 1937. *Something of Myself* first appeared in book form simultaneously in Uniform and Pocket Editions from Macmillan and Co. on 16 February 1937. Publication was followed by correspondence in the *Morning Post* and the *Daily Telegraph* relating to various inaccuracies in the text. Correspondence between Kipling's agent, A. P. Watt, and Macmillan (now in the Macmillan Archive in the British Library) notes that Mrs Kipling asked for these corrections to be incorporated into the text for the Sussex Edition. *Something of Myself* was published (with *Souvenirs of France*) as volume XXXI of the Sussex Edition in 1938. 525 sets were printed, of which 500 were for sale, but, according to Charles Morgan (*The House of Macmillan*, p. 152) most of the edition was destroyed during the Second World War.

I have taken the text of the Sussex Edition, which was seen through the press by Thomas Mark of Macmillan, as my copytext. I have collated it with the text of the first edition and with

Note on the Text

the texts for two other collected editions which Macmillan published in 1938 (the Edition de Luxe and the Bombay Edition). The four texts are different, but the three texts published in 1938 all include the correction of certain factual errors in the first-edition text: 'Sir Edward Grey' is corrected to 'Sir George Grey' (p. 91); 'Arthur Morrison' is changed to 'Alfred Morrison' (p. 115); 'Sir Hercules Ross' becomes 'Sir Hercules Read' (p. 118); 'Pelorus Jack' takes up his true form as a 'dolphin' (p. 91) rather than a 'shark'; and so on. I have also followed the three texts of 1938 in removing a statement about Sir George Grey's activities (p. 91). Mrs Kipling had asked for this cut to be made.

I have generally followed the Sussex Edition in its use of capitals, but with 'the Son' (p. 42) I have followed the other three texts; with 'Sister' (p. 64) I have followed the first edition; and with ''Fifties' (p. 213) and ''Sixties' (p. 141) I have added capitals for consistency. For the spelling of 'carcase' (p. 64), 'bazaar', 'verandah', 'Muhammed', 'Muhammedans' and 'gaol' I have followed the first edition. I have followed Penguin house-style and given the chapters arabic rather than roman numerals.

Robert Hampson

SOMETHING OF MYSELF

Chapter 1

{ A Very Young Person }

1865–1878

Give me the first six years of a child's life and you can have the rest.[1]

Looking back[2] from this my seventieth year, it seems to me that every card in my working life has been dealt me in such a manner that I had but to play it as it came. Therefore, ascribing all good fortune to Allah the Dispenser of Events, I begin:

My first impression is of daybreak, light and colour and golden and purple fruits at the level of my shoulder. This would be the memory of early morning walks to the Bombay fruit-market with my *ayah*[3] and later with my sister[4] in her perambulator, and of our returns with our purchases piled high on the bows of it. Our *ayah* was a Portuguese Roman Catholic who would pray – I beside her – at a wayside Cross. Meeta,[5] my Hindu bearer, would sometimes go into little Hindu temples where, being below the age of caste, I held his hand and looked at the dimly-seen, friendly Gods.

Our evening walks were by the sea in the shadow of palm-groves which, I think, were called the Mahim Woods.[6] When the wind blew the great nuts would tumble, and we fled – my *ayah*, and my sister in her perambulator – to the safety of the open. I have always felt the menacing darkness of tropical eventides, as I have loved the voices of night-winds through palm or banana leaves, and the song of the tree-frogs.

There were far-going Arab dhows on the pearly waters, and gaily dressed Parsees[7] wading out to worship the sunset. Of

33

their creed I knew nothing, nor did I know that near our little house on the Bombay Esplanade were the Towers of Silence, where their Dead are exposed to the waiting vultures on the rim of the towers, who scuffle and spread wings when they see the bearers of the Dead below. I did not understand my Mother's distress when she found 'a child's hand' in our garden, and said I was not to ask questions about it. I wanted to see that child's hand. But my *ayah* told me.

In the afternoon heats before we took our sleep, she or Meeta would tell us stories and Indian nursery songs all unforgotten, and we were sent into the dining-room after we had been dressed, with the caution 'Speak English now to Papa and Mamma.' So one spoke 'English', haltingly translated out of the vernacular idiom that one thought and dreamed in. The Mother sang wonderful songs at a black piano and would go out to Big Dinners. Once she came back, very quickly, and told me, still awake, that 'the big Lord Sahib' had been killed and there was to be no Big Dinner. This was Lord Mayo,[8] assassinated by a native. Meeta explained afterwards that he had been 'hit with a knife'. Meeta unconsciously saved me from any night terrors or dread of the dark. Our *ayah*, with a servant's curious mixture of deep affection and shallow device, had told me that a stuffed leopard's head on the nursery wall was there to see that I went to sleep. But Meeta spoke of it scornfully as 'the head of an animal', and I took it off my mind as a fetish, good or bad, for it was only some unspecified 'animal'.

Far across green spaces round the house was a marvellous place filled with smells of paints and oils, and lumps of clay with which I played. That was the atelier of my Father's School of Art,[9] and a Mr 'Terry Sahib'[10] his assistant, to whom my small sister was devoted, was our great friend. Once, on the way there alone, I passed the edge of a huge ravine a foot deep, where a winged monster as big as myself attacked me, and I fled and wept. My Father drew for me a picture of the tragedy with a rhyme beneath:

> There was a small boy in Bombay
> Who once from a hen ran away.

34

A Very Young Person

When they said: 'You're a baby,'
He replied: 'Well, I may be:
But I don't like these hens of Bombay.'

This consoled me. I have thought well of hens ever since.

Then those days of strong light and darkness passed, and there was a time in a ship[11] with an immense semi-circle blocking all vision on each side of her. (She must have been the old paddle-wheel P. & O. *Ripon*.) There was a train across a desert (the Suez Canal was not yet opened) and a halt in it,[12] and a small girl wrapped in a shawl on the seat opposite me, whose face stands out still. There was next a dark land, and a darker room full of cold, in one wall of which a white woman made naked fire, and I cried aloud with dread, for I had never before seen a grate.

Then came a new small house[13] smelling of aridity and emptiness, and a parting in the dawn with Father and Mother, who said that I must learn quickly to read and write so that they might send me letters and books.

I lived in that house for close on six years. It belonged to a woman who took in children[14] whose parents were in India. She was married to an old Navy Captain, who had been a midshipman at Navarino,[15] and had afterwards been entangled in a harpoon-line while whale-fishing, and dragged down till he miraculously freed himself. But the line had scarred his ankle for life – a dry, black scar, which I used to look at with horrified interest.

The house itself stood in the extreme suburbs of Southsea, next to a Portsmouth unchanged in most particulars since Trafalgar – the Portsmouth of Sir Walter Besant's *By Celia's Arbour*.[16] The timber for a Navy that was only experimenting with ironclads such as the *Inflexible* lay in great booms in the Harbour. The little training-brigs kept their walks opposite Southsea Castle, and Portsmouth Hard was as it had always been. Outside these things lay the desolation of Hayling Island, Lumps Fort, and the isolated hamlet of Milton. I would go for long walks with the Captain, and once he took me to see a ship called the *Alert* (or *Discovery*)[17] returned from Arctic explorations, her decks filled with old sledges and lumber, and her spare rudder being cut up for souvenirs. A sailor gave me a piece, but I lost it. Then the old Captain died, and I was sorry, for he was the only person in that house as far as I can remember who ever threw me a kind word.

It was an establishment run with the full vigour of the Evangelical as revealed to the Woman. I had never heard of Hell, so I was introduced to it in all its terrors – I and whatever luckless little slavey might be in the house, whom severe rationing had led to steal food. Once I saw the Woman beat such a girl who picked up the kitchen poker and threatened retaliation. Myself I was regularly beaten. The Woman had an only son[18] of twelve or thirteen as religious as she. I was a real joy to him, for when his mother had finished with me for the day he (we slept in the same room) took me on and roasted the other side.

If you cross-examine a child of seven or eight on his day's doings (specially when he wants to go to sleep) he will contradict himself very satisfactorily. If each contradiction be set down as a lie and retailed at breakfast, life is not easy. I have known a certain amount of bullying, but this was calculated torture – religious as well as scientific. Yet it made me give attention to the lies I soon found it necessary to tell: and this, I presume, is the foundation of literary effort.

But my ignorance was my salvation. I was made to read without explanation, under the usual fear of punishment. And on a day that I remember it came to me that 'reading' was not 'the Cat lay on the Mat,' but a means to everything that would make me happy. So I read all that came within my reach. As soon as my pleasure in this was known, deprivation from reading was added to my punishments. I then read by stealth and the more earnestly.

There were not many books in that house, but Father and Mother as soon as they heard I could read sent me priceless volumes. One I have still, a bound copy of *Aunt Judy's Magazine*[19] of the early 'Seventies, in which appeared Mrs Ewing's *Six to Sixteen*.[20] I owe more in circuitous ways to that tale than I can tell. I knew it, as I know it still, almost by heart. Here was a history of real people and real things. It was better than

Knatchbull-Hugessen's *Tales at Tea-time*,[21] better even than *The Old Shikarri*[22] with its steel engravings of charging pigs and angry tigers. On another plane was an old magazine with Scott's 'I climbed the dark brow of the mighty Helvellyn.'[23] I knew nothing of its meaning but the words moved and pleased. So did other extracts from the poems of 'A. Tennyson'.[24]

A visitor, too, gave me a little purple book of severely moral tendency called *The Hope of the Katzekopfs*[25] – about a bad boy made virtuous, but it contained verses that began, 'Farewell Rewards and Fairies',[26] and ended with an injunction 'To pray for the "noddle" of William Churne of Staffordshire.' This bore fruit afterwards.

And somehow or other I came across a tale about a lion-hunter[27] in South Africa who fell among lions who were all Freemasons, and with them entered into a confederacy against some wicked baboons. I think that, too, lay dormant until the *Jungle Books* began to be born.

There comes to my mind here a memory of two books of verse about child-life which I have tried in vain to identify. One – blue and fat[28] – described 'nine white wolves' coming 'over the wold' and stirred me to the deeps; and also certain savages who 'thought the name of England was something that could not burn'.

The other book – brown and fat[29] – was full of lovely tales in strange metres. A girl was turned into a water-rat 'as a matter of course'; an Urchin cured an old man of gout by means of a cool cabbage-leaf, and somehow 'forty wicked Goblins' were mixed up in the plot; and a 'Darling' got out on the house-leads with a broom and tried to sweep stars off the skies. It must have been an unusual book for that age, but I have never been able to recover it, any more than I have a song that a nursemaid sang at low-tide in the face of the sunset on Littlehampton Sands when I was less than six. But the impression of wonder, excitement and terror and the red bars of failing light is as clear as ever.

Among the servants in the House of Desolation was one from Cumnor, which name I associated with sorrow and darkness and a raven that 'flapped its wings'. Years later I identified the lines: 'And thrice the Raven flapped her wing Around the towers of Cumnor Hall.'[30] But how and where I first heard the lines that cast the shadow is beyond me – unless it be that the brain holds everything that passes within reach of the senses, and it is only ourselves who do not know this.

When my Father sent me a *Robinson Crusoe* with steel engravings I set up in business alone as a trader with savages (the wreck parts of the tale never much interested me), in a mildewy basement room where I stood my solitary confinements. My apparatus was a coconut shell strung on a red cord, a tin trunk, and a piece of packing-case which kept off any other world. Thus fenced about, everything inside the fence was quite real, but mixed with the smell of damp cupboards. If the bit of board fell, I had to begin the magic all over again. I have learned since from children who play much alone that this rule of 'beginning again in a pretend game' is not uncommon. The magic, you see, lies in the ring or fence that you take refuge in.

Once I remember being taken to a town called Oxford and a street called Holywell, where I was shown an Ancient of Days who, I was told, was the Provost of Oriel;[31] wherefore I never understood, but conceived him to be some sort of idol. And twice or thrice we went, all of us, to pay a day-long visit to an old gentleman[32] in a house in the country near Havant. Here everything was wonderful and unlike my world, and he had an old lady sister who was kind, and I played in hot, sweet-smelling meadows and ate all sorts of things.

After such a visit I was once put through the third degree by the Woman and her son, who asked me if I had told the old gentleman that I was much fonder of him than was the Woman's son. It must have been the tail-end of some sordid intrigue or other – the old gentleman being of kin to that unhappy pair – but it was beyond my comprehension. My sole concern had been a friendly pony in the paddock. My dazed attempts to clear myself were not accepted and, once again, the pleasure that I was seen to have taken was balanced by punishments and humiliation – above all humiliation. That alternation was quite regular. I can but admire the infernal laborious ingenuity of it all. *Exempli gratia.*[33] Coming out of church once I smiled. The Devil-Boy demanded why. I said I didn't know, which was child's truth. He replied that I *must* know. People didn't laugh for nothing. Heaven knows what explanation I put forward; but it was duly reported to the Woman as a 'lie'. Result, afternoon upstairs with the Collect[34] to learn. I learned most of the Collects that way and a great deal of the Bible. The son after three or four years went into a Bank and was generally too tired on his return to torture me, unless things had gone wrong with him. I learned to know what was coming from his step into the house.

But, for a month each year I possessed a paradise which I verily believe saved me. Each December I stayed with my Aunt Georgie,[35] my mother's sister, wife of Sir Edward Burne-Jones, at 'The Grange', North End Road. At first I must have been escorted there, but later I went alone, and arriving at the house would reach up to the open-work iron bell-pull on the wonderful gate that let me into all felicity. When I had a house of my own, and 'The Grange' was emptied of meaning, I begged for and was given that bell-pull for my entrance, in the hope that other children might also feel happy when they rang it.

At 'The Grange' I had love and affection as much as the greediest, and I was not very greedy, could desire. There were most wonderful smells of paints and turpentine whiffing down from the big studio on the first floor where my Uncle worked; there was the society of my two cousins,[36] and a sloping mulberry tree which we used to climb for our plots and conferences. There was a rocking-horse in the nursery and a table that, tilted up on two chairs, made a toboggan-slide of the best. There were pictures finished or half finished of lovely colours; and in the rooms chairs and cupboards such as the world had not yet seen, for William Morris[37] (our Deputy 'Uncle Topsy') was just beginning to fabricate these things. There was an incessant come and go of young people and grown-ups all willing to play with us – except an elderly person called 'Browning', who took no proper interest in the skirmishes which happened to be raging on his entry. Best of all, immeasurably, was the beloved Aunt herself reading us *The Pirate*[38] or *The*

Arabian Nights[39] of evenings, when one lay out on the big
sofas sucking toffee, and calling our cousins 'Ho, Son', or
'Daughter of my Uncle' or 'O True Believer'.

Often the Uncle, who had a 'golden voice', would assist in
our evening play, though mostly he worked at black and white
in the middle of our riots. He was never idle. We made a
draped chair in the hall serve for the seat of 'Norna of the
Fitful Head' and addressed her questions till the Uncle got
inside the rugs and gave us answers which thrilled us with
delightful shivers, in a voice deeper than all the boots in the
world. And once he descended in broad daylight with a tube of
'Mummy Brown'[40] in his hand, saying that he had discovered
it was made of dead Pharaohs and we must bury it accordingly.
So we all went out and helped – according to the rites of
Mizraim and Memphis,[41] I hope – and – to this day I could
drive a spade within a foot of where that tube lies.

At bedtime one hastened along the passages, where unfinished cartoons lay against the walls. The Uncle often painted
in their eyes first, leaving the rest in charcoal – a most effective
presentation. Hence our speed to our own top-landing, where
we could hang over the stairs and listen to the loveliest sound in
the world – deep-voiced men laughing together over dinner.

It was a jumble of delights and emotions culminating in
being allowed to blow the big organ in the studio for the beloved
Aunt, while the Uncle worked, or 'Uncle Topsy' came in full
of some business of picture-frames or stained glass or general
denunciations. Then it was hard to keep the little lead weight on
its string below the chalk-mark, and if the organ ran out in
squeals the beloved Aunt would be sorry. Never, *never* angry!

As a rule Morris took no notice of anything outside what was
in his mind at the moment. But I remember one amazing exception. My cousin Margaret and I, then about eight, were in
the nursery eating pork-dripping on brown bread, which is a
dish for the Gods, when we heard 'Uncle Topsy' in the hall
calling, as he usually did, for 'Ned' or 'Georgie'. The matter
was outside our world. So we were the more impressed when,
not finding the grown-ups, he came in and said he would tell us
a story. We settled ourselves under the table which we used for

a toboggan-slide and he, gravely as ever, climbed on to our big rocking-horse. There, slowly surging back and forth while the poor beast creaked, he told us a tale full of fascinating horrors, about a man who was condemned to dream bad dreams. One of them took the shape of a cow's tail waving from a heap of dried fish. He went away as abruptly as he had come. Long afterwards, when I was old enough to know a maker's pains, it dawned on me that we must have heard the Saga of Burnt Njal,⁴² which was then interesting him. In default of grownups, and pressed by need to pass the story between his teeth and clarify it, he had used us.

But on a certain day – one tried to fend off the thought of it – the delicious dream would end, and one would return to the House of Desolation, and for the next two or three mornings there cry on waking up. Hence more punishments and cross-examinations.

Often and often afterwards, the beloved Aunt would ask me why I had never told anyone how I was being treated. Children tell little more than animals, for what comes to them they accept as eternally established. Also, badly-treated children have a clear notion of what they are likely to get if they betray the secrets of a prison-house before they are clear of it.

In justice to the Woman I can say that I was adequately fed. (I remember a gift to her of some red 'fruit' called 'tomatoes' which, after long consideration, she boiled with sugar; and they were very beastly. The tinned meat of those days was Australian beef with a crumbly fat, and string-boiled mutton, hard to get down.) Nor was my life an unsuitable preparation for my future, in that it demanded constant wariness, the habit of observation, and attendance on moods and tempers; the noting of discrepancies between speech and action; a certain reserve of demeanour; and automatic suspicion of sudden favours. Brother Lippo Lippi,⁴³ in his own harder case, as a boy discovered:

> Why, soul and sense of him grow sharp alike,
> He learns the look of things, and none the less
> For admonition.

So it was with me.

My troubles settled themselves in a few years. My eyes went wrong, and I could not well see to read. For which reason I read the more and in bad lights. My work at the terrible little day-school [44] where I had been sent suffered in consequence, and my monthly reports showed it. The loss of 'reading-time' was the worst of my 'home' punishments for bad school-work. One report was so bad that I threw it away and said that I had never received it. But this is a hard world for the amateur liar. My web of deceit was swiftly exposed – the Son spared time after banking-hours to help in the auto-da-fé [45] – and I was well beaten and sent to school through the streets of Southsea with the placard 'Liar' [46] between my shoulders. In the long run these things, and many more of the like, drained me of any capacity for real, personal hate for the rest of my days. So close must any life-filling passion lie to its opposite. 'Who having known the Diamond will concern himself with glass?' [47]

Some sort of nervous breakdown followed, for I imagined I saw shadows and things that were not there, and they worried me more than the Woman. The beloved Aunt must have heard of it, and a man came down [48] to see me as to my eyes and reported that I was half-blind. This, too, was supposed to be 'showing off', and I was segregated from my sister – another punishment – as a sort of moral leper. Then – I do not remember that I had any warning – the Mother returned [49] from India. She told me afterwards that when she first came up to my room to kiss me good-night, I flung up an arm to guard off the cuff that I had been trained to expect.

I was taken at once from the House of Desolation, and for months ran wild in a little farm-house on the edge of Epping Forest, [50] where I was not encouraged to refer to my guilty past. Except for my spectacles, which were uncommon in those days, I was completely happy with my Mother and the local society, which included for me a gipsy of the name of Saville, who told me tales of selling horses to the ignorant; the farmer's wife; her niece Patty who turned a kind blind eye on our raids into the dairy; the postman; and the farm-boys. The farmer did not approve of my teaching one of his cows to stand and be milked in the field. My Mother drew the line at my return to meals red-booted from assisting at the slaughter of swine, or reeking after the exploration of attractive muck-heaps. These were the only restrictions I recall.

A cousin, afterwards to be a Prime Minister,[51] would come down on visits. The farmer said that we did each other 'no good'. Yet the worst I can remember was our self-sacrificing war against a wasps' nest on a muddy islet in a most muddy pond. Our only weapons were switches of broom, but we defeated the enemy unscathed. The trouble at home centred round an enormous currant roly-poly – a 'spotted dog' a foot long. We took it away to sustain us in action and we heard a great deal about it from Patty in the evening.

Then we went to London and stayed for some weeks in a tiny lodging-house in the semi-rural Brompton Road,[52] kept by an ivory-faced, lordly-whiskered ex-butler and his patient wife. Here, for the first time, it happened that the night got into my head. I rose up and wandered about that still house till daybreak, when I slipped out into the little brick-walled garden and saw the dawn break. All would have been well but for Pluto, a pet toad brought back from Epping Forest, who lived mostly in one of my pockets. It struck me that he might be thirsty, and I stole into my Mother's room and would have given him drink from a water-jug. But it slipped and broke and very much was said. The ex-butler could not understand why I had stayed awake all night. I did not know then that such night-wakings would be laid upon me through my life; or that my fortunate hour would be on the turn of sunrise, with a sou'-west breeze afoot.

The sorely tried Mother got my sister and me season-tickets for the old South Kensington Museum which was only across the road. (No need in those days to caution us against the traffic.) Very shortly we two, on account of our regular attendance (for the weather had turned wet), owned that place and one policeman in special. When we came with any grown-ups he saluted us magnificently. From the big Buddha with the little door in his back, to the towering dull-gilt ancient coaches and carven chariots in long dark corridors – even the places marked 'private' where fresh treasures were always being unpacked – we roved at will, and divided the treasures child-fashion. There were instruments of music inlaid with lapis, beryl and ivories; glorious gold-fretted spinets and clavichords; the bowels of the great Glastonbury clock; mechanical models; steel- and silver-butted pistols, daggers and arquebusses – the labels alone were an education; a collection of precious stones and rings – we quarrelled over those – and a big bluish book which was the manuscript of one of Dickens' novels.[53] That man seemed to me to have written very carelessly; leaving out lots which he had to squeeze in between the lines afterwards.

These experiences were a soaking in colour and design with, above all, the proper Museum smell; and it stayed with me. By the end of that long holiday I understood that my Mother had written verses, that my Father 'wrote things' also; that books and pictures were among the most important affairs in the world; that I could read as much as I chose and ask the meaning of things from anyone I met. I had found out, too, that one could take pen and set down what one thought, and that nobody accused one of 'showing off' by so doing. I read a good deal; *Sidonia the Sorceress*;[54] Emerson's poems;[55] and Bret Harte's stories;[56] and I learned all sorts of verses for the pleasure of repeating them to myself in bed.

Chapter 2

❴ The School before its Time ❵

1878–1882

Then came school at the far end of England. The Head of it
was a lean, slow-spoken, bearded, Arab-complexioned man
whom till then I had known as one of my Deputy-Uncles at
'The Grange' – Cormell Price,[1] otherwise 'Uncle Crom'. My
Mother, on her return to India, confided my sister and me to
the care of three dear ladies[2] who lived off the far end of
Kensington High Street over against Addison Road, in a house
filled with books, peace, kindliness, patience and what today
would be called 'culture'. But it was natural atmosphere.

One of the ladies wrote novels on her knee, by the fireside,
sitting just outside the edge of conversation, beneath two clay
pipes tied with black ribbon, which once Carlyle[3] had smoked.
All the people one was taken to see either wrote or painted
pictures or, as in the case of a Mr and Miss de Morgan,[4]
ornamented tiles. They let me play with their queer, sticky
paints. Somewhere in the background were people called Jean
Ingelow[5] and Christina Rossetti,[6] but I was never lucky
enough to see those good spirits. And there was choice in the
walls of bookshelves of anything one liked from *Firmilian*[7] to
The Moonstone and *The Woman in White*[8] and, somehow, all
Wellington's Indian Despatches,[9] which fascinated me.

These treasures were realized by me in the course of the next
few years. Meantime (Spring of '78), after my experience at
Southsea, the prospect of school did not attract. The United
Services College was in the nature of a company promoted by
poor officers and the like for the cheap education of their sons,

and set up at Westward Ho! near Bideford. It was largely a caste-school – some seventy-five per cent of us had been born outside England and hoped to follow their fathers in the Army. It was but four or five years old when I joined, and had been made up under Cormell Price's hand by drafts from Hailey-bury, whose pattern it followed, and, I think, a percentage of 'hard cases' from other schools. Even by the standards of those days, it was primitive in its appointments, and our food would now raise a mutiny in Dartmoor. I remember no time, after home tips had been spent, when we would not eat dry bread if we could steal it from the trays in the basement before tea. Yet the sick-house was permanently empty except for lawful accidents; I remember not one death of a boy; and only one epidemic – of chicken-pox. Then the Head called us together and condoled with us in such fashion that we expected immedi-ate break-up and began to cheer. But he said that, perhaps, the best thing would be to take no notice of the incident, and that he would 'work us lightly' for the rest of the term. He did and it checked the epidemic.

Naturally, Westward Ho! was brutal enough, but, setting aside the foul speech that a boy ought to learn early and put behind him by his seventeenth year, it was clean with a clean-liness that I have never heard of in any other school. I re-member no cases of even suspected perversion, and am inclined to the theory that if masters did not suspect them, and show that they suspected, there would not be quite so many elsewhere. Talking things over with Cormell Price afterwards, he con-fessed that his one prophylactic against certain unclean microbes was to 'send us to bed dead tired'. Hence the wideness of our bounds, and his deaf ear towards our incessant riots and wars between the Houses.

At the end of my first term, which was horrible, my parents could not reach England for the Easter holidays, and I had to stay up with a few big boys reading for Army Exams.[10] and a batch of youngsters whose people were very far away. I expected the worst, but when we survivors were left in the echoing form-rooms after the others had driven cheering to the station, life suddenly became a new thing (thanks to Cormell

Price). The big remote seniors turned into tolerant elder brothers, and let us small fry rove far out of bounds; shared their delicacies with us at tea; and even took an interest in our hobbies. We had no special work to do and enjoyed ourselves hugely. On the return of the school 'all smiles stopped together',[11] which was right and proper. For compensation I was given a holiday when my Father came home, and with him went to the Paris Exhibition of '78, where he was in charge of Indian Exhibits. He allowed me, at twelve years old, the full freedom of that spacious and friendly city, and the run of the Exhibition grounds and buildings. It was an education in itself; and set my life-long love for France. Also, he saw to it that I should learn to read French at least for my own amusement, and gave me Jules Verne [12] to begin with. French as an accomplishment was not well-seen at English schools in my time, and knowledge of it connoted leanings towards immorality. For myself:

> I hold it truth with him who sung
> Unpublished melodies,
> Who wakes in Paris, being young,
> O' summer, wakes in Paradise.[13]

For those who may be still interested in such matters, I wrote of this part of my life in some *Souvenirs of France*, which are very close to the facts of that time.

My first year and a half was not pleasant. The most persistent bullying comes less from the bigger boys, who merely kick and pass on, than from young devils of fourteen acting in concert against one butt. Luckily for me I was physically some years in advance of my age, and swimming in the big open sea baths, or off the Pebble Ridge, was the one accomplishment that brought me any credit. I played footer (Rugby Union), but here again my sight hampered me. I was not even in the Second Fifteen.

After my strength came suddenly to me about my fourteenth year, there was no more bullying; and either my natural sloth or past experience did not tempt me to bully in my turn. I had by then found me two friends with whom, by a carefully arranged system of mutual aids, I went up the school on co-operative principles.

How we – the originals of Stalky, M'Turk, and Beetle [14] – first came together I do not remember, but our Triple Alliance was well established before we were thirteen. We had been oppressed [15] by a large toughish boy who raided our poor little lockers. We took him on in a long, mixed rough-and-tumble, just this side of the real thing. At the end we were all-out (we worked by pressure and clinging, much as bees 'ball' a Queen) and he never troubled us again.

Turkey possessed an invincible detachment – far beyond mere insolence – towards all the world: and a tongue, when he used it, dipped in some Irish-blue acid. Moreover, he spoke, sincerely, of the masters as 'ushers', which was not without charm. His general attitude was that of Ireland in English affairs at that time.

For executive capacity, the organization of raids, reprisals, and retreats, we depended on Stalky, our Commander-in-Chief and Chief of his own Staff. He came of a household with a stern head, and, I fancy, had training in the holidays. Turkey never told us much about his belongings. He turned up, usually a day or two late, by the Irish packet, aloof, inscrutable, and contradictious. On him lay the burden of decorating our study, for he served a strange God called Ruskin. [16] We fought among ourselves 'regular an' faithful as man an' wife', but any debt which we owed elsewhere was faithfully paid by all three of us.

Our 'socialization of educational opportunities' [17] took us unscathed up the school, till the original of Little Hartopp, [18] asking one question too many, disclosed that I did not know what a cosine was and compared me to 'brute beasts'. [19] I taught Turkey all he ever knew of French, and he tried to make Stalky and me comprehend a little Latin. There is much to be said for this system, if you want a boy to learn anything, because he will remember what he gets from an equal where his master's words are forgotten. Similarly, when it was necessary to Stalky that I should get into the Choir, he taught me how to quaver 'I know a maiden fair to see' [20] by punching me in the kidneys all up and down the cricket-field. (But some small trouble over a solitaire marble pushed from beneath the hem of a robe down the choir-steps into the tiled aisle ended that venture.)

I think it was his infernal impersonality that swayed us all in our wars and peace. He saw not only us but himself from the outside, and in later life, as we met in India and elsewhere, the gift persisted. At long last, when with an equipment of doubtful Ford cars and a collection of most-mixed troops, he put up a monumental bluff against the Bolsheviks somewhere in Armenia (it is written in his *Adventures of Dunsterforce*)[21] and was as nearly as possible destroyed, he wrote to the authorities responsible. I asked him what happened. 'They told me they had no more use for my services,' said he. Naturally I condoled. 'Wrong as usual,' said the ex-Head of Number Five study. 'If any officer under *me* had written what I did to the War Office, I'd have had him broke in two twos.' That fairly sums up the man – and the boy who commanded us. I think I was a buffer state between his drivings and his tongue-lashings and his campaigns in which we were powers; and the acrid, devastating Turkey who, as I have written, 'lived and loved to destroy illusions' yet reached always after beauty. They took up room on tables that I wanted for writing; they broke into my reveries; they mocked my Gods; they stole, pawned or sold my outlying or neglected possessions; and – I could not have gone on a week without them nor they without me.

But my revenge was ample. I have said I was physically precocious. In my last term I had been thrusting an unlovely chin at C— in form. At last he blew up, protested he could no longer abide the sight, and ordered me to shave. I carried this word to my House-master.[22] He, who had long looked on me as a cultivated sink of iniquities, brooded over this confirmation of his suspicions, and gave me a written order on a Bideford barber for a razor, etc. I kindly invited my friends to come and help, and lamented for three miles the burden of compulsory shaving. There were no *ripostes*.[23] There was no ribaldry. But why Stalky and Turkey did not cut their throats experimenting with the apparatus I do not understand.

We will now return to the savage life in which all these prodigious events 'transpired'.

We smoked, of course, but the penalties of discovery were heavy because the Prefects, who were all of the 'Army Class' up for the Sandhurst or Woolwich Preliminary,[24] were allowed under restrictions to smoke pipes. If any of the rank and file were caught smoking, they came up before the Prefects, not on moral grounds, but for usurping the privileges of the Ruling Caste. The classic phrase was: 'You esteem yourself to be a Prefect, do you? *All* right. Come to my study at six, please.' This seemed to work better than religious lectures and even expulsions which some establishments used to deal out for this dread sin.

Oddly enough 'fagging' did not exist, though the name 'fag' was regularly used as a term of contempt and sign of subordination against the Lower School. If one needed a 'varlet' to clean things in a study or run errands, that was a matter for private bargaining in our only currency – food. Sometimes such service gave protection, in the sense that it was distinct cheek to oppress an accredited 'varlet'. I never served thus, owing to my untidiness; but our study entertained one sporadically, and to him we three expounded all housewifely duties. But, as a rule, Turkey would tidy up like the old maid to whom we always compared him.

Games were compulsory unless written excuse were furnished by competent authority. The penalty for wilful shirking was three cuts with a ground-ash from the Prefect of Games. One of the most difficult things to explain to some people is that a boy of seventeen or eighteen can thus beat a boy barely a year his junior, and on the heels of the punishment go for a walk with him; neither party bearing malice or pride.

So too in the War of '14 to '18 young gentlemen found it hard to understand that the Adjutant who poured vitriol on their heads at Parade, but was polite and friendly at Mess, was not sucking up to them to make amends for previous rudeness.

Except in the case of two House-masters I do not recall being lectured or preached at on morals or virtue. It is not always expedient to excite a growing youth's religious emotions, because one set of nerves seems to communicate with others, and Heaven knows what mines a 'pi-jaw'[25] may touch off. But there were no doors to our bare windy dormitories, nor any sort of lock on the form-rooms. Our masters, with one exception [26] who lived outside, were unmarried. The school buildings, originally cheap lodging-houses, made one straight bar against a hillside, and the boys circulated up and down in front of it. A penal battalion could not have been more perfectly policed, though that we did not realize. Mercifully we knew little outside the immediate burden of the day and the necessity for getting into the Army. I think, then, that when we worked we worked harder than most schools.

My House-master was deeply conscientious and cumbered about with many cares for his charges. What he accomplished thereby I know not. His errors sprang from pure and excessive goodness. Me and my companions he always darkly and deeply suspected. Realizing this, we little beasts made him sweat, which he did on slight provocation.

My main interest as I grew older was C—,[27] my English and Classics Master, a rowing-man of splendid physique, and a scholar who lived in secret hope of translating Theocritus [28] worthily. He had a violent temper, no disadvantage in handling boys used to direct speech, and a gift of schoolmaster's 'sarcasm' which must have been a relief to him and was certainly a treasure-trove to me. Also he was a good and House-proud House-master. Under him I came to feel that words could be used as weapons, for he did me the honour to talk at me plentifully; and our year-in year-out form-room bickerings gave us both something to play with. One learns more from a good scholar in a rage than from a score of lucid and laborious drudges; and to be made the butt of one's companions in full form is no bad preparation for later experiences. I think this 'approach' is now discouraged for fear of hurting the soul of youth, but in essence it is no more than rattling tins or firing squibs under a colt's nose. I remember nothing save satisfaction or envy when C— broke his precious ointments over my head.

I tried to give a pale rendering of his style when heated in a 'Stalky' tale, 'Regulus',[29] but I wish I could have presented him as he blazed forth once on the great Cleopatra Ode – the

27th of the Third Book.[30] I had detonated him by a very vile construe of the first few lines. Having slain me, he charged over my corpse and delivered an interpretation of the rest of the Ode unequalled for power and insight. He held even the Army Class breathless.

There must be still masters of the same sincerity; and gramophone records of such good men, on the brink of profanity, struggling with a Latin form, would be more helpful to education than bushels of printed books. C— taught me to loathe Horace[31] for two years; to forget him for twenty, and then to love him for the rest of my days and through many sleepless nights.

After my second year at school, the tide of writing set in. In my holidays the three ladies listened – it was all I wanted – to anything I had to say. I drew on their books, from *The City of Dreadful Night*[32] which shook me to my unformed core, Mrs Gatty's *Parables from Nature*[33] which I imitated and thought I was original, and scores of others. There were few atrocities of form or metre that I did not perpetrate and I enjoyed them all.

I discovered, also, that personal and well-pointed limericks on my companions worked well, and I and a red-nosed boy of uncertain temper exploited the idea – not without dust and heat; next, that the metre of *Hiawatha*[34] saved one all bother about rhyme: and that there had been a man called Dante[35] who, living in a small Italian town at general issue with his neighbours, had invented for most of them lively torments in a nine-ringed Hell, where he exhibited them to after-ages. C— said, 'He must have made himself infernally unpopular.' I combined my authorities.

I bought a fat, American–cloth-bound note-book, and set to work on an *Inferno*, into which I put, under appropriate torture, all my friends and most of the masters. This was really remunerative because one could chant his future doom to a victim walking below the windows of the study which I with my two companions now possessed. Then, 'as rare things will',[36] my book vanished, and I lost interest in the *Hiawatha* metre.

Tennyson and *Aurora Leigh*[37] came in the way of nature to me in the holidays, and C— in form once literally threw *Men and Women* at my head. Here I found 'The Bishop orders his Tomb', 'Love among the Ruins' and 'Fra Lippo Lippi', a not too remote – I dare to think – ancestor of mine.

Swinburne's poems I must have come across first at the Aunt's. He did not strike my very young mind as 'anything in particular' till I read *Atalanta in Calydon*,[38] and one verse of verses which exactly set the time for my side-stroke when I bathed in the big rollers off the Ridge. As thus:

> Who shall *seek* thee and *bring*
>   And *restore* thee thy *day* [*Half roll*]
> When the *dove* dipt her *wing*
>   And the *oars* won their *way* [*Other half roll*]
> Where the narrowing Symplegades whitened the
>   Straits of Propontis with spray? [*Carry on with the impetus*]

If you can time the last line of it to end with a long roller crashing on your head, the cadence is complete. I even forgave Bret Harte, to whom I owed many things, for taking that metre in vain in his 'Heathen Chinee'. But I never forgave C— for bringing the fact to my notice.

Not till years later – talking things over with my 'Uncle Crom'– did I realize that injustices of this sort were not without intention. 'You needed a tight hand in those days,' he drawled. 'C— gave it to you.' 'He did,' said I, 'and so did H—,' the married master whom the school thoroughly feared.

'I remember *that*,' Crom answered. 'Yes, that was me too.' This had been an affair of an Essay – 'A Day in the Holidays,' or something of that nature. C— had set it but the papers were to be marked by H—. My essay was of variegated but constant vileness, modelled, I fancy, on holiday readings of a journal called *The Pink 'Un*.[39] Even I had never done anything worse. Normally H—'s markings would have been sent in to C— without comment. On this occasion, however (I was in Latin form at the time), H— entered and asked for the floor. C— yielded it to him with a grin. H— then told me off before my delighted companions in his best style, which was acid and contumelious. He wound up by a few general remarks about dying as a 'scurrilous journalist'. (I think now that H—

too may have read *The Pink 'Un*.) The tone, matter, and setting of his discourse were as brutal as they were meant to be – brutal as the necessary wrench on the curb that fetches up a too-flippant colt. C— added a rider or two after H— had left.

(But it pleased Allah to afflict H— in after years. I met him in charge of a 'mixed' College in New Zealand, where he taught a class of young ladies Latinity. 'And when they make false quantities, like *you* used to, they make – eyes at me!' I thought of my chill mornings at Greek Testament under his ready hand, and pitied him from the bottom of my soul.)

Yes – I must have been 'nursed' with care by Crom and under his orders. Hence, when he saw I was irretrievably committed to the ink-pot, his order that I should edit the School Paper[40] and have the run of his Library Study. Hence, I presume, C—'s similar permission, granted and withdrawn as the fortunes of our private war varied. Hence the Head's idea that I should learn Russian with him (I got as far as some of the cardinal numbers) and, later, *précis*-writing. This latter meant severe compression of dry-as-dust material, no essential fact to be omitted. The whole was sweetened with reminiscences of the men of Crom's youth,[41] and throughout the low, soft drawl and the smoke of his perpetual Vevey[42] he shed light on the handling of words. Heaven forgive me! I thought these privileges were due to my transcendent personal merits.

Many of us loved the Head for what he had done for us, but I owed him more than all of them put together; and I think I loved him even more than they did. There came a day when he told me that a fortnight after the close of the summer holidays of '82, I would go to India to work on a paper in Lahore, where my parents lived, and would get one hundred silver rupees a month! At term-end he most unjustly devised a prize poem – subject 'The Battle of Assaye'[43] which, there being no competitor, I won in what I conceived was the metre of my latest 'infection' – Joaquin Miller.[49] And when I took the prize-book, Trevelyan's *Competition Wallah*,[45] Crom Price said that if I went on I might be heard of again.

I spent my last few days before sailing with the beloved Aunt in the little cottage that the Burne-Joneses had bought for a holiday house at Rottingdean. There I looked across the village green and the horse-pond at a house called 'The Elms' behind a flint wall, and at a church opposite; and – had I known it – at 'The bodies of those to be In the Houses of Death and of Birth.'[46]

Chapter 3

❴ Seven Years' Hard [1] ❵

> I am poor Brother Lippo by your leave.
> You need not clap your torches to my face.
> *Fra Lippo Lippi.*

So, at sixteen years and nine months, but looking four or five years older, and adorned with real whiskers which the scandalized Mother abolished within one hour of beholding, I found myself at Bombay [2] where I was born, moving among sights and smells that made me deliver in the vernacular sentences whose meaning I knew not. Other Indian-born boys have told me how the same thing happened to them.

There were yet three or four days' rail to Lahore, where my people lived. After these, my English years fell away, nor ever, I think, came back in full strength.

That was a joyous home-coming. For – consider! – I had returned to a Father and Mother of whom I had seen but little since my sixth year. I might have found my Mother 'the sort of woman *I* don't care for', as in one terrible case that I know; and my Father intolerable. But the Mother proved more delightful than all my imaginings or memories. My Father was not only a mine of knowledge and help, but a humorous, tolerant, and expert fellow-craftsman. I had my own room in the house; my servant, handed over to me by my father's servant, whose son he was, with the solemnity of a marriage-contract; my own horse, cart, and groom; my own office-hours and direct responsibilities; and – oh, joy! – my own office-box, just like my Father's, which he took daily to the Lahore Museum and School of Art. [3] I do not remember the smallest friction in any detail of our lives. We delighted more in each other's society than in that of strangers; and when my sister came out, a little later, our cup was filled to the brim. Not only were we happy, but we knew it.

But the work was heavy. I represented fifty per cent of the 'editorial staff' of the one daily paper [4] of the Punjab – a small sister of the great *Pioneer* at Allahabad under the same proprietorship. And a daily paper comes out every day even though fifty per cent of the staff have fever.

My Chief took me in hand, and for three years or so I loathed him. He had to break me in, and I knew nothing. What he suffered on my account I cannot tell; but the little that I ever acquired of accuracy, the habit of trying at least to verify references, and some knack of sticking to desk-work, I owed wholly to Stephen Wheeler.

I never worked less than ten hours and seldom more than fifteen per diem;[5] and as our paper came out in the evening did not see the midday sun except on Sundays. I had fever too, regular and persistent, to which I added for a while chronic dysentery. Yet I discovered that a man can work with a temperature of 104, even though next day he has to ask the office who wrote the article. Our native Foreman, on the News side, Mian Rukn Din, a Muhammedan gentleman of kind heart and infinite patience, whom I never saw unequal to a situation, was my loyal friend throughout. From the modern point of view I suppose the life was not fit for a dog, but my world was filled with boys, but a few years older than I, who lived utterly alone, and died from typhoid mostly at the regulation age of twenty-two. As regarding ourselves at home, if there were any dying to be done, we four were together. The rest was in the day's work, with love to sweeten all things.

Books, plays, pictures, and amusements, outside what games the cold weather allowed, there were none. Transport was limited to horses and such railways as existed. This meant that one's normal radius of travel would be about six miles in any direction, and – one did not meet new white faces at every six miles. Death was always our near companion. When there was an outbreak [6] of eleven cases of typhoid in our white community of seventy, and professional nurses had not been invented, the men sat up with the men and the women with the women. We lost four of our invalids and thought we had done well. Otherwise, men and women dropped where they stood. Hence our custom of looking up anyone who did not appear at our daily gatherings.

The dead of all times were about us – in the vast forgotten Muslim cemeteries round the Station, where one's horse's hoof of a morning might break through to the corpse below; skulls and bones tumbled out of our mud garden walls, and were turned up among the flowers by the Rains; and at every point were tombs of the dead. Our chief picnic rendezvous and some of our public offices had been memorials to desired dead women; and Fort Lahore,[7] where Runjit Singh's wives[8] lay, was a mausoleum of ghosts.

This was the setting in which my world revolved. Its centre for me – a member at seventeen – was the Punjab Club, where bachelors, for the most part, gathered to eat meals of no merit among men whose merits they knew well. My Chief was married and came there seldom, so it was mine to be told every evening of the faults of that day's issue in very simple language. Our native compositors 'followed copy' without knowing one word of English. Hence glorious and sometimes obscene misprints. Our proof-readers (sometimes we had a brace of them) drank, which was expected; but systematic and prolonged D.T.[9] on their part gave me more than my share of their work. And in that Club and elsewhere I met none except picked men at their definite work – Civilians, Army, Education, Canals, Forestry, Engineering, Irrigation, Railways, Doctors, and Lawyers – samples of each branch and each talking his own shop. It follows then that that 'show of technical knowledge' for which I was blamed later came to me from the horse's mouth, even to boredom.

So soon as my paper could trust me a little, and I had behaved well at routine work, I was sent out, first for local reportings; then to race-meetings which included curious nights in the lottery-tent. (I saw one go up in flame once, when a heated owner hove an oil-lamp at the handicapper on the night the owner was coming up for election at the Club. That was the first and last time I had seen every available black ball expended and members begging for more.) Later I described openings of big bridges [10] and such-like, which meant a night or two with the engineers; floods on railways [11] – more nights in the wet with wretched heads of repair gangs; village festivals and consequent outbreaks of cholera or small-pox; communal riots [12] under the shadow of the Mosque of Wazir Khan, [13] where the patient waiting troops lay in timber-yards or side-alleys till the order came to go in and hit the crowds on the feet with the gun-butt (killing in Civil Administration was then reckoned confession of failure), and the growling, flaring, creed-drunk city would be brought to hand without effusion of blood, or the appearance of any agitated Viceroy; visits of Viceroys [14] to neighbouring Princes on the edge of the great Indian Desert, where a man might have to wash his raw hands and face in soda-water; reviews of Armies expecting to move against Russia [15] next week; receptions of an Afghan Potentate, [16] with whom the Indian Government wished to stand well (this included a walk into the Khyber, where I was shot at, but without malice, by a rapparee [17] who disapproved of his ruler's foreign policy); murder and divorce trials, and (a really filthy job) an inquiry [18] into the percentage of lepers among the butchers who supplied beef and mutton to the European community of Lahore. (Here I first learned that crude statements of crude facts are not well-seen by responsible official authorities.) It was Squeers' method [19] of instruction, but how could I fail to be equipped with more than all I might need? I was saturated with it, and if I tripped over detail, the Club attended to me.

My first bribe [20] was offered to me at the age of nineteen when I was in a Native State where, naturally, one concern of the Administration was to get more guns of honour added to the Ruler's official salute when he visited British India, and even a roving correspondent's good word might be useful. Hence in the basket of fruits (*dali* is its name) laid at my tent door each morning, a five-hundred-rupee note and a Cashmere shawl. As the sender was of high caste I returned the gift at the hands of the camp-sweeper, who was not. Upon this my servant, responsible to his father, and mine, for my well-being, said without emotion: 'Till we get home you eat and drink from my hands.' This I did.

On return to work I found my Chief had fever, and I was in sole charge. Among his editorial correspondence was a letter from this Native State setting forth the record during a few days' visit of 'your reporter, a person called Kipling'; who had broken, it seemed, the Decalogue [21] in every detail from rape to theft. I wrote back that as Acting-Editor I had received the complaints and would investigate, but they must expect me to be biassed because I was the person complained of.

I visited the State more than once later, and there was not a cloud on our relations. I had dealt with the insult *more Asiatico* [22] – which *they* understood; the ball had been returned *more Asiatico* – which *I* understood; and the incident had been closed.

My second bribe came when I worked under Stephen Wheeler's successor, Kay Robinson, [23] brother of Phil Robinson who wrote *In My Indian Garden*. With him, thanks to his predecessor having licked me into some shape, my relations were genial. It was the old matter of gun-salutes again; the old machinery of the basket of fruit and shawls and money for us both, but this time left impudently on the office verandah. Kay and I wasted a happy half-hour pricking '*Timeo Danaos et dona ferentes*' [24] into the currency notes, mourned that we could not take either them or the shawls, and let the matter go.

My third and most interesting bribe was when reporting a divorce case in Eurasian [25] society. An immense brown woman penned me in a corner and offered 'if I would but keep her name out of it' to give me most intimate details, which she began at once to do. I demanded her name before bargaining. 'Oah! I am the Respondent. Thatt is why I ask you.' It is hard to report some dramas without Ophelias if not Hamlets. But I was repaid for her anger when Counsel asked her if she had ever expressed a desire to dance on her husband's grave. Till then she had denied everything. 'Yess,' she hissed, 'and I jolly-damn-well *would* too.'

A soldier of my acquaintance had been sentenced to life-imprisonment for a murder which, on evidence not before the court, seemed to me rather justified. I saw him later in Lahore gaol at work on some complicated arrangement of nibs with different coloured inks, stuck into a sort of loom which, drawn over paper, gave the ruling for the blank forms of financial statements. It seemed wickedly monotonous. But the spirit of man is undefeatable. 'If I made a mistake of an eighth of an inch in spacing these lines, I'd throw out *all* the accounts of the Upper Punjab,' said he.

As to our reading public, they were at the least as well educated as fifty per cent of our 'staff'; and by force of their lives could not be stampeded or much 'thrilled'. Double head-lines we had never heard of, nor special type, and I fear that the amount of 'white' in the newspapers today would have struck us as common cheating. Yet the stuff we dealt in would have furnished modern journals of enterprise with almost daily sensations.

My legitimate office-work was sub-editing, which meant eternal cuttings-down of unwieldly contributions – such as discourses on abstruse questions of Revenue and Assessment from a great and wise Civilian who wrote the vilest hand that even our compositors ever saw; literary articles about Milton. (And how was I to know that the writer was a relative of one of our proprietors, who thought our paper existed to air his theories?) Here Crom Price's training in *précis*-work helped me to get swiftly at what meat there might be in the disorderly messes. There were newspaper exchanges from Egypt to Hong Kong to be skimmed nearly every morning and, once a week, the English papers on which one drew in time of need; local correspondence from out-stations to vet for possible libels in their innocent allusions; 'spoofing' letters from subalterns to be guarded against (twice I was trapped here); always, of course, the filing of cables, and woe betide an error then! I took them down from the telephone – a primitive and mysterious power whose native operator broke every word into monosyllables. One cut-and-come-again affliction was an accursed Muscovite paper, the *Novoie Vremya*,[26] written in French, which, for weeks and weeks, published the war diaries of Alikhanoff, a Russian General then harrying the Central Russian Khanates. He gave the name of every camp he halted at, and regularly reported that his troops warmed themselves at fires of *sax-aul*,[27] which I suppose is perhaps sage-brush. A week after I had translated the last of the series every remembrance of it passed from my normal memory.

Ten or twelve years later,[28] I fell sick in New York and passed through a long delirium which, by ill-chance, I remembered when I returned to life. At one stage of it I led an enormous force of cavalry mounted on red horses with brand-new leather saddles, under the glare of a green moon, across steppes so vast that they revealed the very curve of earth. We would halt at one of the camps named by Alikhanoff in his diary (I would see the name of it heaving up over the edge of the planet), where we warmed ourselves at fires of *sax-aul*, and where, scorched on one side and frozen on the other, I sat till my infernal squadrons went on again to the next fore-known halt; and so through the list.

In the early 'Eighties a Liberal Government[29] had come into power at Home and was acting on liberal 'principle', which so far as I have observed ends not seldom in bloodshed. Just then, it was a matter of principle[30] that Native Judges should try white women. Native in this case meant overwhelmingly Hindu; and the Hindu's idea of women is not lofty. No one had asked for any such measure – least of all the Judiciary concerned. But principle is principle, though the streets swim. The European community were much annoyed. They went to the extremity of revolt – that is to say even the officials of the Service and their wives very often would not attend the functions and levées of the then Viceroy,[31] a circular and bewildered recluse of religious tendencies. A pleasant English gentleman called C. P. Ilbert[32] had been imported to father and god-father the Bill. I think he, too, was a little bewildered. Our paper, like most of the European Press, began with stern disapproval of the measure, and, I fancy, published much comment and correspondence which would now be called 'disloyal'.

One evening, while putting the paper to bed, I looked as

usual over the leader. It was the sort of false-balanced, semi-judicial stuff that some English journals wrote about the Indian White Paper [33] from 1932 to '34, and like them it furnished a barely disguised exposition of the Government's high ideals. In after-life one got to know that touch better, but it astonished me at the time, and I asked my Chief what it all meant. He replied, as I should have done in his place: 'None of your dam' business,' and, being married, went to his home. I repaired to the Club which, remember, was the whole of my outside world.

As I entered the long, shabby dining-room where we all sat at one table, everyone hissed. I was innocent enough to ask: 'What's the joke? Who are they hissing?' 'You,' said the man at my side. 'Your dam' rag has ratted over the Bill.'

It is not pleasant to sit still when one is twenty [34] while all your universe hisses you. Then uprose a Captain, our Adjutant of Volunteers, and said: 'Stop that! The boy's only doing what he's paid to do.' The demonstration tailed off, but I had seen a great light. The Adjutant was entirely correct. I was a hireling, paid to do what I was paid to do, and – I did not relish the idea. Someone said kindly: 'You damned young ass! Don't you know that your paper has the Government printing-contract?' I *did* know it, but I had never before put two and two together.

A few months later one of my two chief proprietors received the decoration [35] that made him a Knight. Then I began to take much interest in certain smooth Civilians, who had seen good in the Government measure and had somehow been shifted out of the heat to billets in Simla. [36] I followed under shrewd guidance, often native, the many pretty ways by which a Government can put veiled pressure on its employees in a land where every circumstance *and* relation of a man's life is public property. So, when the great and epoch-making India Bill [37] turned up fifty years later, I felt as one re-treading the tortuous byways of his youth. One recognized the very phrases and assurances of the old days still doing good work, and waited, as in a dream, for the very slightly altered formulas in which those who were parting with their convictions excused themselves. Thus: 'I may act as a brake, you know. At any rate I'm keeping a more extreme man out of the game.' 'There's no sense running counter to the inevitable,' – and all the other Devil-provided camouflage for the sinner-who-faces-both-ways.

In '85 I was made a Freemason[38] by dispensation (Lodge Hope and Perseverance 782 E.C.), being under age, because the Lodge hoped for a good Secretary. They did not get him, but I helped, and got the Father to advise, in decorating the bare walls of the Masonic Hall with hangings after the prescription of Solomon's Temple. Here I met Muslims, Hindus, Sikhs, members of the Arya and Brahmo Samaj,[39] and a Jew Tyler,[40] who was priest and butcher to his little community in the city. So yet another world opened to me which I needed.

My Mother and Sister would go up to the Hills[41] for the hot weather, and in due course my Father too. My own holiday came when I could be spared. Thus I often lived alone in the big house, where I commanded by choice native food, as less revolting than meat-cookery, and so added indigestion to my more intimate possessions.

In those months – mid-April to mid-October – one took up one's bed and walked[42] about with it from room to room, seeking for less heated air; or slept on the flat roof with the waterman to throw half-skinfuls of water on one's parched carcase. This brought on fever but saved heat-stroke.

Often the night got into my head as it had done in the boarding-house in the Brompton Road, and I would wander till dawn in all manner of odd places – liquor-shops, gambling- and opium-dens, which are not a bit mysterious, wayside entertainments such as puppet-shows, native dances; or in and about the narrow gullies under the Mosque of Wazir Khan for the sheer sake of looking. Sometimes, the Police would challenge, but I knew most of their officers, and many folk in some quarters knew me for the son of my Father, which in the East more than anywhere else is useful. Otherwise, the word 'News-paper' sufficed; though I did not supply my paper with many accounts of these prowls. One would come home, just as the light broke, in some night-hawk of a hired carriage which stank of hookah-fumes, jasmine-flowers, and sandalwood; and if the driver were moved to talk, he told one a good deal. Much of real Indian life goes on in the hot-weather nights. That is why the native staff of the offices are not much use next morning. All native offices aestivate from May at least till September. Files and correspondence are then as a matter of course pitched unopened into corners, to be written up or faked when the weather gets cooler. But the English who go Home on leave, having imposed the set hours of a northern working day upon the children of children, are surprised that India does not work as they do. This is one of the reasons why autonomous India will be interesting.

And there were 'wet' nights too at the Club [43] or one Mess, when a table-ful of boys, half-crazed with discomfort, but with just sense enough to stick to beer and bones which seldom betray, tried to rejoice and somehow succeeded. I remember one night when we ate tinned haggis with cholera in the cantonments 'to see what would happen', and another when a savage stallion in harness was presented with a very hot leg of roast mutton, as he snapped. Theoretically this is a cure for biting, but it only made him more of a cannibal.

I got to meet the soldiery of those days in visits to Fort Lahore and, in a less degree, at Mian Mir Cantonments. [44] My first and best beloved Battalion was the 2nd Fifth Fusiliers, with whom I dined in awed silence a few weeks after I came out. When they left I took up with their successors, the 30th East Lancashire, another North-country regiment; and, last, with the 31st East Surrey – a London recruited confederacy of skilful dog-stealers, some of them my good and loyal friends. There were ghostly dinners, too, with Subalterns in charge of the Infantry Detachment at Fort Lahore, where, all among marble-inlaid, empty apartments of dead Queens, or under the domes of old tombs, meals began with the regulation thirty grains of quinine in the sherry, and ended – as Allah pleased!

I am, by the way, one of the few civilians who have turned out a Quarter-Guard of Her Majesty's troops. It was on a chill winter morn, about 2 a.m. at the Fort, and though I suppose I had been given the countersign on my departure from the Mess, I forgot it ere I reached the Main Guard, and when challenged announced myself spaciously as 'Visiting Rounds'. When the men had clattered out I asked the Sergeant if he had ever seen a finer collection of scoundrels. That cost me beer by the gallon, but it was worth it.

Having no position to consider, and my trade enforcing it, I could move at will in the fourth dimension.[45] I came to realize the bare horrors of the private's life, and the unnecessary torments he endured on account of the Christian doctrine which lays down that 'the wages of sin is death'.[46] It was counted impious that bazaar prostitutes should be inspected; or that the men should be taught elementary precautions in their dealings with them. This official virtue cost our Army in India nine thousand expensive white men a year always laid up from venereal disease. Visits to Lock Hospitals[47] made me desire, as earnestly as I do today, that I might have six hundred priests – Bishops of the Establishment for choice – to handle for six months precisely as the soldiers of my youth were handled.

Heaven knows the men died fast enough from typhoid, which seemed to have something to do with water, but we were not sure; or from cholera, which was manifestly a breath of the Devil that could kill all on one side of a barrack-room and spare the others; from seasonal fever; or from what was described as 'blood-poisoning'.

Lord Roberts,[48] at that time Commander-in-Chief in India, who knew my people, was interested in the men, and – I had by then written one or two stories about soldiers[49] – the proudest moment of my young life was when I rode up Simla Mall beside him on his usual explosive red Arab, while he asked me what the men thought about their accommodation, enter-tainment-rooms and the like. I told him, and he thanked me as gravely as though I had been a full Colonel.

My month's leave at Simla, or whatever Hill Station my people went to, was pure joy – every golden hour counted. It began in heat and discomfort, by rail and road. It ended in the cool evening, with a wood fire in one's bedroom, and next morn – thirty more of them ahead! – the early cup of tea, the Mother who brought it in, and the long talks of us all together again. One had leisure to work, too, at whatever play-work was in one's head, and that was usually full.

Simla was another new world. There the Hierarchy lived,

and one saw and heard the machinery of administration stripped bare. There were the Heads of the Viceregal and Military staffs and their Aides-de-Camp; and playing whist with Great Ones, who gave him special news, was the Correspondent [50] of our big sister-paper the *Pioneer*, then a power in the land.

The dates, but not the pictures, of those holidays are blurred. At one time our little world was full of the aftermaths of Theosophy as taught by Madame Blavatsky [51] to her devotees. My Father knew the lady and, with her, would discuss wholly secular subjects; she being, he told me, one of the most interesting and unscrupulous impostors he had ever met. This, with his experience, was a high compliment. I was not so fortunate, but came across queer, bewildered, old people, who lived in an atmosphere of 'manifestations' running about their houses. But the earliest days of Theosophy devastated the *Pioneer*, whose Editor [52] became a devout believer, and used the paper for propaganda to an extent which got on the nerves not only of the public but of a proof-reader, who at the last moment salted an impassioned leader on the subject with, in brackets: *'What do you bet this is a dam' lie?'* The Editor was most untheosophically angry!

On one of my Simla leaves [53] – I had been ill with dysentery again – I was sent off for rest along the Himalaya–Tibet road in the company of an invalid officer and his wife. My equipment was my servant – he from whose hands I had fed in the Native State before-mentioned; Dorothea Darbishoff, *alias* Dolly Bobs, a temperamental she-pony; and four baggage-coolies who were recruited and changed at each stage. I knew the edge of the great Hills both from Simla and Dalhousie, but had never marched any distance into them. They were to me a revelation of 'all might, majesty, dominion, and power, henceforth and for ever', [54] in colour, form, and substance indescribable. A little of what I realized then came back to me in *Kim*.

On the day I turned back for Simla – my companions were going further – my servant embroiled himself with a new quartette of coolies and managed to cut the eye of one of them. I was a few score miles from the nearest white man, and did not wish to be haled before any little Hill Rajah, knowing as I did that the coolies would unitedly swear that I had directed the outrage. I therefore paid blood-money, and strategically withdrew – on foot for the most part because Dolly Bobs objected to every sight and most of the smells of the landscape. I had to keep the coolies, who, like the politicians, would not stay put, in front of me on the six-foot-wide track, and, as is ever the case when one is in difficulties, it set in to rain. My urgent business was to make my first three days' march in one – a matter of thirty odd miles. My coolies wanted to shy off to their village and spend their ill-gotten silver. On me developed the heart-breaking job of shepherding a retreat. I do not think my mileage that day could have been much less than forty miles of sheer up-hill and down-dale slogging. But it did me great good, and enabled me to put away bottles of strong Army beer at the wet evening's end in the resthouse. On our last day, a thunderstorm, which had been at work a few thousand feet below us, rose to the level of the ridge we were crossing and exploded in our midst. We were all flung on our faces, and when I was able to see again I observed the half of a well-grown pine, as neatly split lengthwise as a match by a penknife, in the act of hirpling down the steep hillside by itself. The thunder drowned everything, so that it seemed to be posturing in dumb show, and when it began to hop – horrible vertical hops – the effect was of pure D.T. My coolies, however, who had had the tale of my misdeeds from their predecessors, argued that if the local Gods missed such a sitting shot as I had given them, I could not be altogether unlucky.

It was on this trip that I saw a happy family of four bears out for a walk together, all talking at the tops of their voices; and also – the sun on his wings, a thousand feet below me – I stared long at a wheeling eagle, himself thousands of feet above the map-like valley he was quartering.

On my return I handed my servant over to his father, who dealt faithfully with him for having imperilled my Father's son. But what I did *not* tell him was that my servant, a Punjabi Muslim, had in his first panic embraced the feet of the injured hill-coolie, a heathen, and begged him to 'show mercy'. A servant, precisely because he is a servant, has his *izzat* – his honour – or, as the Chinese say, his 'face'. Save that, and he is yours. One should never rate one's man before others; nor, if he knows that you know the implication of the words that you are using on him, should you ever use certain words and phrases. But to a young man raw from England, or to an old one in whose service one has grown grey, anything is permitted. In the first case: 'He is a youngster. He slangs as his girl has taught him,' and the man keeps his countenance even though his master's worst words are inflected woman-fashion. In the second case, the aged servitor and deputy-conscience says: 'It is naught. We were young men together. Ah! you should have heard him *then*!'

The reward for this very small consideration is service of a kind that one accepted as a matter of course – till one was without it. My man would go monthly to the local Bank and draw my pay in coined rupees, which he would carry home raw in his waist-band, as the whole bazaar knew, and decant into an old wardrobe, whence I would draw for my needs till there remained no more.

Yet, it was necessary to his professional honour that he should present me monthly a list of petty disbursements on my personal behalf – such as oil for the buggy-lamps, bootlaces, thread for darning my socks, buttons replaced and the like – all written out in bazaar-English by the letter-writer at the corner of the road. The total rose, of course, with my pay, and on each rupee of this bill my man took the commission of the East, say one-sixteenth or perhaps one-tenth of each rupee.

For the rest, till I was in my twenty-fourth year, I no more dreamed of dressing myself than I did of shutting an inner door or – I was going to say turning a key in a lock. But we had no locks. I gave myself indeed the trouble of stepping into the garments that were held out to me after my bath, and out of them as I was assisted to do. And – luxury of which I dream still – I was shaved before I was awake!

One must set these things against the taste of fever in one's mouth, and the buzz of quinine in one's ears; the temper frayed by heat to breaking-point but for sanity's sake held back from the break; the descending darkness of intolerable dusks; and the less supportable dawns of fierce, stale heat through half of the year.

When my people were at the Hills and I was alone, my Father's butler took command. One peril of solitary life is going to seed in details of living. As our numbers at the Club shrank between April and mid-September, men grew careless, till at last our conscience-stricken Secretary, himself an offender, would fetch us up with a jerk, and forbid us dining in little more than singlet and riding-breeches.

This temptation was stronger in one's own house, though one knew if one broke the ritual of dressing for the last meal one was parting with a sheet-anchor. (Young gentlemen of larger views today consider this 'dress-for-dinner' business as an affectation ranking with 'the old school tie'. I would give some months' pay for the privilege of enlightening them.) Here the butler would take charge. 'For the honour of the house there must be a dinner. It is long since the Sahib has bidden friends to eat.' I would protest like a fretful child. He would reply: 'Except for the names of the Sahibs to be invited all things are on *my* head.' So one dug up four or five companions in discomfort; the pitiful, scorched marigold blooms would appear on the table and, to a full accompaniment of glass, silver, and napery, the ritual would be worked through, and the butler's honour satisfied for a while.

At the Club, sudden causeless hates flared up between friends and died down like straw fires; old grievances were recalled and brooded over aloud; the complaint-book bristled with accusations and inventions. All of which came to nothing when the first Rains fell, and after a three days' siege of creeping and crawling things, whose bodies stopped our billiards and almost put out the lamps they sizzled in, life picked up in the blessed cool.

But it was a strange life. Once, suddenly, in the Club ante-room a man asked a neighbour to pass him the newspaper. 'Get it yourself,' was the hot-weather answer. The man rose but on his way to the table dropped and writhed in the first grip of cholera. He was carried to his quarters, the Doctor came, and for three days he went through all the stages of the disease even to the characteristic baring of discoloured gums. Then he returned to life and, on being condoled with, said: 'I remember getting up to get the paper, but after that, give you my word, I don't remember a thing till I heard Lawrie say that I was coming out of it.' I have heard since that oblivion is sometimes vouchsafed.

Though I was spared the worst horrors, thanks to the pressure of work, a capacity for being able to read, and the pleasure of writing what my head was filled with, I felt each succeeding hot weather more and more, and cowered in my soul as it returned.

This is fit place for a 'pivot' experience to be set side by side with the affair of the Adjutant of Volunteers at the Club. It happened one hot-weather evening, in '86 or thereabouts, when I felt that I had come to the edge of all endurance. As I entered my empty house in the dusk there was no more in me except the horror of a great darkness, that I must have been fighting for some days. I came through that darkness alive, but how I do not know. Late at night I picked up a book by Walter Besant which was called *All in a Garden Fair*.[55] It dealt with a young man who desired to write; who came to realize the possibilities of common things seen, and who eventually succeeded in his desire. What its merits may be from today's 'literary' standpoint I do not know. But I *do* know that that book was my salvation in sore personal need, and with the reading and re-reading it became to me a revelation, a hope and strength. I was certainly, I argued, as well equipped as the hero and – and – after all, there was no need for me to stay here for ever. I could go away and measure myself against the doorsills of London as soon as I had money. Therefore I would begin to save money, for I perceived there was absolutely no reason outside myself why I should not do exactly what to me seemed good. For proof of my revelation I did, sporadically but sincerely, try to save money, and I built up in my head – always with the book to fall back upon – a dream of the future that sustained me. To Walter Besant singly and solely do I owe this – as I told him when we met, and he laughed, rolled in his chair, and seemed pleased.

In the joyous reign of Kay Robinson, my second Chief, our paper changed [56] its shape and type. This took up for a week or so all hours of the twenty-four and cost me a breakdown due to lack of sleep. But we two were proud of the results. One new feature was a daily 'turnover' – same as the little pink *Globe* [57] at Home – of one column and a quarter. Naturally, the 'office' had to supply most of them and once more I was forced to 'write short'.

All the queer outside world [58] would drop into our workshop sooner or later – say a Captain just cashiered for horrible drunkenness, who reported his fall with a wry, appealing face, and then – disappeared. Or a man old enough to be my father, on the edge of tears because he had been overpassed for Honours in the *Gazette*. Or three troopers of the Ninth Lancers, one of whom was an old schoolmate [59] of mine who became a General with an expedition of his own in West Africa in the Great War. The other two also were gentlemen-rankers who rose to high commands. One met men going up and down the ladder in every shape of misery and success.

There was a night at the Club when some silly idiot found a half-dead viper and brought it to dinner in a pickle-bottle. One man of the company kept messing about with the furious little beast on the table-cloth till he had to be warned to take his hands away. A few weeks after, some of us realized it would have been better had he accomplished what had been in his foreboding mind that night.

But the cold weather brought ample amends. The family were together again and – except for my Mother's ukase against her men bringing bound volumes of the *Illustrated London News* to meals (a survival of hot-weather savagery) – all was bliss. So, in the cold weather of '85 we four made up a Christmas annual called *Quartette*,[60] which pleased us a great deal and attracted a certain amount of attention. (Later, much later, it became a 'collector's piece' in the US book-market, and to that extent smudged the happy memories of its birth.) In '85 I began a series of tales [61] in the *Civil and Military Gazette* which were called *Plain Tales from the Hills*. They came in when and as padding was needed. In '86 also I published a collection of newspaper verses on Anglo-Indian life, called *Departmental Ditties*, which, dealing with things known and suffered by many people, were well received. I had been allowed, further, to send stuff that we, editorially, had no use for, to far-off Calcutta papers, such as the *Indigo Planters' Gazette*,[62] and elsewhere. These things were making for me the beginnings of a name even unto Bengal.

But mark how discreetly the cards were being dealt me. Up till '87 my performances had been veiled in the decent obscurity of the far end of an outlying province, among a specialized community who did not interest any but themselves. I was like a young horse entered for small, up-country events where I could get used to noise and crowds, fall about till I found my feet, and learn to keep my head with the hoofs drumming behind me. Better than all, the pace of my office-work was 'too good to inquire', and its nature – that I should realize all sorts and conditions of men and make others realize them – gave me no time to 'realize' myself.

Here was my modest notion of my own position at the end of my five years' Viceroyalty on the little *Civil and Military Gazette*. I was still fifty per cent of the editorial staff, though for a while I rose to have a man under me. But – just are the Gods! – that varlet was 'literary' and must needs write Elia-like[63] 'turnovers' instead of sticking to the legitimate! Any fool, I knew to my sorrow, could write. My job was to sub-edit him or her into some sort of shape. Any other fool could review (I myself on urgent call have reviewed the later works of a writer called Browning,[64] and what my Father said about *that* was unpublishable). Reporting was a minor 'feature', although we did not use that word. I myself *qua*[65] reporter could turn in stuff one day and *qua* sub-editor knock it remorselessly into cocked hats the next. The difference, then, between me and the vulgar herd who 'write for papers' was, as I saw it, the gulf that divides the beneficed clergyman from ladies and gentlemen who contribute pumpkins and dahlias to Harvest Festival[66] decorations. To say that I magnified my office is to understate. But this may have saved me from magnifying myself beyond decency.

In '87 orders came for me to serve on the *Pioneer*, our big sister-paper at Allahabad, hundreds of miles to the southward, where I should be one of four at least and a new boy at a big school.

But the North-West Provinces, as they were then, being largely Hindu, were strange 'air and water' to me. My life had lain among Muslims, and a man leans one way or other according to his first service. The large, well-appointed Club,[67] where Poker had just driven out Whist and men gambled seriously, was full of large-bore officials, and of a respectability all new. The Fort where troops were quartered had its points; but one bastion jutted out into a most holy river.[68] Therefore, partially burned corpses made such a habit of stranding just below the Subalterns' quarters that a special expert was entertained to pole them off and onward. In Fort Lahore we dealt in nothing worse than ghosts.

Moreover, the *Pioneer* lived under the eye of its chief proprietor,[69] who spent several months of each year in his bungalow over the way. It is true that I owed him my chance in life, but when one has been second-in-command of even a third-class cruiser, one does not care to have one's Admiral permanently moored at a cable's length. His love for his paper, which his single genius and ability had largely created, led him sometimes to 'give the boys a hand'. On those hectic days (for he added and subtracted to the last minute) we were relieved when the issue caught the down-country mail.

But he was patient with me, as were the others, and through him again I got a wider field for 'outside stuff'. There was to be a weekly edition[70] of the *Pioneer* for Home consumption. Would I edit it, additional to ordinary work? Would I not? There would be fiction – syndicated serial-matter bought by the running foot from agencies at Home. That would fill one whole big page. The 'sight of means to do ill deeds'[71] had the usual effect. Why buy Bret Harte, I asked, when I was prepared to supply home-grown fiction on the hoof? And I did.

My editing of the *Weekly* may have been a shade casual – it was but a re-hash of news and views after all. My head was full

74

of, to me, infinitely more important material. Henceforth no mere twelve-hundred Plain Tales jammed into rigid frames, but three- or five-thousand-word cartoons once a week. So did young Lippo Lippi, whose child I was, look on the blank walls of his monastery when he was bidden decorate them! 'Twas 'ask and have, Choose for more's ready,'[72] with a vengeance.

I fancy my change of surroundings and outlook precipitated the rush. At the beginning of it I had an experience which, in my innocence, I mistook for the genuine motions of my Daemon.[73] I must have been loaded more heavily than I realized with 'Gyp',[74] for there came to me in scenes as stereoscopically clear as those in the crystal an Anglo-Indian *Autour du Mariage*.[75] My pen took charge and I, greatly admiring, watched it write for me far into the nights. The result I christened *The Story of the Gadsbys*,[76] and when it first appeared in England I was complimented on my 'knowledge of the world'. After my indecent immaturity came to light, I heard less of these gifts. Yet, as the Father said loyally: 'It wasn't *all* so dam' bad, Ruddy.'

At any rate it went into the *Weekly*, together with soldier tales, Indian tales, and tales of the opposite sex. There was one of this last which, because of a doubt, I handed up to the Mother, who abolished it and wrote me: *Never you do that again*. But I did and managed to pull off, not unhandily, a tale called 'A Wayside Comedy',[77] where I worked hard for a certain 'economy of implication', and in one phrase of less than a dozen words believed I had succeeded. More than forty years later a Frenchman,[78] browsing about some of my old work, quoted this phrase as the *clou*[79] of the tale and the key to its method. It was a belated 'workshop compliment' that I appreciated. Thus, then, I made my own experiments in the weights, colours, perfumes, and attributes of words in relation to other words, either as read aloud so that they may hold the ear, or, scattered over the page, draw the eye. There is no line of my verse or prose which has not been mouthed till the tongue has made all smooth, and memory, after many recitals, has mechanically skipped the grosser superfluities.

These things occupied and contented me, but – outside of

them – I felt that I did not quite fit the *Pioneer's* scheme of things and that my superiors were of the same opinion. My work on the *Weekly* was not legitimate journalism. My flippancy in handling what I was trusted with was not well-seen by the Government or the departmental officialism, on which the *Pioneer* rightly depended for advance and private news, gathered in at Simla or Calcutta by our most important Chief Correspondent. I fancy my owners thought me safer on the road than in my chair; for they sent me out to look at Native State mines, mills, factories and the like. Here I think they were entirely justified. My proprietor at Allahabad had his own game to play (it brought him his well-deserved knighthood in due course) and, to some extent, my vagaries might have embarrassed him. One, I know, did. The *Pioneer* editorially, but cautiously as a terrier drawing up to a porcupine, had hinted that some of Lord Roberts' military appointments at that time verged on nepotism. It was a regretful and wellbalanced allocution. My rhymed comment (and why my Chief passed it I know not!) said just the same thing, but not quite so augustly. All I remember of it are the last two flagrant lines:

> And if the *Pioneer* is wrath
> Oh Lord, what must *you* be!

I don't think Lord Roberts was pleased with it, but I know he was not half so annoyed as my chief proprietor.

On my side I was ripe for change and, thanks always to *All in a Garden Fair*, had a notion now of where I was heading. My absorption in the *Pioneer Weekly* stories, which I wanted to finish, had put my plans to the back of my head, but when I came out of that furious spell of work towards the end of '88 I rearranged myself. I wanted money for the future. I counted my assets. They came to one book of verse; one ditto prose; and – thanks to the *Pioneer's* permission – a set of six small paperbacked railway-bookstall volumes embodying most of my tales in the *Weekly* – copyright of which the *Pioneer* might well have claimed. The man who then controlled the Indian railway bookstalls [80] came of an imaginative race, used to taking chances. I sold him the six paper-backed books for £200 and a small royalty. *Plain Tales from the Hills* I sold for £50, and I forget how much the same publisher gave me for *Departmental Ditties*. (This was the first and last time I ever dealt direct with publishers.)

Fortified with this wealth, and six months' pay in lieu of notice, I left India[81] for England by way of the Far East and the United States, after six and a half years of hard work and a reasonable amount of sickness. My God-speed came from the managing director, a gentleman of sound commercial instincts, who had never concealed his belief that I was grossly overpaid, and who, when he paid me my last wages, said: 'Take it from me, you'll never be worth more than four hundred rupees a month to anyone.' Common pride bids me tell that at that time I was drawing seven hundred a month.

Accounts were squared between us curiously soon. When my notoriety fell upon me, there was a demand for my old proofs, signed and unsigned stuff not included in my books, and a general turning-out of refuse-bins for private publication and sale. This upset my hopes of editing my books decently and responsibly, and wrought general confusion. But I was told later that the *Pioneer* had made as much out of its share in this remnant-traffic as it had paid me in wages since I first landed. (Which shows how one cannot get ahead of gentlemen of sound commercial instincts.)

Yet a man must needs love anything that he has worked and suffered under. When, at long last, the *Pioneer* – India's greatest and most important paper which used to pay twenty-seven per cent to its shareholders – fell on evil days and, after being bedevilled and bewitched, was sold to a syndicate, and I received a notification beginning: 'We think you may be interested to know that', etc., I felt curiously alone and unsponsored. But my first mistress and most true love, the little *Civil and Military Gazette*, weathered the storm. Even if I wrote them, these lines are true:

> Try as he will, no man breaks wholly loose
>   From his first love, no matter who she be.

Something of Myself

> Oh, was there ever sailor free to choose,
>   That didn't settle somewhere near the sea?
>
> Parsons in pulpits, tax-payers in pews,
>   Kings on your thrones, you know as well as me,
> We've only one virginity to lose,
>   And where we lost it there our hearts will be![82]

And, besides, there is, or was, a tablet in my old Lahore office asserting that here I 'worked'. And Allah knows that is true also!

Chapter 4

⟨ The Interregnum ⟩

The youth who daily further from the East
Must travel . . .[1]

Wordsworth

And, in the autumn of '89,[2] I stepped into a sort of waking dream when I took, as a matter of course, the fantastic cards that Fate was pleased to deal me.

The ancient landmarks of my boyhood still stood. There were the beloved Aunt and Uncle, the little house of the Three Old Ladies, and in one corner of it the quiet figure by the fireplace composedly writing her next novel on her knee. It was at the quietest of tea-parties, in this circle, that I first met Mary Kingsley,[3] the bravest woman of all my knowledge. We talked a good deal over the cups, and more while walking home afterwards – she of West African cannibals and the like. At last, the world forgetting, I said: 'Come up to my rooms and we'll talk it out there.' She agreed, as a man would, then suddenly remembering said: 'Oh, I forgot I was a woman. 'Fraid I mustn't.' So I realized that my world was all to explore again.

A few – a very few – people in it had died, but no one expected to do so for another twenty years. White women stood and waited on one behind one's chair. It was all whirlingly outside my comprehension.

But my small stock-in-trade of books had become known in certain quarters; and there was an evident demand for my stuff. I do not recall that I stirred a hand to help myself. Things happened to me. I went, by invitation, to Mowbray

Morris,[4] the editor of *Macmillan's Magazine*, who asked me how old I was and, when I told him I hoped to be twenty-four at the end of the year, said: 'Good God!' He took from me an Indian tale and some verses,[5] which latter he wisely edited a little. They were both published in the same number of the *Magazine* – one signed by my name and the other 'Yussuf'. All of this confirmed the feeling (which has come back at intervals through my life), 'Lord ha' mercy on me, this is none of I.'[6]

Then more tales were asked for, and the editor[7] of the *St James's Gazette*[8] wanted stray articles, signed and unsigned. My 'turnover' training on the *Civil and Military* made this easy for me, and somehow I felt easier with a daily paper under my right elbow.

About this time was an interview in a weekly paper,[9] where I felt myself rather on the wrong side of the counter and that I ought to be questioning my questioner. Shortly after, that same weekly made me a proposition which I could not see my way to accept, and then announced that I was 'feeling my oats',[10] of which, it was careful to point out, it had given me my first sieveful. Since, at that time, I was overwhelmed, not to say scared, by the amazing luck that had come to me, the pronouncement gave me confidence. If that was how I struck the external world – good! For naturally I considered the whole universe was acutely interested in me only – just as a man who strays into a skirmish is persuaded he is the pivot of the action.

Meantime, I had found me quarters in Villiers Street,[11] Strand, which forty-six years ago was primitive and passionate in its habits and population. My rooms were small, not over-clean or well-kept, but from my desk I could look out of my window through the fanlight of Gatti's Music-Hall entrance, across the street, almost on to its stage. The Charing Cross trains rumbled through my dreams on one side, the boom of the Strand on the other, while, before my windows, Father Thames under the Shot Tower walked up and down with his traffic.

At the outset I had so muddled and mismanaged my affairs that, for a while, I found myself with some money owing me for work done, but no funds in hand. People who ask for money, however justifiably, have it remembered against them. The beloved Aunt, or any one of the Three Old Ladies, would have given to me without question; but that seemed too like confessing failure at the outset. My rent was paid; I had my dress-suit; I had nothing to pawn save a collection of unmarked shirts picked up in all the ports; so I made shift to manage on what small cash I had in pocket.

My rooms were above an establishment of Harris the Sausage King, who, for tuppence, gave as much sausage and mash as would carry one from breakfast to dinner when one dined with nice people who did not eat sausage for a living. Another tuppence found me a filling supper. The excellent tobacco of those days was, unless you sank to threepenny 'Shag' or soared to sixpenny 'Turkish', tuppence the half-ounce: and fourpence, which included a pewter of beer or porter, was the price of admission to Gatti's.

It was here, in the company of an elderly but upright barmaid from a pub near by, that I listened to the observed and compelling songs of the Lion and Mammoth Comiques,[12] and the shriller strains – but equally 'observed' – of the Bessies and Bellas,[13] whom I could hear arguing beneath my window with their cab-drivers, as they sped from Hall to Hall. One lady sometimes delighted us with *viva-voce*[14] versions of – 'what 'as just 'appened to me outside 'ere, if you'll believe it.' Then she would plunge into brilliant improvisations. Oh, we believed! Many of us had, perhaps, taken part in the tail of that argument at the doors, ere she stormed in.

Those monologues I could never hope to rival, but the smoke, the roar, and the good-fellowship of relaxed humanity at Gatti's 'set' the scheme for a certain sort of song. The Private Soldier in India I thought I knew fairly well. His English brother (in the Guards mostly) sat and sang at my elbow any night I chose; and, for Greek chorus, I had the comments of my barmaid – deeply and dispassionately versed in all knowledge of evil as she had watched it across the zinc she was always swabbing off. (Hence, some years later, verses called 'Mary, pity Women',[15] based on what she told me about 'a friend o' mine 'oo was mistook in 'er man'.) The outcome was the first of some verses

81

called *Barrack-Room Ballads* which I showed to Henley[16] of the *Scots*, later *National Observer*, who wanted more; and I became for a while one of the happy company[17] who used to gather in a little restaurant off Leicester Square and regulate all literature till all hours of the morning.

I had the greatest admiration for Henley's verse and prose and, if such things be merchandise in the next world, will cheerfully sell a large proportion of what I have written for a single meditation – illumination – inspiration or what you please – that he wrote on the *Arabian Nights* in a tiny book of Essays and Reviews.[18]

As regards his free verse[19] I – plus some Chianti – once put forward the old notion that free verse was like fishing with barbless hooks. Henley replied volcanically. It was, said he, 'the cadences that did it'. That was true; but he alone, to my mind, could handle them aright, being a Master Craftsman who had paid for his apprenticeship.

Henley's demerits were, of course, explained to the world by loving friends after his death. I had the fortune to know him only as kind, generous, and a jewel of an editor, with the gift of fetching the very best out of his cattle, with words that would astonish oxen. He had, further, an organic loathing of Mr Gladstone[20] and all Liberalism. A Government Commission of Enquiry[21] was sitting in those days on some unusually blatant traffic in murder among the Irish Land Leaguers;[22] and had whitewashed the whole crowd. Whereupon, I wrote some impolite verses called 'Cleared!'[23] which at first *The Times* seemed ready to take but on second thoughts declined. I was recommended to carry them to a monthly review of sorts edited by a Mr Frank Harris,[24] whom I discovered to be the one human being that I could on no terms get on with. He, too, shied at the verses, which I referred to Henley, who, having no sense of political decency, published them in his *Observer*, and – after a cautious interval – *The Times* quoted them in full. This was rather like some of my experiences in India, and gave me yet more confidence.

To my great pride I was elected a Member of the Savile[25] – 'the little Savile' then in Piccadilly – and, on my introduction, dined with no less than Hardy and Walter Besant. My debts to the latter grew at once, and you may remember that I owed him much indeed. He had his own views on publishers, and was founding, or had just founded, the Authors' Society.[26] He advised me to entrust my business to an agent and sent me to his own – A. P. Watt, whose son was about my own age. The father took hold of my affairs at once and most sagely; and on his death his son succeeded. In the course of forty-odd years I do not recall any difference between us that three minutes' talk could not clear up. This, also, I owed to Besant.

Nor did his goodness halt there. He would sit behind his big, frosted beard and twinkling spectacles, and deal me out wisdom concerning this new incomprehensible world. One heard very good talk at the Savile. Much of it was the careless give-and-take of the atelier when the models are off their stands, and one throws bread-pellets at one's betters, and makes hay of all schools save one's own. But Besant saw deeper. He advised me to 'keep out of the dog-fight'. He said that if I were 'in with one lot' I would have to be out with another; and that, at last, 'things would get like a girls' school where they stick out their tongues at each other when they pass'. That was true too. One heard men vastly one's seniors wasting energy and good oaths in recounting 'intrigues' against them, and of men who had 'their knife into' their work, or whom they themselves wished to 'knife'. (This reminded me somehow of the elderly officials who opened their hearts in my old office when they were disappointed over anticipated Honours.) It seemed best to stand clear of it all. For that reason, I have never directly or indirectly criticized any fellow-craftsman's output, or encouraged any man or woman to do so; nor have I approached any persons that they might be led to comment on my output. My acquaintance with my contemporaries has from first to last been very limited.

At 'the little Savile' I remember much kindness and toleration. There was Gosse,[27] of course, sensitive as a cat to all atmospheres, but utterly fearless when it came to questions of good workmanship; Hardy's grave and bitter humour; Andrew Lang,[28] as detached to all appearances as a cloud, but – one

learned to know – never kinder in your behalf than when he
seemed least concerned with you; Eustace Balfour,[29] a large,
lovable man, and one of the best of talkers, who died too soon:
Herbert Stephen,[30] very wise and very funny when he chose:
Rider Haggard,[31] to whom I took at once, he being of the
stamp adored by children and trusted by men at sight; and he
could tell tales, mainly against himself, that broke up the tables:
Saintsbury,[32] a solid rock of learning and geniality whom I
revered all my days; profoundly a scholar and versed in the art
of good living. There was a breakfast with him and Walter
Pollock of the *Saturday Review*[33] in the Albany,[34] when he
produced some specially devilish Oriental delicacy which we
cooked by the light of our united ignorances. It was splendid!
Why those two men took the trouble to notice me, I never
knew; but I learned to rely on Saintsbury's judgment in the
weightier matters of the Laws of Literature. At his latter end
he gave me inestimable help in a little piece of work called
'Proofs of Holy Writ',[35] which without his books could never
have been handled. I found him at Bath, compiling with eru-
dition equal to his earnestness the Cellar-book[36] of the Queen's
Doll's House. He produced a bottle of real Tokay,[37] which I
tasted, and lost my number badly by saying that it reminded me
of some medicinal wine. It is true he merely called me a blas-
phemer of the worst, but what he thought I do not care to
think!

There were scores of other good men at the Savile, but
the tones and the faces of those I have named come back
clearest.

My home life – it was a far cry from Piccadilly to Villiers
Street – was otherwise, through the months of amazement
which followed my return to England. That period was all, as I
have said, a dream, in which it seemed that I could push down
walls, walk through ramparts and stride across rivers. Yet I was
so ignorant, I never guessed when the great fogs fell that trains
could take me to light and sunshine a few miles outside London.
Once I faced the reflection of my own face in the jet-black
mirror of the window-panes for five days. When the fog
thinned, I looked out and saw a man standing opposite the pub

where the barmaid lived. Of a sudden his breast turned dull red like a robin's, and he crumpled, having cut his throat. In a few minutes – seconds it seemed – a hand-ambulance arrived and took up the body. A pot-boy with a bucket of steaming water sluiced the blood off into the gutter, and what little crowd had collected went its way.

One got to know that ambulance [38] (it lived somewhere at the back of St Clement Danes [39]) as well as the Police of the E Division, and even as far as Piccadilly Circus, where, any time after 10.30 p.m., the forces might be found at issue with 'real ladies'. And through all this shifting, shouting brotheldom the pious British householder [40] and his family bored their way back from the theatres, eyes-front and fixed, as though not seeing.

Among my guests in chambers was a Lion Comique [41] from Gatti's – an artist with sound views on art. According to him, 'it was all right to keep on knockin' 'em' [42] ('puttin' it across' came later) 'but, outside o' *that*, a man wants something to lay *hold* of. I'd ha' got it, I think, but for this dam' whisky. But, take it from me, life's all a bloomin' kick-up.' [43] Certainly my life was; but, to some extent, my Indian training served to ballast me.

I was plentifully assured, *viva voce* and in the Press-cuttings – which is a drug that I do not recommend to the young – that 'nothing since Dickens' [44] compared with my 'meteoric rise to fame', etc. (But I was more or less inoculated, if not immune, to the coarser sorts of print.) And there was my portrait [45] to be painted for the Royal Academy as a notoriety. (But I had a Muhammedan's objection to having my face taken, as likely to draw the Evil Eye. So I was not too puffed up.) And there were letters and letters of all sorts of tendencies. (But if I answered them all I might as well be back at my old table.) And there were proposals from 'certain people of importance', insistent and unscrupulous as horse-copers, telling me how 'the ball was at my feet' and that I had only to kick it – by repeating the notes I had already struck and trailing characters I had already 'created' through impossible scenes – to achieve all sorts of desirable things. But I had seen men as well as horses foundered in my lost world behind me. One thing only stood fast through this welter. I was making money – much more than four hundred rupees a month – and when my Bank-book told me I had one thousand whole pounds saved, the Strand was hardly wide enough for my triumph. I had intended a book 'to take advantage of the market'. This I had just sense enough to countermand. What I most needed was that my people should come over and see what had overtaken their son. This they did on a flying visit,[46] and then my 'kick-up' had some worth.

As always, they seemed to suggest nothing and interfere nowhere. But they were there – my Father with his sage Yorkshire outlook and wisdom; my Mother, all Celt[47] and three-parts fire – both so entirely comprehending that except in trivial matters we had hardly need of words.

I think I can with truth say that those two made for me the only public for whom then I had any regard whatever till their deaths, in my forty-fifth year. Their arrival simplified things, and 'set' in my head a notion that had been rising at the back of it. It seemed easy enough to 'knock 'em' – but to what end beyond the heat of the exercise? (That both my grandfathers had been Wesleyan Ministers did not strike me till I was, familiarly, reminded of it.) I had been at work on the rough of a set of verses called later 'The English Flag'[48] and had boggled at a line which had to be a key-line but persisted in going 'soft'. As was the custom between us, I asked into the air: 'What am I trying to get *at*?' Instantly the Mother, with her quick flutter of the hands: 'You're *trying* to say: "What do they know of England who only England know?"' The Father confirmed. The rest of the rhetoric came away easily; for it was only pictures seen, as it were, from the deck of a long fourteen-footer, a craft that will almost sail herself.

In the talks that followed, I exposed my notion of trying to tell to the English something of the world outside England – not directly but by implication.

They understood. Long before the end the Mother, summarizing, said: '*I* see. "Unto them did he discover His swan's nest among the reeds."[49] Thank you for telling us, dear.' That settled that; and when Lord Tennyson (whom alas! I never had the good fortune to meet) expressed his approval of the verses when they appeared, I took it for a lucky sign. Most men properly broke to a trade pick up some sort of workshop facility which gives them an advantage over their untrained fellows. My office-work had taught me to think out a notion in detail, pack it away in my head, and work on it by snatches in any surroundings. The lurch and surge of the old horse-drawn buses made a luxurious cradle for such ruminations. Bit by bit, my original notion grew into a vast, vague conspectus – Army and Navy Stores List[50] if you like – of the whole sweep and meaning of things and effort and origins throughout the Empire. I visualized it, as I do most ideas, in the shape of a semi-circle of buildings and temples projecting into a sea – of dreams. At any rate, after I had got it straight in my head, I felt there need be no more 'knockin' 'em' in the abstract.

Likewise, in my wanderings beyond Villiers Street, I had met several men and an occasional woman, whom I by no means loved. They were overly soft-spoken or blatant, and dealt in pernicious varieties of safe sedition. For the most part they seemed to be purveyors of luxuries to the 'Aristocracy', whose destruction by painful means they loudly professed to desire. They derided my poor little Gods of the East, and asserted that the British in India spent violent lives 'oppressing' the Native. (This in a land where white girls of sixteen, at twelve or fourteen pounds per annum, hauled thirty and forty pounds weight of bath-water at a time up four flights of stairs!)

The more subtle among them had plans, which they told me, for 'snatching away England's arms when she isn't looking – just like a naughty child – so that when she wants to fight she'll find she can't.' (We have come far on that road since.) Meantime, their aim was peaceful, intellectual penetration and the formation of what today would be called 'cells' in unventilated corners. Collaborating with these gentry was a mixed crowd of wide-minded, wide-mouthed Liberals, who darkened counsel with pious but disintegrating catch-words, and took care to live very well indeed. Somewhere, playing up to them, were various journals, not at all badly written, with a most enviable genius for perverting or mistaking anything that did not suit their bilious doctrine. The general situation, as I saw it,

promised an alluring 'dog-fight', in which I had no need to take
aggressive part because, as soon as the first bloom had faded
off my work, my normal output seemed to have the gift of
arriding *per se* [51] the very people I most disliked. And I had the
additional luck not to be taken seriously for some time. People
talked, quite reasonably, of rockets and sticks; and that genius,
J.K.S.,[52] brother to Herbert Stephen, dealt with Haggard and
me in some stanzas which I would have given much to have
written myself. They breathed a prayer for better days when:

> The world shall cease to wonder
>   At the genius of an Ass,
> And a boy's eccentric blunder
>   Shall not bring success to pass . . .
> When there stands a muzzled stripling,
>   Mute, beside a muzzled bore:
> When the Rudyards cease from Kipling
>   And the Haggards Ride no more.

It ran joyously through all the papers. It still hangs faintly in
the air and, as I used to warn Haggard, may continue as an
aroma when all but our two queer names are forgotten.

Several perfectly good reviewers also helped me by demon-
strating how I had arrived at my effects by a series of happy
accidents. One kind man even went to some trouble, including
a good dinner, to discover personally whether I had 'ever read
much'. I could not do less than confirm his worst suspicions,
for I had been 'taken on' in that way at the Punjab Club, till my
examiner found out that I was pulling his leg, and chased me
all round the compound. (The greatest reverence is due to the
young. They have, when irritated, little of their own.)

But in all this jam of work done or devising, demands, distractions, excitements, and promiscuous confusions, my health
cracked again. I had broken down twice in India from straight
overwork, plus fever and dysentery, but this time the staleness
and depression came after a bout of real influenza, when all my
Indian microbes joined hands and sang for a month in the
darkness of Villiers Street.

So I took ship to Italy,[53] and there chanced to meet Lord

Dufferin,[54] our Ambassador, who had been Viceroy of India and had known my people. Also, I had written some verses called 'The Song of the Women'[55] about Lady Dufferin's maternity work for women in India, which both she and he liked. He was kindness itself, and made me his guest at his Villa near Naples where, one evening between lights, he talked – at first to me directly, then sliding into a reverie – of his work in India, Canada, and the world at large. I had seen administrative machinery from beneath, all stripped and overheated. This was the first time I had listened to one who had handled it from above. And unlike the generality of Viceroys, Lord Dufferin *knew*. Of all his revelations and reminiscences, the sentence that stays with me is: 'And so, you see, there can be no room' (or was it 'allowance'?) 'for good intentions in one's work.'

Italy, however, was not enough. My need was to get clean away and re-sort myself. Cruises were then unknown; but my dependence was Cook. For the great J.M. himself[56] – the man with the iron mouth and domed brow – had been one of my Father's guests at Lahore when he was trying to induce the Indian Government to let him take over the annual pilgrimage to Mecca[57] as a business proposition. Had he succeeded some lives, and perhaps a war or two, might have been saved. His home offices took friendly interest in my plans and steamer connections.

I sailed first to Cape Town[58] in a gigantic three-thousand-ton liner called *The Moor*, not knowing I was in the hands of Fate. Aboard her, I met a Navy Captain[59] going to a new Command at Simon's Town. At Madeira he desired to lay in wine for his two-year commission. I assisted him through a variegated day and fluctuating evening, which laid the foundations of life-long friendship.

Cape Town in '91 was a sleepy, unkempt little place, where the stoeps[60] of some of the older Dutch houses still jutted over the pavement. Occasional cows strolled up the main streets, which were full of coloured people of the sort that my *ayah* had pointed out to me were curly-haired (*hubshees*)[61] who slept in such posture as made it easy for the devils to enter their bodies. But there were also many Malays who were Muslims of a sort and had their own Mosques, and whose flamboyantly-attired women sold flowers on the kerb, and took in washing. The dry, spiced smell of the land and the smack of the clean sunshine were health-restoring. My Navy Captain introduced me to the Naval society of Simon's Town, where the south-easter blows five days a week, and the Admiral of the Cape Station lived in splendour, with at least a brace of live turtles harnessed to the end of a little wooden jetty, swimming about till due to be taken up for turtle soup. The Navy Club there and the tales of the junior officers delighted me beyond words. There I witnessed one of the most comprehensive 'rags' [62] I had ever seen. It rose out of a polite suggestion to a newly-appointed Lieutenant-Commander [63] that the fore-topmast of his tiny gunboat 'wanted staying forward'. It went on till all the furniture was completely rearranged all over the room. (How was I to guess that in a few years I should know Simon's Town like the inside of my own pocket, and should give much of my life and love to the glorious land around it?)

We parted, my Captain and I, after a farewell picnic, among white, blowing sand where natives were blasting and where, of a sudden, a wrathful baboon came down the rock-face and halted waist-deep in a bed of arum-lilies. 'We'll meet again,' said my Captain, 'and if ever you want a cruise, let me know.'

A day or so before my departure for Australia, I lunched at an Adderley Street [64] restaurant next to three men. One of them, I was told, was Cecil Rhodes, [65] who had made the staple of our passengers' talk on *The Moor* coming out. It never occurred to me to speak to him; and I have often wondered why . . .

Her name was *The Doric*. She was almost empty, and she spent twenty-four consecutive days and nights trying, all but successfully, to fill her boats at one roll and empty them down the saloon skylight the next. Sea and sky were equally grey and naked on that weary run to Melbourne. [66] Then I found myself in a new land with new smells and among people who insisted a little too much that they also were new. But there are no such things as new people in this very old world.

The leading paper offered me the most distinguished honour

of describing the Melbourne Cup,[67] but I had reported races before and knew it was not in my line. I was more interested in the middle-aged men who had spent their lives making or managing the land. They were direct of speech among each other, and talked a political slang new to me. One learned, as one always does, more from what they said to each other or took for granted in their talk, than one could have got at from a hundred questions. And on a warm night I attended a Labour Congress, where Labour debated whether some much-needed life-boats should be allowed to be ordered from England, or whether the order should be postponed till life-boats could be built in Australia under Labour direction at Labour prices.

Hereafter my memories of Australian travel are mixed up with trains transferring me, at unholy hours, from one too-exclusive State gauge to another; of enormous skies and primitive refreshment-rooms, where I drank hot tea and ate mutton, while now and then a hot wind, like the *loo* of the Punjab, boomed out of the emptiness. A hard land, it seemed to me, and made harder for themselves by the action of its inhabitants, who – it may have been the climate – always seemed a bit on edge.

I went also to Sydney, which was populated by leisured multitudes all in their shirt-sleeves and all picnicking all the day. They volunteered that they were new and young, but would do wonderful things some day, which promise they more than kept. Then to Hobart, in Tasmania, to pay my respects to Sir George Grey,[68] who had been Governor at Cape Town in the days of the Mutiny. He was very old, very wise and fore-seeing, with the gentleness that accompanies a certain sort of strength.

Then came New Zealand by steamer (one was always taking small and rickety coastwise craft across those big seas), and at Wellington I was met, precisely where warned to expect him, by 'Pelorus Jack',[69] the big, white-marked dolphin, who held it his duty to escort shipping up the harbour. He enjoyed a special protection of the Legislature proclaiming him sacred, but, years later, some animal shot and wounded him and he was no more seen. Wellington opened another world of kindly people, more homogeneous, it struck me, than the Australian, large, long-eyelashed, and extraordinarily good-looking. Maybe I was prejudiced, because no less than ten beautiful maidens took me for a row in a big canoe by moonlight on the still waters of Wellington Harbour, and everyone generally put aside everything for my behoof, instruction, amusement, and comfort. So, indeed, it has always been. For which reason I deserve no credit when my work happens to be accurate in detail. A friend long ago taxed me with having enjoyed the 'income of a Prince and the treatment of an Ambassador',[70] and with not appreciating it. He even called me, among other things, 'an ungrateful hound'. But what, I ask you, could I have done except go on with my work and try to add to the pleasure of those that had found it pleasant? One cannot repay the unrepayable by grins and handshakes.

From Wellington I went north towards Auckland in a buggy with a small grey mare, and a most taciturn driver. It was bush country after rain. We crossed a rising river[71] twenty-three times in one day, and came out on great plains where wild horses stared at us, and caught their feet in long blown manes as they stamped and snorted. At one of our halts I was given for dinner a roast bird with a skin like pork crackling, but it had no wings nor trace of any. It was a kiwi[72] – an apteryx. I ought to have saved its skeleton, for few men have eaten apteryx. Hereabouts my driver – I had seen the like happen in lonely places before – exploded, as sometimes solitaries will. We passed a horse's skull beside the track, at which he began to swear horribly but without passion. He had, he said, driven and ridden past that skull for a very long time. To him it meant the lock on the chain of his bondage to circumstance, and why the hell did I come along talking about all those foreign, far places I had seen? Yet he made me go on telling him.

I had had some notion of sailing from Auckland to visit Robert Louis Stevenson at Samoa,[73] for he had done me the honour to write me about some of my tales; and moreover I was Eminent Past Master R.L.S. Even today I would back myself to take seventy-five per cent marks in written or *viva-voce* examination on *The Wrong Box*[74] which, as the Initiated know, is the Test Volume of that Degree. I read it first in a small hotel in Boston in '89,[75] when the negro waiter nearly turned me out of the dining-room for spluttering over my meal.

But Auckland, soft and lovely in the sunshine, seemed the end of organized travel; for the captain of a fruit-boat, which might or might not go to Samoa at some time or other, was so devotedly drunk that I decided to turn south, and work back to India. All I carried away from the magic town of Auckland was the face and voice of a woman who sold me beer at a little hotel there. They stayed at the back of my head till ten years later when, in a local train of the Cape Town suburbs, I heard a petty officer from Simon's Town telling a companion about a woman in New Zealand who 'never scrupled to help a lame duck or put her foot on a scorpion'. Then – precisely as the removal of the key-log in a timber-jam starts the whole pile – those words gave me the key to the face and voice at Auckland, and a tale called 'Mrs Bathurst'[76] slid into my mind, smoothly and orderly as floating timber on a bank-high river.

The South Island, mainly populated by Scots, their sheep, and the Devil's own high winds, I tackled in another small steamer, among colder and increasing seas. We cleared it at the Last Lamp-post in the World – Invercargill – on a boisterous dark evening, when General Booth[77] of the Salvation Army came on board. I saw him walking backward in the dusk over the uneven wharf, his cloak blown upwards, tulip-fashion, over his grey head, while he beat a tambourine in the face of the singing, weeping, praying crowd who had come to see him off.

We stood out, and at once took the South Pacific. For the better part of a week we were swept from end to end, our poop was split, and a foot or two of water smashed through the tiny saloon. I remembered no set meals. The General's cabin was near mine, and in the intervals between crashes overhead and cataracts down below he sounded like a wounded elephant; for he was in every way a big man.

I saw no more of him till I had picked up my P. & O.,[78] which also happened to be his, for Colombo at Adelaide. Here all the world came out in paddle-boats and small craft to speed him on his road to India. He spoke to them from our upper deck, and one of his gestures – an imperative, repeated, downward sweep of the arm – puzzled me, till I saw that a woman crouching on the paddle-box of a crowded boat had rucked her petticoats well up to her knees. In those days righteous woman ended at the neck and instep. Presently, she saw what was troubling the General. Her skirts were adjusted and all was peace and piety. I talked much with General Booth during that voyage. Like the young ass I was, I expressed my distaste at his appearance on Invercargill wharf. 'Young feller,' he replied, bending great brows at me, 'if I thought I could win *one* more soul to the Lord by walking on my head and playing the tambourine with my toes, I'd – I'd learn how.'

He had the right of it ('if by any means I can save some'[79]) and I had decency enough to apologize. He told me about the beginnings of his mission, and how surely he would be in gaol[80] were his accounts submitted to any sort of official inspection; and how his work *must* be a one-man despotism with only the Lord for supervisor. (Even so spoke Paul and, I am well sure, Muhammed.)

'Then why,' I asked, 'can't you stop your Salvation lassies from going out to India and living alone native-fashion among natives?' I told him something of village conditions in India. The despot's defence was very human. 'But what *am* I to do?' he demanded. 'The girls *will* go, and one *can't* stop 'em.'

I think this first flare of enthusiasm was rationalized later, but not before some good lives had been expended. I conceived great respect and admiration for this man with the head of Isaiah and the fire of the Prophet,[81] but, like the latter, rather at sea among women. The next time I met him was at Oxford[82] when Degrees were being conferred. He strode across to me in his Doctor's robes, which magnificently became him, and, 'Young feller,' said he, 'how's your soul?'

I have always liked the Salvation Army, of whose work outside England I have seen a little. They are, of course, open to all the objections urged against them by science and the regular creeds: but it seems to me that when a soul conceives itself as being reborn it may go through agonies both unscientific and unregulated. Haggard, who had worked with him [83] and for the Army on several occasions, told me that for sheer luxury of attendance, kindliness, and good-will, nothing compared with travel under their care.

From Colombo I crossed over to the India of the extreme south which I did not know, and for four days and four nights in the belly [84] of the train could not understand one word of the speech around me. Then came the open north and Lahore, where I was snatching a few days' visit with my people. They were coming 'Home' for good soon: so this was my last look round the only real home I had yet known.

Chapter 5

⑆ The Committee of Ways and Means [1] ⑄

Then down to Bombay where my *ayah*, so old but so unaltered, met me with blessings and tears; and then to London to be married [2] in January '92 in the thick of an influenza epidemic, when the undertakers had run out of black horses and the dead had to be content with brown ones. The living were mostly abed. (We did not know then that this epidemic was the first warning that the plague – forgotten for generations – was on the move out of Manchuria. [3])

All of which touched me as much as it would any other young man under like circumstances. My concern was to get out of the pest-house as soon as might be. For was I not a person of substance? Had I not several – more than two at least – thousand pounds in Fixed Deposits? Had not my own Bank's Manager himself suggested that I might invest some of my 'capital' in, say, indigo? But I preferred to invest once more in Cook's tickets – for two – on a voyage round the world. It was all arranged beyond any chance of failure.

So we were married in the church [4] with the pencil-pointed steeple at Langham Place – Gosse, Henry James, and my cousin Ambrose Poynter being all the congregation present [5] – and we parted at the church door to the scandal of the Beadle, my wife to administer medicine to her mother, and I to a wedding breakfast [6] with Ambrose Poynter; after which, on returning to collect my wife, I saw, pinned down by weights on the rainy pavement as was the custom of those untroubled days, a newspaper poster announcing my marriage, which made me feel uncomfortable and defenceless.

And a few days afterwards we were on our magic carpet [7] which was to take us round the earth, beginning with Canada deep in snow. Among our wedding gifts was a generous silver flask filled with whisky, but of incontinent habit. It leaked in the valise where it lay with flannel shirts. And it scented the entire Pullman from end to end ere we arrived at the cause. But by that time all our fellow-passengers were pitying that poor girl who had linked her life to this shameless inebriate. Thus in a false atmosphere all of our innocent own, we came to Vancouver,[8] where with an eye to the future and for proof of wealth we bought, or thought we had, twenty acres of a wilderness called North Vancouver, now part of the City. But there was a catch in the thing, as we found many years later when, after paying taxes on it for ever so long, we discovered it belonged to someone else. All the consolation we got then from the smiling people of Vancouver was: 'You bought that from Steve, did you? Ah-ah, *Steve*! You hadn't ought to ha' bought from Steve. No! Not from *Steve*.' And thus did the good Steve cure us of speculating in real estate.

Then to Yokohama,[9] where we were treated with all the kindliness in the world by a man and his wife on whom we had no shadow of any claim. They made us more than welcome in their house, and saw to it that we should see Japan in wistaria and peony time. Here an earthquake[10] (prophetic as it turned out) overtook us one hot break of dawn, and we fled out into the garden, where a tall cryptomeria waggled its insane head back and forth with an 'I told you so' expression; though not a breath was stirring. A little later I went to the Yokohama branch of my Bank on a wet forenoon to draw some of my solid wealth. Said the Manager to me: 'Why not take more? It will be just as easy.' I answered that I did not care to have too much cash at one time in my careless keeping, but that when I had looked over my accounts I might come again in the afternoon. I did so; but in that little space my Bank, the notice on its shut door explained, had suspended payment.[11] (Yes, I should have done better to have invested my 'capital' as its London Manager had hinted.)

I returned with my news to my bride of three months and a child to be born.[12] Except for what I had drawn that morning – the Manager had sailed as near to the wind as loyalty permitted – and the unexpended Cook vouchers, and our personal possessions in our trunks, we had nothing whatever. There was an instant Committee of Ways and Means, which advanced our understanding of each other more than a cycle of solvent matrimony. Retreat – flight, if you like – was indicated. What would Cook return for the tickets, not including the price of lost dreams? 'Every pound you've paid, of course,' said Cook of Yokohama. 'These things are all luck and – here's your refund.'

Back again, then, across the cold North Pacific, through Canada on the heels of the melting snows, and to the outskirts of a little New England town [13] where my wife's paternal grandfather (a Frenchman) had made his home and estate many years before. The country was large-boned, mountainous, wooded, and divided into farms of from fifty to two hundred barren acres. Roads, sketched in dirt, connected white, clapboarded farm-houses, where the older members of the families made shift to hold down the eating mortgages. The younger folk had gone elsewhere. There were many abandoned houses too; some decaying where they stood; others already reduced to a stone chimney-stack or mere green dimples still held by an undefeated lilac-bush. On one small farm was a building known as the Bliss Cottage, generally inhabited by a hired man. It was of one storey and a half; seventeen feet high to the roof-tree; seventeen feet deep and, including the kitchen and wood-shed, twenty-seven feet wide over all. Its water-supply was a single half-inch lead pipe connecting with a spring in the neighbourhood. But it was habitable, and it stood over a deep if dampish cellar. Its rent was ten dollars or two pounds a month.

We took it. We furnished it with a simplicity that fore-ran the hire-purchase system. We bought, second or third hand, a huge, hot-air stove which we installed in the cellar. We cut generous holes in our thin floors for its eight-inch tin pipes (why we were not burned in our beds each week of the winter I never can understand) and we were extraordinarily and self-centredly content.

As the New England summer flamed into autumn I piled cut spruce boughs all round the draughty cottage sill, and helped to put up a tiny roofless verandah along one side of it for future needs. When winter shut down and sleigh-bells rang all over the white world that tucked us in, we counted ourselves secure. Sometimes we had a servant. Sometimes she would find the solitude too much for her and flee without warning, one even leaving her trunk. This troubled us not at all. There are always two sides to a plate, and the cleaning of frying- and saucepans is as little a mystery as the making of comfortable beds. When our lead pipe froze, we would slip on our coon-skin coats and thaw it out with a lighted candle. There was no space in the attic bedroom for a cradle, so we decided that a trunk-tray would be just as good. We envied no one – not even when skunks wandered into our cellar and, knowing the nature of the beasts, we immobilized ourselves till it should please them to depart.

But our neighbours saw no humour in our proceedings. Here was a stranger of an unloved race, currently reported to 'make as much as a hundred dollars out of a ten-cent bottle of ink', and who had 'pieces in the papers' about him, who had married a 'Balestier girl'. Did not her grandmother still live on the Balestier place, where 'old Balestier' instead of farming had built a large house, and there had dined late in special raiment, and drunk red wines after the custom of the French instead of decent whisky? And behold this Britisher, under pretext of having lost money, had settled his wife down 'right among her own folk' in the Bliss Cottage. It was not seemly on the face of it; so they watched as secretively as the New England or English peasant can, and what toleration they extended to the 'Britisher' was solely for the sake of 'the Balestier girl'.

But we had received the first shock of our young lives at the first crisis in them. The Committee of Ways and Means passed a resolution, never rescinded, that henceforth, at any price, it must own its collective self.

As money came in from the sale of books and tales, the first use we made of it was to buy back *Departmental Ditties*, *Plain Tales*, and the six paper-backed books that I had sold to get me funds for leaving India in '89. They cost something, but, owning them, the Bliss Cottage breathed more comfortably.

Not till much later did we realize the terrible things that 'folks thought of your doin's'. From their point of view they were right. Also, they were practical as the following will show.

One day a stranger drove up to the Bliss Cottage. The palaver opened thus:

'Kiplin', ain't ye?'

That was admitted.

'Write, don't ye?'

That seemed accurate. (Long pause.)

'Thet bein' so, you've got to live to please folk, hain't ye?'

That indeed was the raw truth. He sat rigid in the buggy and went on.

'Thet bein' so, you've got to please to live, I reckon?'

It was true. (I thought of my Adjutant of Volunteers[14] at Lahore.)

'Puttin' it thet way,' he pursued, 'we'll 'low thet, by and by, ye *can't* please. Sickness – accident – any darn thing. *Then –* what's liable to happen ye – both of ye?'

I began to see, and he to fumble in his breast pocket.

'Thet's where Life Insurance comes in. Na-ow, *I* repre-sent,' etc. etc. It was beautiful salesmanship. The Company was reputable, and I effected my first American insurance, Leuconoë agreeing with Horace[15] to trust the future as little as possible.

Other visitors were not so tactful. Reporters came from papers in Boston, which I presume believed itself to be civilized, and demanded interviews. I told them I had nothing to say. 'If ye hevn't, guess we'll *make* ye say something.' So they went away and lied copiously, their orders being to 'get the story'. This was new to me at the time; but the Press had not got into its full free stride of later years.

My workroom in the Bliss Cottage was seven feet by eight, and from December to April the snow lay level with its window-sill. It chanced that I had written a tale[16] about Indian Forestry work which included a boy who had been brought up by wolves. In the stillness, and suspense, of the winter of '92 some memory of the Masonic Lions[17] of my childhood's magazine, and a phrase in Haggard's *Nada the Lily*,[18] combined with the echo of this tale. After blocking out the main idea in my head, the pen took charge, and I watched it begin to write stories [19] about Mowgli and animals, which later grew into the *Jungle Books*.

Once launched there seemed no particular reason to stop, but I had learned to distinguish between the peremptory motions of my Daemon,[20] and the 'carry-over' or induced electricity, which comes of what you might call mere 'frictional' writing. Two tales, I remember, I threw away and was better pleased with the remainder. More to the point, my Father thought well of the workmanship.

My first child[21] and daughter was born in three foot of snow on the night of December 29th, 1892. Her Mother's birthday being the 31st and mine the 30th of the same month, we congratulated her on her sense of the fitness of things, and she throve in her trunk-tray in the sunshine on the little plank verandah. Her birth brought me into contact with the best friend I made in New England – Dr Conland.

It seemed that the Bliss Cottage might be getting a little congested, so, in the following spring, the Committee of Ways and Means 'considered a field and bought it' – as much as ten whole acres – on a rocky hillside looking across a huge valley to Wantastiquet, the wooded mountain across the Connecticut river.

That summer there came out of Quebec Jean Pigeon with nine other *habitants* who put up a wooden shed for their own accommodation in what seemed twenty minutes, and then set to work to build us a house which we called 'Naulakha'.[22] Ninety feet was the length of it and thirty the width, on a high foundation of solid mortared rocks which gave us an airy and a skunk-proof basement. The rest was wood, shingled, roof and sides, with dull green hand-split shingles, and the windows were lavish and wide. Lavish, too, was the long open attic, as I realized when too late. Pigeon asked me whether I would have it finished in ash or cherry. Ignorant that I was, I chose ash, and so missed a stretch of perhaps the most satisfying interior wood that is grown. Those were opulent days, when timber was nothing regarded, and the best of cabinet-work could be had for little money.

Next, we laid out a long drive to the road. This needed dynamite to soften its grades and a most mellow plumber brought up many sticks of it all rattling about under his buggy-seat among the tamping-rods. We dived, like woodchucks, into the nearest deepest hole. Next, needing water, we sunk a five-inch shaft three hundred foot into the New England granite, which nowhere was less than three, though some say thirty, thousand foot thick. Over that we set a windmill, which gave us not enough water and moaned and squeaked o' nights. So we knocked out its lowest bolts, hitched on two yoke of bullocks, and overthrew it, as it might have been the Vendôme Column:[23] thus spiritually recouping ourselves for at least half the cost of erection. A low-power atmospheric pump, which it was my disgustful duty to oil, was its successor. These experiences gave us both a life-long taste for playing with timber, stone, concrete, and such delightful things.

Horses were an integral part of our lives, for the Bliss Cottage was three miles from the little town, and half a mile from the house in building. Our permanent servitor was a big, philo-sophical black called Marcus Aurelius,[24] who waited in the buggy as cars wait today, and when weary of standing up would carefully lie down and go to sleep between his shafts. After we had finished with him, we tied his reins short and sent him in charge of the buggy alone down the road to his stable-door, where he resumed his slumbers till someone came to undress him and put him to bed. There was a small mob of other horses about the landscape, including a meek old stallion with a permanently lame leg, who passed the evening of his days in a horse-power machine which cut wood for us.

I tried to give something of the fun and flavour of those days in a story called 'A Walking Delegate'[25] where all the characters are from horse-life.

The wife's passion, I discovered, was driving trotters. It chanced that our first winter in 'Naulakha' she went to look at the new patent safety heating-stove, which blew flame in her face and burnt it severely. She recovered slowly, and Dr Conland suggested that she needed a tonic. I had been in treaty for a couple of young, seal-brown, full brother and sister

Morgans,[26] good for a three-mile clip, and, on Conland's hint, concluded the deal. When I told the wife, she thought it would console her to try them and, that same afternoon, leaving one eye free of the bandages, she did so in three foot of snow and a failing light, while I suffered beside her. But Nip and Tuck were perfect roadsters and the 'tonic' succeeded. After that they took us all over the large countryside.

It would be hard to exaggerate the loneliness and sterility of life on the farms. The land was denuding itself of its accustomed inhabitants, and their places had not yet been taken by the wreckage of Eastern Europe or the wealthy city folk who later bought 'pleasure farms'. What might have become characters, powers, and attributes perverted themselves in that desolation as cankered trees throw out branches akimbo, and strange faiths and cruelties, born of solitude to the edge of insanity, flourished like lichen on sick bark.

One day-long excursion up the flanks of Wantastiquet, our guardian mountain across the river, brought us to a farm-house where we were welcomed by the usual wild-eyed, flat-fronted woman of the place. Looking over sweeps of emptiness, we saw our 'Naulakha' riding on its hillside like a little boat on the flank of a far wave. Said the woman, fiercely: 'Be you the new lights 'crost the valley yonder? Ye don't know what a comfort they've been to me this winter. Ye aren't ever goin' to shroud 'em up – or *be* ye?' So, as long as we lived there, that broad side of 'Naulakha' which looked her-ward was always nakedly lit.

In the little town where we shopped there was another atmosphere. Vermont was by tradition a 'Dry' State.[27] For that reason, one found in almost every office the water-bottle and thick tooth-glass displayed openly, and in discreet cupboards or drawers the whisky bottle. Business was conducted and concluded with gulps of raw spirit, followed by a pledget of ice-cold water. Then, both parties chewed cloves, but whether to defeat the Law, which no one ever regarded, or to deceive their women-folk, of whom they went in great fear (they were mostly educated up to College age by spinsters), I do not know.

But a promising scheme for a Country Club had to be abandoned because many men who would by right belong to it could not be trusted with a full whisky bottle. On the farms, of course, men drank cider, of various strengths, and sometimes achieved almost maniacal forms of drunkenness. The whole business seemed to me as unwholesomely furtive and false as many aspects of American life at that time.

Administratively, there was unlimited and meticulous legality, with a multiplication of semi-judicial offices and titles; but of law-abidingness, or of any conception of what that implied, not a trace. Very little in business, transportation, or distribution, that I had to deal with, was sure, punctual, accurate, or organized. But this they neither knew nor would have believed though angels affirmed it. Ethnologically, immigrants were coming into the States at about a million head a year. They supplied the cheap – almost slave – labour, lacking which all wheels would have stopped, and they were handled with a callousness that horrified me. The Irish had passed out of the market into 'politics' which suited their instincts of secrecy, plunder, and anonymous denunciation. The Italians were still at work, laying down trams, but were moving up, *via* small shops and curious activities, to the dominant position which they now occupy in well-organized society. The German, who had preceded even the Irish, counted himself a full-blooded American, and looked down gutturally on what he called 'foreign trash'. Somewhere in the background, though he did not know it, was the 'representative' American, who traced his blood through three or four generations and who, controlling nothing and affecting less, protested that the accepted lawlessness of life was not 'representative' of his country, whose moral, aesthetic, and literary champion he had appointed himself. He said, too, almost automatically, that all foreign elements could and would soon be 'assimilated' into 'good Americans'. And not a soul cared what he said or how he said it! They were making or losing money.

The political background of the land was monotonous. When the people looked, which was seldom, outside their own borders, England was still the dark and dreadful enemy to be feared and guarded against. The Irish, whose other creed is Hate; the history books in the Schools; the Orators; the eminent Senators;

and above all the Press; saw to that. Now John Hay,[28] one of the very few American Ambassadors to England with two sides to their heads, had his summer house a few hours north by rail from us. On a visit to him,[29] we discussed the matter. His explanation was convincing. I quote the words which stayed textually in my memory. 'America's hatred of England is the hoop round the forty-four (as they were then) staves of the Union.' He said it was the only standard possible to apply to an enormously variegated population. 'So – when a man comes up out of the sea, we say to him: "See that big bully over there in the East? He's England! Hate him, and you're a good American."'

On the principle, 'if you can't keep a love affair going, start a row', this is reasonable. At any rate the belief lifted on occasion the overwhelming vacuity of the national life into some contact with imponderable externals.

But how thoroughly the doctrine was exploited I did not realize till we visited Washington in '95, where I met Theodore Roosevelt,[30] then Under-Secretary (I never caught the name of the Upper) to the US Navy. I liked him from the first and largely believed in him. He would come to our hotel, and thank God in a loud voice that he had not one drop of British blood in him; his ancestry being Dutch, and his creed conforming-Dopper,[31] I think it is called. Naturally I told him nice tales about his Uncles and Aunts in South Africa – only I called them Ooms and Tanties – who esteemed themselves the sole lawful Dutch under the canopy and dismissed Roosevelt's stock for 'Verdomder Hollanders'.[32] Then he became really eloquent, and we would go off to the Zoo together, where he talked about grizzlies that he had met. It was laid on him, at that time, to furnish his land with an adequate Navy; the existing collection of unrelated types and casual purchases being worn out. I asked him how he proposed to get it, for the American people did not love taxation. 'Out of *you*,' was the disarming reply. And so – to some extent – it was. The obedient and instructed Press explained how England – treacherous and jealous as ever – only waited round the corner to descend on the unprotected coasts of Liberty, and to that end was preparing, etc. etc. etc. (This in

'95 when England had more than enough hay on her own trident to keep her busy!) But the trick worked, and all the Orators and Senators gave tongue, like the Hannibal Chollops [33] that they were. I remember the wife of a Senator who, apart from his politics, was very largely civilized, invited me to drop into the Senate and listen to her spouse 'twisting the Lion's tail'.[34] It seemed an odd sort of refreshment to offer a visitor. I could not go, but I read his speech. [At the present time (autumn '35) I have also read with interest the apology offered by an American Secretary of State to Nazi Germany for unfavourable comments on that land by a New York Police Court Judge.[35]] But those were great and spacious and friendly days in Washington which – politics apart – Allah had not altogether deprived of a sense of humour; and the food was a thing to dream of.

Through Roosevelt I met Professor Langley [36] of the Smithsonian,[37] an old man who had designed a model aeroplane driven – for petrol had not yet arrived – by a miniature flash-boiler engine, a marvel of delicate craftsmanship. It flew on trial over two hundred yards, and drowned itself in the waters of the Potomac, which was cause of great mirth and humour to the Press of his country. Langley took it coolly enough and said to me that, though he would never live till then, I should see the aeroplane established.

The Smithsonian, specially on the ethnological side, was a pleasant place to browse in. Every nation, like every individual, walks in a vain show – else it could not live with itself – but I never got over the wonder of a people who, having extirpated the aboriginals of their continent more completely than any modern race had ever done, honestly believed that they were a godly little New England community, setting examples to brutal mankind. This wonder I used to explain to Theodore Roosevelt, who made the glass cases of Indian relics shake with his rebuttals.

The next time I met him was in England, not long after his country had acquired the Philippines,[38] and he – like an elderly lady with one babe – yearned to advise England on colonial administration. His views were sound enough, for his subject was Egypt [39] as it was beginning to be then, and his text 'Govern or get out.' He consulted several people as to how far he could go. I assured him that the English would take anything from him, but were racially immune to advice.

I never met him again, but we corresponded through the years when he 'jumped' Panama [40] from a brother-President [41] there whom he described as 'Pithecanthropoid', [42] and also during the War, in the course of which I met two of his delightful sons. [43] My own idea of him was that he was a much bigger man than his people understood or, at that time, knew how to use, and that he and they might have been better off had he been born twenty years later.

Meantime, our lives went on at the Bliss Cottage and, so soon as it was built, at 'Naulakha'. To the former one day came Sam McClure, [44] credited with being the original of Stevenson's Pinkerton in *The Wrecker*, but himself, far more original. He had been everything from a pedlar to a tin-type photographer along the highways, and had held intact his genius and simplicity. He entered, alight with the notion for a new Magazine to be called 'McClure's'. I think the talk lasted some twelve – or it may have been seventeen – hours, before the notion was fully hatched out. He, like Roosevelt, was in advance of his age, for he looked rather straightly at practices and impostures which were in the course of being sanctified because they paid. People called it 'muck-raking' at the time, and it seemed to do no sort of good. I liked and admired McClure more than a little, for he was one of the few with whom three and a half words serve for a sentence, and as clean and straight as spring water. Nor did I like him less when he made a sporting offer to take all my output for the next few years at what looked like fancy rates. But the Committee of Ways and Means decided that futures were not to be dealt in. (I here earnestly commend to the attention of the ambitious young a text in the thirty-third chapter of Ecclesiasticus [45] which runs: '*As long as thou livest and hast breath in thee, give not thyself over to any.*')

To 'Naulakha', on a wet day, came from Scribner's of New York a large young man called Frank Doubleday, with a proposal, among other things, for a complete edition of my then works. One accepts or refuses things that really matter on personal and illogical grounds. We took to that young man at sight, and he and his wife became of our closest friends. In due time, when he was building up what turned into the great firm of Doubleday, Page & Co., and later Doubleday, Doran & Co.,[46] I handed over the American side of my business to him. Whereby I escaped many distractions for the rest of my life. Thanks to the large and intended gaps in the American Copyright law,[47] much could be done by the enterprising not only to steal, which was natural, but to add to and interpolate and embellish the thefts with stuff I had never written. At first this annoyed me, but later I laughed; and Frank Doubleday chased the pirates up with cheaper and cheaper editions, so that their thefts became less profitable. There no more pretence to morality in these gentlemen than in their brethren, the bootleggers[48] of later years. As a pillar of the Copyright League[49] (even *he* could not see the humour of it) once said, when I tried to bring him to book for a more than usually flagrant trespass: 'We thought there was money in it, so we did it.' It was, you see, his religion. By and large I should say that American pirates have made, say, half as many dollars out of my stuff as I am occasionally charged with having 'made' out of the legitimate market in that country.

Into this queer life the Father came to see how we fared, and we two went wandering into Quebec, where, the temperature being 95 and all the world dressed all over after the convention of those days, the Father was much amazed. Then we visited at Boston his old friend, Charles Eliot Norton[50] of Harvard, whose daughters I had known at 'The Grange' in my boyhood and since. They were Brahmins[51] of the Boston Brahmins, living delightfully, but Norton himself, full of forebodings as to the future of his land's soul, felt the established earth sliding under him, as horses feel coming earth-tremors.

He told us a tale of old days in New England. He and another Professor, wandering round the country in a buggy and discussing high and moral matters, halted at the farm of an elderly farmer well known to them, who, in the usual silence of New England, set about getting the horse a bucket of water.

The Committee of Ways and Means

The two men in the buggy went on with their discussion, in the course of which one of them said: 'Well, according to Montaigne,' and gave a quotation. Voice from the horse's head, where the farmer was holding the bucket: ''Tweren't Montaigne said that. 'Twere Mon-tes-ki-ew.'[52] And 'twas.

That, said Norton, was in the middle or late 'Seventies. We two wandered about the back of Shady Hill in a buggy, but nothing of that amazing kind befell us. And Norton spoke of Emerson and Wendell Holmes and Longfellow and the Alcotts[53] and other influences of the past as we returned to his library, and he browsed aloud among his books; for he was a scholar among scholars.

But what struck me, and he owned to something of the same feeling, was the apparent waste and ineffectiveness, in the face of the foreign inrush, of all the indigenous effort of the past generation. It was then that I first began to wonder whether Abraham Lincoln[54] had not killed rather too many autochthonous 'Americans' in the Civil War, for the benefit of their hastily imported Continental supplanters. This is black heresy, but I have since met men and women who have breathed it. The weakest of the old-type immigrants had been sifted and salted by the long sailing-voyage of those days. But steam began in the late 'Sixties and early 'Seventies, when human cargoes could be delivered with all their imperfections and infections in a fortnight or so. And one million[55] more-or-less acclimatized Americans had been killed.

Somehow or other, between '92 and '96 we managed to pay two flying visits[56] to England, where my people were retired and lived in Wiltshire; and we learned to loathe the cold North Atlantic more and more. On one trip our steamer came almost atop of a whale, who submerged just in time to clear us, and looked up into my face with an unforgettable little eye the size of a bullock's. Eminent Masters R.L.S. will remember what William Dent Pitman[57] saw of 'haughty and indefinable' in the hairdresser's waxen model. When I was illustrating the *Just So Stories*, I remembered and strove after that eye.

We went once or twice[58] to Gloucester, Mass., on a summer visit, when I attended the annual Memorial Service to the men drowned or lost in the cod-fishing schooners fleet. Gloucester was then the metropolis of that industry.

Now our Dr Conland had served in that fleet when he was young. One thing leading to another, as happens in this world, I embarked on a little book which was called *Captains Courageous*. My part was the writing; his the details. This book took us (he rejoicing to escape from the dread respectability of our little town) to the shore-front, and the old T-wharf of Boston Harbour, and to queer meals in sailors' eating-houses, where he renewed his youth among ex-shipmates or their kin. We assisted hospitable tug-masters to help haul three- and four-stick schooners of Pocahontas coal[59] all round the harbour; we boarded every craft that looked as if she might be useful, and we delighted ourselves to the limit of delight. Charts we got – old and new – and the crude implements of navigation such as they used off the Banks,[60] and a battered boat-compass, still a treasure with me. (Also, by pure luck, I had sight of the first sickening uprush and vomit of iridescent coal-dusted water into the hold of a ship, a crippled iron hulk, sinking at her moorings.) And Conland took large cod and the appropriate knives with which they are prepared for the hold, and demonstrated anatomically and surgically so that I could make no mistake about treating them in print. Old tales, too, he dug up, and the lists of dead and gone schooners whom he had loved, and I revelled in profligate abundance of detail – not necessarily for publication but for the joy of it. And he sent me – may he be forgiven! – out on a pollock-fisher, which is ten times fouler than any cod-schooner, and I was immortally sick, even though they tried to revive me with a fragment of unfresh pollock.

As though this were not enough, when, at the end of my tale, I desired that some of my characters should pass from San Francisco to New York in record time, and wrote to a railway magnate[61] of my acquaintance asking what he himself would do, that most excellent man sent a fully worked-out time-table, with watering halts, changes of engine, mileage, track conditions, and climates, so that a corpse could not have gone wrong in the schedule. My characters arrived triumphantly; and, then, a real live railway magnate was so moved after reading the book that he called out his engines and called out his men, hitched up his own private car, and set himself to beat *my* time on paper over the identical route, and succeeded. Yet the book was not all reporterage. I wanted to see if I could catch and hold something of a rather beautiful localized American atmosphere that was already beginning to fade. Thanks to Conland I came near this.

A million – or it may have been only forty – years later, a Super-film Magnate [62] was in treaty with me for the film rights of this book. At the end of the sitting, my Daemon led me to ask if it were proposed to introduce much 'sex appeal' into the great work. 'Why, certainly,' said he. Now a happily married lady cod-fish lays about three million eggs at one confinement. I told him as much. He said: 'Is that so?' And went on about 'ideals' . . . Conland had been long since dead, but I prayed that wherever he was, he might have heard.

And so, in this unreal life, indoors and out, four years passed, and a good deal of verse and prose saw the light. Better than all, I had known a corner of the United States as a householder, which is the only way of getting at a country. Tourists may carry away impressions, but it is the seasonal detail of small things and doings (such as putting up fly-screens and stove-pipes, buying yeast-cakes and being lectured by your neighbours) that bite in the lines of mental pictures. They were an interesting folk, but behind their desperate activities lay always, it seemed to me, immense and unacknowledged boredom – the dead-weight of material things passionately worked up into Gods, that only bored their worshippers more and worse and longer. The intellectual influences of their Continental immigrants were to come later. At this time they were still more or less connected with the English tradition and schools, and the Semitic strain had not yet been uplifted in a too-much-at-ease Zion. So far as I was concerned, I felt the atmosphere was to some extent hostile. [63] The idea seemed to be that I was 'making money' out of America – witness the new house and the horses – and was not sufficiently grateful for my privileges. My visits to England and the talk there persuaded me that the English scene might be shifting to some new developments, which would be worth watching. A meeting of the Committee of Ways and Means came to the conclusion that 'Naulakha', desirable as it was, meant only 'a house' and not '*The* House' of our dreams. So we loosed hold and, with another small daughter,[64] born in the early spring snows and beautifully tanned in a sumptuous upper verandah, we took ship for England, after clearing up all our accounts. As Emerson wrote:

> Wilt thou seal up the avenues of ill?
> Pay every debt as if God wrote the bill.[65]

The spring of '96 saw us in Torquay,[66] where we found a house for our heads that seemed almost too good to be true. It was large and bright, with big rooms each and all open to the sun, the grounds embellished with great trees and the warm land dipping southerly to the clean sea under the Marychurch cliffs. It had been inhabited for thirty years by three old maids. We took it hopefully. Then we made two notable discoveries. Everybody was learning to ride things called 'bicycles'. In Torquay there was a circular cinder-track where, at stated hours, men and women rode solemnly round and round on them. Tailors supplied special costumes for this sport. Someone – I think it was Sam McClure from America – had given us a tandem bicycle, whose double steering-bars made good dependence for continuous domestic quarrel. On this devil's toast-rack we took exercise, each believing that the other liked it. We even rode it through the idle, empty lanes, and would pass or overtake without upset several carts in several hours. But, one fortunate day, it skidded, and decanted us on to the road-metal. Almost before we had risen from our knees, we made mutual confession of our common loathing of wheels, pushed the Hell-Spider home by hand, and rode it no more.

The other revelation came in the shape of a growing depression which enveloped us both – a gathering blackness of mind and sorrow of the heart, that each put down to the new, soft climate and, without telling the other, fought against for long weeks. It was the Feng-shui – the Spirit of the house itself – that darkened the sunshine and fell upon us every time we entered, checking the very words on our lips.

A talk about a doubtful cistern brought another mutual confession. 'But I thought *you* liked the place?' 'But I made sure *you* did,' was the burden of our litanies. Using the cistern for a stalking-horse, we paid forfeit and fled.[67] More than thirty years later on a motor-trip we ventured down the steep little road to that house, and met, almost unchanged, the gardener and his wife in the large, open, sunny stable-yard, and, quite unchanged, the same brooding Spirit of deep, deep Despondency within the open, lit rooms.

But while we were at Torquay there came to me the idea of beginning some tracts or parables on the education of the young. These, for reasons honestly beyond my control, turned themselves into a series of tales called *Stalky & Co.* My very dear Headmaster, Cormell Price, who had now turned into 'Uncle Crom' or just 'Crommy', paid a visit at the time[68] and we discussed school things generally. He said, with the chuckle that I had reason to know, that my tracts would be some time before they came to their own. On their appearance they were regarded as irreverent, not true to life, and rather 'brutal'. This led me to wonder, not for the first time, at which end of their carcasses grown men keep their school memories.

Talking things over with 'Crommy', I reviled him for the badness and scantiness of our food at Westward Ho! To which he replied: 'We-el! For one thing, we were all as poor as church mice. Can you remember anyone who had as much as a bob a week pocket-money? *I* can't. For another, a boy who is always hungry is more interested in his belly than in anything else.' (In the Boer War I learned that the virtue in a battalion living on what is known as 'Two and a half' – Army biscuits – a day is severe.) Speaking of sickness and epidemics, which were unknown to us, he said: 'I expect you were healthy because you lived in the open almost as much as Dartmoor ponies.' *Stalky & Co.* became the illegitimate ancestor of several stories of school-life whose heroes lived through experiences mercifully denied to me. It is still read ('35) and I maintain it is a truly valuable collection of tracts.

Our flight from Torquay ended almost by instinct at Rottingdean[69] where the beloved Aunt and Uncle had their holiday house, and where I had spent my very last days before sailing for India fourteen years back. In 1882 there had been but one daily bus from Brighton, which took forty minutes; and when a stranger appeared on the village green the native young would stick out their tongues at him. The Downs poured almost direct into the one village street and lay out eastward unbroken to Russia Hill above Newhaven. It was little altered in '96. My cousin, Stanley Baldwin, had married the eldest daughter of the Ridsdales[70] out of 'The Dene' – the big house that flanked one side of the green. My Uncle's 'North End House' commanded the other, and a third house opposite the church was waiting to be taken according to the decrees of Fate. The Baldwin marriage, then, made us free of the joyous young brotherhood and sisterhood of 'The Dene', and its friends.

The Aunt and the Uncle had said to us: 'Let the child that is coming to you be born in our house,' and had effaced themselves till my son John[71] arrived on a warm August night of '97, under what seemed every good omen. Meantime, we had rented by direct interposition of Fate that third house opposite the church on the green. It stood in a sort of little island behind flint walls which we then thought were high enough, and almost beneath some big ilex trees. It was small, none too well built, but cheap, and so suited us who still remembered a little affair at Yokohama. Then there grew up great happiness between 'The Dene', 'North End House', and 'The Elms'. One could throw a cricket-ball from any one house to the other, but, beyond turning out at 2 a.m. to help a silly foxhound puppy who had stuck in a drain, I do not remember any violent alarms and excursions other than packing farm-carts filled with mixed babies – Stanley Baldwin's and ours – and despatching them into the safe clean heart of the motherly Downs for jam-smeared picnics. Those Downs moved me to write some verses called 'Sussex'.[72] Today, from Rottingdean to Newhaven is almost fully developed suburb, of great horror.

When the Burne-Joneses returned to their own 'North End House', all was more than well. My Uncle's world was naturally not mine, but his heart and brain were large enough to take in any universe, and in the matter of doing one's own work in one's own way he had no doubts. His golden laugh, his delight in small things, and the perpetual war of practical jokes that waged between us, was refreshment after working hours. And when we cousins, Phil, his son, Stanley Baldwin and I, went to the beach and came back with descriptions of fat bathers, he would draw them, indescribably swag-bellied, wallowing in the surf. Those were exceedingly good days, and one's work came easily and fully.

Now even in the Bliss Cottage I had a vague notion of an Irish boy, born in India and mixed up with native life. I went as far as to make him the son of a private in an Irish Battalion, and christened him 'Kim of the 'Rishti – short, that is, for Irish. This done, I felt like Mr Micawber[73] that I had as good as paid that I O U on the future, and went after other things for some years.

In the meantime my people had left India for good, and were established in a small stone house near Tisbury, Wilts. It possessed a neat little stone-walled stable with a shed or two, all perfectly designed for clay and plaster of Paris works, which are not desired indoors. Later, the Father put up a tin tabernacle which he had thatched, and there disposed his drawing port-folios, big photo and architectural books, gravers, modelling-tools, paints, siccatives, varnishes, and the hundred other don't-you-touch-'ems that every right-minded man who works with his hands naturally collects. (These matters are detailed because they all come into the story.)

Within short walk of him lay 'Fonthill', the great house of Alfred Morrison,[74] millionaire and collector of all manner of beautiful things, his wife contenting herself with mere precious and sub-precious stones. And my Father was free of all these treasures and many others in such houses as 'Clouds', where the Wyndhams[75] lived, a few miles away. I think that both he and my Mother were happy in their English years, for they knew exactly what they did not want; and I knew that when I came over to see them I had no need to sing: 'Backward, turn backward, O Time, in your flight.'[76]

In a gloomy, windy autumn *Kim* came back to me with

insistence, and I took it to be smoked over with my Father. Under our united tobaccos it grew like the Djinn released from the brass bottle,[77] and the more we explored its possibilities the more opulence of detail did we discover. I do not know what proportion of an iceberg is below water-line, but *Kim* as it finally appeared was about one-tenth of what the first lavish specification called for.

As to its form there was but one possible to the author, who said that what was good enough for Cervantes[78] was good enough for him. To whom the Mother: 'Don't you stand in your wool-boots hiding behind Cervantes with *me*! You *know* you couldn't make a plot to save your soul.'

So I went home much fortified and *Kim* took care of himself. The only trouble was to keep him within bounds. Between us, we knew every step, sight, and smell on his casual road, as well as all the persons he met. Once only, as I remember, did I have to bother the India Office,[79] where there are four acres of books and documents in the basements, for a certain work on Indian magic which I always sincerely regret that I could not steal. They fuss about receipts there.

At 'The Elms', Rottingdean, the sou'-wester raged day and night, till the silly windows jiggled their wedges loose. (Which was why the Committee vowed never to have a house of their own with up-and-down windows. Cf. Charles Reade[80] on that subject.) But I was quite unconcerned. I had my Eastern sunlight and if I wanted more I could get it at 'The Gables', Tisbury. At last I reported *Kim* finished. 'Did *it* stop, or you?' the Father asked. And when I told him that it was *It*, he said: 'Then it oughtn't to be too bad.'

He would take no sort of credit for any of his suggestions, memories, or confirmations – not even for that single touch of the low-driving sunlight which makes luminous every detail in the picture of the Grand Trunk Road[81] at eventide. The Himalayas I painted *all* by myself, as the children say. So also the picture of the Lahore Museum of which I had once been Deputy Curator for six weeks – unpaid but immensely important. And there was a half-chapter of the Lama sitting down in the blue-green shadows at the foot of a glacier, telling Kim stories out of the Jatakas,[82] which was truly beautiful but, as my old Classics master[83] would have said, 'otiose', and it was removed almost with tears.

But the crown of the fun came when (in 1902) was issued an illustrated edition of my works,[84] and the Father attended to *Kim*. He had the notion of making low-relief plaques and photographing them afterwards. Here it was needful to catch the local photographer, who, till then, had specialized in privates of the Line with plastered hair and skin-tight uniforms, and to lead him up the strenuous path of photographing dead things so that they might show a little life. The man was a bit bewildered at first, but he had a teacher of teachers, and so grew to understand. The incidental muck-heaps in the stable-yard were quite noticeable, though a loyal housemaid fought them broom-and-bucket, and Mother allowed messy half-born 'sketches' to be dumped by our careless hands on sofas and chairs. Naturally when he got his final proofs he was sure that 'it all ought to be done again from the beginning', which was rather how I felt about the letterpress, but, if it be possible, he and I will do that in a better world, and on a scale to amaze Archangels.

There is one picture that I remember of him in the tin tabernacle, hunting big photos of Indian architecture for some utterly trivial detail in a corner of some plaque. He looked up as I came in and, rubbing his beard and carrying on his own thought, quoted: 'If you get simple beauty and naught else, You get about the best thing God invents.'[85] It is the greatest of my many blessings that I was given grace to know them at the time, instead of having them brought to my remorseful notice too late.

I expect that is why I am perhaps a little impatient over the Higher Cannibalism[86] as practised today.

And so much for *Kim* which has stood up for thirty-five years. There was a good deal of beauty in it, and not a little wisdom; the best in both sorts being owed to my Father.

A great, but frightening, honour came to me when I was thirty-three (1897) and was elected to the Athenaeum[87] under Rule Two, which provides for admitting distinguished persons without ballot. I took counsel with Burne-Jones as to what to do. 'I don't dine there often,' said he. 'It frightens *me* rather, but we'll tackle it together.' And on a night appointed we went to that meal. So far as I recall we were the only people in that big dining-room, for in those days the Athenaeum, till one got to know it, was rather like a cathedral between services. But at any rate I had dined there, and hung my hat on Peg 33. (I have shifted it since.) Before long I realized that if one wanted to know anything from forging an anchor to forging antiquities one would find the world's ultimate expert in the matter at lunch. I managed to be taken into a delightful window-table, pre-empted by an old General,[88] who had begun life as a Middy in the Crimea before he entered the Guards. In his later years he was a fearless yachtsman, as well as several other things, and he dealt faithfully with me when I made technical errors in any tale of mine that interested him. I grew very fond of him, and of four or five others who used that table.

One afternoon, I remember, Parsons[89] of the *Turbinia* asked if I would care to see a diamond burned. The demonstration took place in a room crammed with wires and electric cells (I forget what their aggregate voltage was) and all went well for a while. The diamond's tip bubbled like cauliflower *au gratin*.[90] Then there was a flash and a crash, and we were on the floor in darkness. But, as Parsons said, that was not the diamond's fault.

Among other pillars of the dear, dingy, old downstairs billiard-room was Hercules Read,[91] of the British Museum on the Eastern Antiquities side. Externally, he was very handsome, but his professional soul was black, even for that of a Curator – and my Father had been a Curator. (*Note.* It is entirely right that the English should mistrust and disregard all the Arts and most of the Sciences, for on that indifference rests their moral grandeur, but their starvation in their estimates is sometimes too marked.)

At this present age I do not lunch very often at the Athenaeum, where it has struck me that the bulk of the members are scandalously young, whether elected under Rule Two or by ballot of their fellow-infants. Nor do I relish persons of forty calling me 'Sir'.

The Committee of Ways and Means

My life made me grossly dependent on Clubs for my spiritual comfort. Three English ones, the Athenaeum, Carlton, and Beefsteak,[92] met my wants, but the Beefsteak gave me most. Our company there was unpredictable, and one could say what one pleased at the moment without being taken at the foot of the letter. Sometimes one would draw a full house of five different professions, from the Bench to the Dramatic Buccaneer. Otherwhiles, three of a kind, chance-stranded in Town, would drift into long, leisurely talk that ranged half earth over, and separate well pleased with themselves and their table-companions. And once, when I feared that I might have to dine alone, there entered a member whom I had never seen before, and have never met since, full of bird-preservation. By the time we parted what I did not know about bird sanctuaries was scarcely worth knowing. But it was best when of a sudden someone or something plunged us all in what you might call a general 'rag',[93] each man's tongue guarding his own head.

There is no race so dowered as the English with the gift of talking real, rich, allusive, cut-in-and-out 'skittles'.[94] Americans are too much anecdotards; the French too much orators for this light-handed game, and neither race delivers itself so unreservedly to mirth as we do.

When I lived in Villiers Street, I picked up with the shore-end of a select fishing-club, which met in a tobacconist's back-parlour. They were mostly small tradesmen, keen on roach, dace, and such, but they too had that gift, as I expect their forebears had in Addison's time.[95]

The late Doctor Johnson[96] once observed that 'we shall receive no letters in the grave.' I am perfectly sure, though Boswell never set it down, that he lamented the lack of Clubs in that same place.

Chapter 6

⦃ South Africa ⦄

But at the back of my head there was an uneasiness, based on things that men were telling me about affairs outside England. (The inhabitants of that country never looked further than their annual seaside resorts.) There was trouble, too, in South Africa after the Jameson Raid[1] which promised, men wrote me, further trouble. Altogether, one had a sense of 'a sound of a going in the tops of the mulberry trees'[2] – of things moving into position as troops move. And into the middle of it all came the Great Queen's Diamond Jubilee,[3] and a certain optimism that scared me. The outcome, as far as I was concerned, took the shape of a set of verses called 'Recessional',[4] which were published in *The Times* in '97 at the end of the Jubilee celebrations. It was more in the nature of a *nuzzur-wattu* (an averter of the Evil Eye), and – with the conservatism of the English – was used in choirs and places where they sing long after our Navy and Army alike had in the name of 'peace' been rendered innocuous. It was written just before I went off on Navy manœuvres with my friend Captain E. H. Bayly.[5] When I returned it seemed to me that the time was ripe for its publication, so, after making one or two changes in it, I gave it to *The Times*. I say 'gave' because for this kind of work I did not take payment. It does not much matter what people think of a man after his death, but I should not like the people whose good opinion I valued to believe that I took money for verses on Joseph Chamberlain, Rhodes, Lord Milner,[6] or any of my South African verse in *The Times*.

It was this uneasiness of mine which led us down to the Cape in the winter of '97,[7] taking the Father with us. There we lived in a boarding-house at Wynberg,[8] kept by an Irishwoman, who faithfully followed the instincts of her race and spread miseries and discomforts round her in return for good monies. But the children throve, and the colour, light, and half-Oriental manners of the land bound chains round our hearts for years to come.

It was here that I first met Rhodes to have any talk with. He was as inarticulate as a schoolboy of fifteen. Jameson and he, as I perceived later, communicated by telepathy. But Jameson was not with him at that time. Rhodes had a habit of jerking out sudden questions as disconcerting as those of a child – or the Roman Emperor he so much resembled. He said to me apropos of nothing in particular: 'What's your dream?' I answered that he was part of it, and I think I told him that I had come down to look at things. He showed me some of his newly established fruit-farms in the peninsula, wonderful old Dutch houses, stalled in deep peace, and lamented the difficulty of getting sound wood for packing-cases and the shortcomings of native labour. But it was his wish and his will that there should be a fruit-growing industry in the Colony, and his chosen lieutenants made it presently come to pass. The Colony then owed no thanks to any Dutch Ministry[9] in that regard. The racial twist of the Dutch (they had taken that title to themselves and called the inhabitants of the Low Countries 'Hollanders') was to exploit everything they could which was being done for them, to put every obstacle in the way of any sort of development, and to take all the cash they could squeeze out of it. In which respect they were no better and no worse than many of their brethren. It was against their creed to try and stamp out cattle-plagues, to dip their sheep, or to combat locusts, which in a country overwhelmingly pastoral had its drawbacks. Cape Town, as a big distributing centre, was dominated in many ways by rather nervous shopkeepers, who wished to stand well with their customers up-country, and who served as Mayors and occasional public officials. And the aftermath of the Jameson Raid had scared many people.

During the South African War[10] my position among the rank and file came to be unofficially above that of most Generals. Money was wanted to procure small comforts for the troops at the Front and, to this end, the *Daily Mail* started what must have been a very early 'stunt'. It was agreed that I should ask the public for subscriptions. That paper charged itself with the rest. My verses ('The Absent-minded Beggar'[11]) had some elements of direct appeal but, as was pointed out, lacked 'poetry'. Sir Arthur Sullivan[12] wedded the words to a tune guaranteed to pull teeth out of barrel-organs. Anybody could do what they chose with the result, recite, sing, intone, or reprint, etc., on condition that they turned in all fees and profits to the main account – 'The Absent-minded Beggar Fund' – which closed at about a quarter of a million. Some of this was spent in tobacco. Men smoked pipes more than cigarettes at that epoch, and the popular brand was a cake – chewable also – called 'Hignett's True Affection'. My note-of-hand at the Cape Town depot was good for as much as I cared to take about with me. The rest followed. My telegrams were given priority by sweating RE sergeants[13] from all sorts of congested depots. My seat in the train was kept for me by British Bayonets in their shirt-sleeves. My small baggage was fought for and ser-vilely carried by Colonial details, who are not normally meek, and I was *persona gratissima*[14] at certain Wynberg Hospitals[15] where the nurses found I was good for pyjamas. Once I took a bale of them to the wrong nurse (the red capes confused me) and, knowing the matter to be urgent, loudly announced: 'Sister, I've got your pyjamas.' That one was neither grateful nor very polite.

My attractions led to every sort of delightful or sometimes sorrowful wayside intimacies with all manner of men: and only once did I receive a snub. I was going up to Bloemfontein[16] just after its capture in a carriage taken from the Boers, who had covered its floors with sheep's guts and onions, and its side with caricatures of 'Chamberlain' on a gallows. Otherwise, there was nothing much except woodwork. Behind us was an open truck of British troops whom the Company wag was enter-taining by mimicking their officers telling them how to pile horseshoes. As evening fell, I got from him a couple of three-wicked, signal-lamp candles, which gave us at least light to eat by. I naturally wanted to know how he had come by these desirable things. He replied: 'Look 'ere, Guv'nor, *I* didn't ask *you* 'ow you come by the baccy you dished out just now. *Can't* you bloody well leave me alone?'

In this same ghost-train an Indian officer's servant (Muhammedan) was worried on a point of conscience. 'Would this Government-issued tin of bully-beef be lawful food for a Muslim?' I told him that, when Islam wars with unbelievers, the Koran permits reasonable latitude of ceremonial obligations; and he need not hesitate. Next dawn, he was at my bunk-side with Anglo-India's morning cup of tea. (He must have stolen the hot water from the engine, for there was not a drop in the landscape.) When I asked how the miracle had come about, he replied, with a smile of my own Kadir Baksh:[17] '*Millar*, Sahib,' signifying that he had found (or 'made') it.

My Bloemfontein trip was on Lord Roberts' order[18] to report and do what I was told. This was explained at the station by two strangers, who grew into my friends for life, H. A. Gwynne,[19] then Head Correspondent of Reuters', and Perceval Landon[20] of *The Times*. 'You've got to help us edit a paper for the troops,' they said, and forthwith inducted me into the newly captured 'office', for Bloemfontein had fallen – Boer fashion – rather like an outraged Sunday School a few days before.

The compositors and the plant were also captives of our bow and spear and rather cross about it – especially the ex-editor's wife, a German with a tongue. When one saw a compositor, one told him to compose Lord Roberts' Official Proclamation to the deeply injured enemy. I had the satisfaction of picking up from the floor a detailed account of how Her Majesty's Brigade of Guards had been driven into action by the fire of our artillery; and a proof of a really rude leader about myself.

There was in that lull a large trade in proclamations – and butter at half a crown the pound. We used all the old stereos,[21] advertising long-since-exhausted comestibles, coal and groceries (face-powder, I think, was the only surviving commodity in the Bloemfontein shops), and we enlivened their interstices with our own contributions, supplemented by the works of dusty men, who looked in and gave us very fine copy – mostly libellous.

Julian Ralph,[22] the very best of Americans, was a co-editor
also. And he had a grown son who went down with a fever
unpleasantly like typhoid. We searched for a competent doctor,
and halted a German who, so great was the terror of our arms
after the 'capture', demanded haughtily: 'But who shall pay me
for my trouble if I come?' No one seemed to know, but several
men explained who would pay him if he dallied on the way.
He took one look at the boy's stomach, and said happily: 'Of
course it is typhoid.' Then came the question how to get the
case over to hospital, which was rank with typhoid, the Boers
having cut the water-supply. The first thing was to fetch down
the temperature with an alcohol swabbing. Here we were at a
standstill till some genius – I think it was Landon – said: 'I've
noticed there's an officer's wife in the place who's wearing a
fringe.'[23] On this hint a man went forth into the wide dusty
streets, and presently found her, fringe and all. Heaven knows
how she had managed to wangle her way up, but she was a
sportswoman of purest water. 'Come to my room,' said she,
and in passing over the priceless bottle, only sighed: 'Don't use
it *all* – unless you have to.' We ran the boy down from 103 to a
generous 99 and pushed him into hospital, where it turned out
that it was not typhoid after all but only bad veldt-fever.

First and last there were, I think, eight thousand cases of
typhoid in Bloemfontein. Often to my knowledge both 'ceremonial' Union Jacks in a battalion would be 'in use' at the same
time. Extra corpses went to the grave under the Service
blanket.

Our own utter carelessness, officialdom, and ignorance were
responsible for much of the death-rate.[24] I have seen a Horse
Battery 'dead to the wide'[25] come in at midnight in raging rain
and be assigned, by some idiot saving himself trouble, the site
of an evacuated typhoid-hospital. Result – thirty cases after a
month. I have seen men drinking raw Modder-river a few
yards below where the mules were staling; and the organization
and siting of latrines seemed to be considered 'nigger-work'.
The most important medical office in any battalion ought to be
Provost-Marshal of Latrines.

To typhoid was added dysentery, the smell of which is even

more depressing than the stench of human carrion. One could wind the dysentery tents a mile off. And remember that, till we planted disease, the vast sun-baked land was antiseptic and sterilized – so much so that a clean abdominal Mauser-wound [26] often entailed no more than a week of abstention from solid food. I found this out on a hospital-train, where I had to head off a mob of angry 'abdominals' from regular rations. That was when we were picking up casualties after a small affair called Paardeberg,[27] and the lists – really about two thousand – were carefully minimized to save the English public from 'shock'. During this work I happened to fall unreservedly, in darkness, over a man near the train, and filled my palms with gravel. He explained in an even voice that he was 'fractured 'ip, sir. 'Ope you ain't 'urt yourself, sir.' I never got at this unknown Philip Sidney's name.[28] They were wonderful even in the hour of death – these men and boys – lodge-keepers and ex-butlers of the Reserve and raw town-lads of twenty.

But to return to Bloemfontein. In an interval of our editorial labours, I went out of the town and presently met the 'solitary horseman' of the novels.[29] He was a Conductor – Commissariat Sergeant – who reported that the 'flower of the British Army' had been ambushed and cut up at a place called 'Sanna's Post',[30] and passed on obviously discomposed. I had imagined the flower of that Army to be busied behind me reading our paper; but, a short while after, I met an officer who, in the old Indian days, was nicknamed 'the Sardine'. He was calm, but rather fuzzy as to the outlines of his uniform, which was frayed and ripped by bullets. Yes, there had been trouble where he came from, but he was fuller for the moment of professional admiration.

'What was it like? They got us in a donga.[31] Just like going into a theatre. "Stalls left, dress-circle right," don't you know? We just dropped into the trap, and it was "Infantry this way, please. Guns to the right, *if* you please." Beautiful bit of work! How many did they get of us? About twelve hundred, I think, and four – maybe six – guns. Expert job they made of it. *That's* the result of bill-stickin' expeditions.' And with more compliments to the foe, he too passed on.

By the time that I returned to Bloemfontein the populace had it that eighty thousand Boers were closing in on the town at once, and the Press Censor (Lord Stanley, now Derby) was besieged with persons anxious to telegraph to Cape Town. To him a non-Aryan pushed a domestic wire 'weather here change-able'. Stanley, himself a little worried for the fate of some of his friends in that ambuscaded column, rebuked the gentleman.

'The Sardine' was right about the 'bill-sticking' expeditions. Wandering columns had been sent round the country to show how kind the British desired to be to the misguided Boer. But the Transvaal Boer, not being a town-bird, was unimpressed by the 'fall' of the Free State capital, and ran loose on the veldt with his pony and Mauser.

So there had to be a battle, which was called the Battle of Kari Siding.[32] All the staff of the *Bloemfontein Friend* attended. I was put in a Cape cart, with native driver, containing most of the drinks, and with me was a well-known war-correspondent.[33] The enormous pale landscape swallowed up seven thousand troops without a sign, along a front of seven miles. On our way we passed a collection of neat, deep, and empty trenches well undercut for shelter on the shrapnel side. A young Guards officer, recently promoted to *Brevet*-Major – and rather sore with the paper that we had printed it *Branch* – studied them interestedly. They were the first dim lines of the dug-out, but his and our eyes were held. The Hun had designed them *secundum artem*,[34] but the Boer had preferred the open within reach of his pony. At last we came to a lone farm-house in a vale adorned with no less than five white flags. Beyond the ridge was a sputter of musketry and now and then the whoop of a field-piece. 'Here,' said my guide and guardian, 'we get out and walk. Our driver will wait for us at the farm-house.' But the driver loudly objected. 'No, sar. They shoot. They shoot me.' 'But they are white-flagged all over,' we said. 'Yess, sar. That *why*,' was his answer, and he preferred to take his mules down into a decently remote donga and wait our return.

The farm-house (you will see in a little why I am so detailed) held two men and, I think, two women, who received us dis-interestedly. We went on into a vacant world full of sunshine and distances, where now and again a single bullet sang to himself. What I most objected to was the sensation of being under aimed fire – being, as it were, required as a head. 'What are they doing this for?' I asked my friend. 'Because they think we are the Something Light Horse. They ought to be just under this slope.' I prayed that the particularly Something Light Horse would go elsewhere, which they presently did, for the aimed fire slackened and a wandering Colonial, bored to extinction, turned up with news from a far flank. 'No; nothing doing and no one to see.' Then more cracklings and a most cautious move forward to the lip of a large hollow where sheep were grazing. Some of them began to drop and kick. 'That's both sides trying sighting-shots,' said my companion. 'What range do you make it?' I asked. 'Eight hundred, at the nearest. That's close quarters nowadays. You'll never see anything closer than this. Modern rifles make it impossible. We're hung up till something cracks somewhere.' There was a decent lull for meals on both sides, interrupted now and again by sputters. Then one indubitable shell – ridiculously like a pip-squeak in that vastness but throwing up much dirt. 'Krupp![35] Four or six pounder at extreme range,' said the expert. 'They still think we're the— Light Horse. They'll come to be fairly regular from now on.' Sure enough, every twenty minutes or so, one judgmatic shell pitched on our slope. We waited, seeing nothing in the emptiness, and hearing only a faint murmur as of wind along gas-jets, running in and out of the unconcerned hills.

Then pom-poms opened. These were nasty little one-pounders, ten in a belt (which usually jammed about the sixth round). On soft ground they merely thudded. On rock-face the shell breaks up and yowls like a cat. My friend for the first time seemed interested. 'If these are *their* pom-poms, it's Pretoria for us,' was his diagnosis. I looked behind me – the whole length of South Africa down to Cape Town – and it seemed very far. I felt that I could have covered it in five minutes under fair conditions, but – *not* with those aimed shots up my back. The pom-poms opened again at a bare rock-reef that gave the shells full value. For about two minutes a file of racing ponies, their tails and their riders' heads well down, showed

and vanished northward. 'Our pom-poms,' said the correspondent. 'Le Gallais,[36] I expect. *Now* we shan't be long.'
All this time the absurd Krupp was faithfully feeling for us,
vice[37]—Light Horse, and, given a few more hours, might
perhaps hit one of us. Then to the left, almost under us, a small
piece of hanging woodland filled and fumed with our shrapnel
much as a man's moustache fills with cigarette-smoke. It was
most impressive and lasted for quite twenty minutes. Then
silence; then a movement of men and horses from our side up
the slope, and the hangar our guns had been hammering spat
steady fire at them. More Boer ponies on more skylines; a last
flurry of pom-poms on the right and a little frieze of far-off
meek-tailed ponies, already out of rifle range.

'*Maffeesh*,'[38] said the correspondent, and fell to writing on
his knee. 'We've shifted 'em.'

Leaving our infanty to follow men on pony-back towards the
Equator, we returned to the farm-house. In the donga where he
was waiting someone squibbed off a rifle just after we took our
seats, and our driver flogged out over the rocks to the danger of
our sacred bottles.

Then Bloemfontein, and Gwynne storming in late with his
accounts complete – one hundred and twenty-five casualties,
and the general opinion that 'French[39] was a bit of a butcher'
and a tale of the General commanding the cavalry who absolutely refused to break up his horses by galloping them across
raw rock – 'not for any dam' Boer.'

Months later, I got a cutting from an American paper, on
information from Geneva – even then a pest-house of propaganda – describing how I and some officers – names, date, and
place correct – had entered a farm-house where we found two
men and three women. We had dragged the women from under
the bed where they had taken refuge (I assure you that no
Tantie Sannie[40] of that day could bestow herself beneath any
known bed) and, giving them a hundred yards' start, had shot
them down as they ran.

Even then, the beastliness struck me as more comic than
significant. But by that time I ought to have known that it was
the Hun's reflection of his own face as he spied at our back-

windows. He had thrown in the 'hundred yards' start' touch as a tribute to our national sense of fair play.

From the business point of view the war was ridiculous. We charged ourselves step by step with the care and maintenance of all Boerdom – women and children included. Whence horrible tales of our atrocities in the concentration-camps.

One of the most widely exploited charges was our deliberate cruelty in making prisoners' tents and quarters open to the north. A Miss Hobhouse[41] among others was loud in this matter, but she was to be excused.

We were showing off our newly-built little 'Woolsack'[42] to a great lady on her way up-country, where a residence was being built for her. At the larder the wife pointed out that it faced south – that quarter being the coldest when one is south of the Equator. The great lady considered the heresy for a moment. Then, with the British sniff which abolishes the absurd, 'Hmm! I shan't allow *that* to make any difference to *me*.'

Some Army and Navy Stores Lists were introduced into the prisoners' camps, and the women returned to civil life with a knowledge of corsets, stockings, toilet-cases, and other accessories frowned upon by their clergymen and their husbands. *Qua* women they were not very lovely, but they made their men fight, and they knew well how to fight on their own lines.

In the give-and-take of our work our troops got to gauge the merits of the commando-leaders they were facing. As I remember the scale, De Wet,[43] with two hundred and fifty men, was to be taken seriously. With twice that number he was likely to fall over his own feet. Smuts[44] (of Cambridge), warring, men assured me, in a black suit, trousers rucked to the knees, and a top-hat, could handle five hundred but, beyond that, got muddled. And so with the others. I had the felicity of meeting Smuts as a British General, at the Ritz during the Great War. Meditating on things seen and suffered, he said that being hunted about the veldt on a pony made a man think quickly, and that perhaps Mr Balfour[45] (as he was then) would have been better for the same experience.

Each commando had its own reputation in the field, and the grizzlier their beards the greater our respect. There was an elderly contingent from Wakkerstroom which demanded most cautious handling. They shot, as you might say, for the pot.[46] The young men were not so good. And there were foreign contingents who insisted on fighting after the manner of Europe. These the Boers wisely put in the forefront of the battle and kept away from. In one affair the Zarps – the Transvaal Police – fought brilliantly and were nearly all killed. But they were Swedes for the most part, and we were sorry.

Occasionally foreign prisoners were gathered in. Among them I remember a Frenchman who had joined for pure logical hatred of England, but, being a professional, could not resist telling us how we ought to wage the war. He was quite sound but rather cantankerous.

The 'war' became an unpleasing compost of 'political considerations', social reform, and housing; maternity-work and variegated absurdities. It is possible, though I doubt it, that first and last we may have killed four thousand Boers. Our own casualties, mainly from preventible disease, must have been six times as many.

The junior officers agreed that the experience ought to be a 'first-class dress-parade for Armageddon',[47] but their practical conclusions were misleading. Long-range, aimed rifle-fire would do the work of the future: troops would never get nearer each other than half a mile, and Mounted Infantry would be vital. This was because, having found men on foot cannot overtake men on ponies, we created eighty thousand of as good Mounted Infantry as the world had seen. For these Western Europe had no use. Artillery preparation of wire-works, such as were not at Magersfontein,[48] was rather overlooked in the re-formers' schemes, on account of the difficulty of bringing up ammunition by horse-power. The pom-poms, and Lord Dundonald's[49] galloping light gun-carriages, ate up their own weight in shell in three or four minutes.

In the ramshackle hotel at Bloemfontein, where the correspondents lived and the officers dropped in, one heard free and fierce debate as points came up, but – since no one dreamt of the internal-combustion engine that was to stand the world on its thick head, and since our wireless apparatus did not work in those landscapes – we were all beating the air.

Eventually the 'war' petered out on political lines. Brother Boer – and all ranks called him that – would do everything except die. Our men did not see why they should perish chasing stray commandoes, or festering in block-houses, and there followed a sort of demoralizing 'handy-pandy'[50] of alternate surrenders complicated by exchange of Army tobacco for Boer brandy which was bad for both sides.

At long last, we were left apologizing to a deeply-indignant people, whom we had been nursing and doctoring for a year or two; and who now expected, and received, all manner of free gifts and appliances for the farming they had never practised. We put them in a position to uphold and expand their primitive lust for racial domination, and thanked God we were 'rid of a knave'.

Into these shifts and changes we would descend yearly for five or six months from the peace of England to the deeper peace of 'The Woolsack', and life under the oak-trees overhanging the patio, where mother-squirrels taught their babies to climb, and in the stillness of hot afternoons the fall of an acorn was almost like a shot. To one side of us was a pine and eucalyptus grove, heavy with mixed scent; in front our garden, where anything one planted out in May became a blossoming bush by December. Behind all tiered the flank of Table Mountain and its copses of silver-trees, flanking scarred ravines. To get to Rhodes' house, 'Groote Schuur', one used a path through a ravine set with hydrangeas, which in autumn (England's spring) were one solid packed blue river. To this Paradise we moved each year-end from 1900 to 1907 – a complete equipage of governess, maids, and children, so that the latter came to know and therefore, as children will, to own the Union Castle Line – stewards and all: and on any change of governess to instruct the new hand how cabins were set away for a long voyage and 'what went where'. Incidentally we lost two governesses and one loved cook by marriage, the tepid seas being propitious to such things.

Ship-board life, going and coming, was a mere prolongation of South Africa and its interests. There were Jews a plenty from the Rand; Pioneers; Native Commissioners dealing with Basutos or Zulus; men of the Matabele Wars [51] and the opening of Rhodesia; prospectors; politicians of all stripes, all full of their business; Army officers also, and from one of these, [52] when I expected no such jewel, I got a tale called 'Little Foxes' – so true in detail that an awed Superintendent of Police wrote me out of Port Sudan, demanding how I had come to know the very names of the hounds in the very pack to which he had been Whip in his youth. But, as I wrote him back, I had been talking with the Master.

Jameson, too, once came home with us, and disgraced himself at the table which we kept for ourselves. A most English lady with two fair daughters had been put there our first day out, and when she rightly enough objected to the quality of the food, and called it prison fare, Jameson said: 'Speaking as one of the criminal classes, [53] I assure you it is worse.' At the next meal the table was all our own.

But the outward journey was the great joy because it always included Christmas near the Line, [54] where there was no room for memories; seasonable inscriptions written in soap on the mirrors by skilly stewards; and a glorious fancy-dress ball. Then, after the Southern Cross had well risen above the bows, the packing away of heavy kit, secure it would not be needed till May, the friendly, well-known Mountain and the rush to the garden to see what had happened in our absence; the flying barefoot visit to our neighbours the Strubens at 'Struben-heim', [55] where the children were regularly and lovingly spoiled; the large smile of the Malay laundress, and the easy pick-up-again of existence.

Life went well then, and specially for the children, who had all the beasts on the Rhodes estate to play with. Uphill lived the lions, Alice and Jumbo, whose morning voices were the signal for getting up. The zebra paddock, which the emus also used, was immediately behind 'The Woolsack' – a slope of scores of acres. The zebras were always play-fighting like Lions and Unicorns on the Royal Arms; the game being to grab the other's fore-leg below the knee if it could not snatch it away. No fence could hold them when they cared to shift. Jameson and I once saw a family of three returning from an excursion. A heavy sneeze-wood-post fence and wires lay in the path, blind-tight except where the lowest wire spanned a small ditch. Here Papa kneeled, snouted under the wire till it slid along his withers, hove it up, and so crawled through. Mamma and Baby followed in the same fashion. At this, an aged lawn-mower pony who was watching conceived he might also escape, but got no further than backing his fat hind-quarters against one of the posts, and turning round from time to time in wonder that it had not given way. It was, as Jameson said, the complete allegory of the Boer and the Briton.

In another paddock close to the house lived a spitting llama, whose peculiarity the children learned early. But their little visitors did not, and, if they were told to stand close to the fence and make noises, they did – once. You can see the rest.

But our most interesting visitor was a bull-kudu of some eighteen hands. He would jump the seven-foot fence round our little peach orchard, hook a loaded branch in the great rings of his horns, rend it off with a jerk, eat the peaches, leaving the stones, and lift himself over the wires, like a cloud, up the flank of Table Mountain. Once, coming home after dinner, we met him at the foot of the garden, gigantic in the moonlight, and fetched a compass round him, walking delicately, the warm red dust in our shoes: because we knew that a few days before the keepers had given him a dose of small shot in his stern for chasing somebody's cook.

The children's chaperon on their walks was a bulldog – Jumbo – of terrific aspect, to whom all Kaffirs [56] gave full right of way. There was a legend that he had once taken hold of a native and, when at last removed, came away with his mouth full of native. Normally, he lay about the house and apologized abjectly when anyone stepped on him. The children fed him with currant buns and then, remembering that currants were indigestible, would pick them out of his back teeth while he held his dribbling jaws carefully open.

A baby lion [57] was another of our family for one winter. His mother, Alice, desiring to eat him when born, he was raked out with broomsticks from her side and taken to 'Groote Schuur' where, in spite of the unwilling attentions of a she-dog foster-mother (he had of course the claws of a cat) he pined. The wife hinted that, with care, he might recover. 'Very good,' said Rhodes. 'I'll send him over to "The Woolsack" and you can try.' He came, with corrugated-iron den and foster-mother complete. The latter the wife dismissed; went out and bought stout motor-gloves, and the largest of babies' bottles, and fed him forthwith. He highly approved of this, and ceased not to pull at the bottle till it was all empty. His tummy was then slapped, as it might have been a water-melon, to be sure that it rang full, and he went to sleep. Thus he lived and throve in his den, which the children were forbidden to enter, lest their caresses should injure him.

When he was about the size of a large rabbit, he cut little pins of teeth, and made coughing noises which he was persuaded were genuine roars. Later, he developed rickets, and I was despatched to an expert at Cape Town to ask for a cure. 'Too much milk,' said the expert. 'Give him real, not cold-storage, boiled mutton-broth.' This at first he refused to touch in the saucer, but was induced to lick the wife's dipped finger, whence he removed the skin. His ears were boxed, and he was left alone with the saucer to learn table-manners. He wailed all night, but in the morning lapped like a lion among Christians, and soon got rid of his infirmity. For three months he was at large among us, incessantly talking to himself as he wandered about the house or in the garden where he stalked butterflies. He dozed on the stoep, I noticed, due north and south, looking with slow eyes up the length of Africa – always a little aloof, but obedient to the children, who at that time wore little more than one garment apiece. We returned him in perfect condition on our departure for England, and he was then the size of a bull-terrier but not so high. Rhodes and Jameson were both away. He was put in a cage, fed, like his family, on imperfectly thawed cold-storage meats fouled in the grit of his floor, and soon died of colic. But M'Slibaan, which we made Matabele for 'Sullivan', as fitted his Matabele ancestry, was always honoured among the many kind ghosts that inhabited 'The Woolsack'.

Lions, as pets, are hardly safe after six months old; but here is an exception. A man kept a lioness up-country till she was a full year old, and then, with deep regret on both sides, sent her to Rhodes' Zoo. Six months later he came down, and with a girl who did not know what fear was entered her cage, where she received him fawning, rolling, crooning – almost weeping with love and delight. Theoretically, of course, he and the girl ought to have been killed, but they took no hurt at all.

During the war, by some luck our water-supply had not been restricted, and our bath was of the type you step down into and soak in at full length. Hence also Gwynne, filthy after months of the veldt, standing afar off like a leper. ('I say, I want a bath and – there's my kit in the garden. No, I haven't left it on the stoep. It's crawling.') Many came. As the children put it: 'There's always a lot of dirty ones.'

When Rhodes was hatching his scheme of the Scholarships,[58] he could come over and, as it were, think aloud or discuss, mainly with the wife, the expense side of the idea. It was she who suggested that £250 a year was not enough for scholars who would have to carry themselves through the long intervals of an Oxford 'year'. So he made it three hundred. My use to him was mainly as a purveyor of words; for he was largely inarticulate. After the idea had been presented – and one had to know his code for it – he would say: 'What am I trying to express? Say it, *say* it.' So I would say it, and if the phrase suited not, he would work it over, chin a little down, till it satisfied him.

The order of his life at 'Groote Schuur' was something like this. The senior guest allotted their rooms to men who wished to 'see' him. They did not come except for good reason connected with their work, and they stayed till Rhodes 'saw' them, which might be two or three days. His heart[59] compelled him to lie down a good deal on a huge couch on the marble-flagged verandah facing up Table Mountain towards the four-acre patch of hydrangeas, which lay out like lapis-lazuli on the lawns. He would say: 'Well, So-and-so. I see you. What is it?' And the case would be put.

There was a man[60] laying the Cape-to-Cairo telegraph, who

had come to a stretch of seventy miles beside a lake, where the ladies of those parts esteemed copper above gold, and took it from the poles for their adornment. What to do? When he had finished his exposition Rhodes, turning heavily on his couch, said: 'You've got some sort of lake there, haven't you? Lay it like a cable. Don't bother me with a little thing like that.' Palaver done set, and at his leisure the man returned.

One met interesting folk at 'Groote Schuur' meals, which often ended in long talks of the days of building up Rhodesia.

During the Matabele War Rhodes, with some others, under a guide, had wandered on horseback beyond the limits of safety, and had to take refuge in some caves. The situation was eminently unhealthy, and in view of some angry Matabeles hunting them they had to spur out of it. But the guide, just when the party were in the open, was foolish enough to say something to the effect that Rhodes's 'valuable life' was to be considered. Upon which Rhodes pulled up and said: 'Let's get this straight before we go on. *You* led us into this mess, didn't you?' 'Yes, sir, yes. But *please* come on.' 'No. Wait a minute. Consequently you're running to save your own hide, aren't you?' 'Yes, sir. We all are.' 'That's all right. I only wanted to have it settled. *Now* we'll come on.' And they did, but it was a close shave. I heard this at his table, even as I heard his delayed reply to a query by a young officer [61] who wished to know what Rhodes thought of him and his career. Rhodes postponed his answer till dinner and then, in his characteristic voice, laid down that the young man would eminently succeed, but only to a certain point, because he was always thinking of his career and not of the job he was doing. Thirty later years proved the truth of his verdict.

Chapter 7

⟨ The Very-Own House ⟩

How can I turn from any fire
On any man's hearth-stone?
I know the wonder and desire
That went to build my own.

The Fires[1]

All this busy while the Committee of Ways and Means kept before them the hope of a house of their very own – a real House in which to settle down for keeps – and took trains on rails and horsed carriages of the age to seek it. Our adventures were many and sometimes grim – as when a 'comfortable nursery' proved to be a dark padded cell at the end of a discreet passage! Thus we quested for two or three years, till one summer day a friend cried at our door: 'Mr Harmsworth[2] has just brought round one of those motor-car things. Come and try it!'

It was a twenty-minute trip. We returned white with dust and dizzy with noise. But the poison worked from that hour. Somehow, an enterprising Brighton agency hired us a victoria-hooded,[3] carriage-sprung, carriage-braked, single-cylinder, belt-driven, fixed-ignition Embryo which, at times, could cover eight miles an hour. Its hire, including 'driver', was three and a half guineas a week. The beloved Aunt, who feared nothing created, said 'Me too!' So we three house-hunted together taking risks of ignorance that made me shudder through after-years. But we went to Arundel and back, which was sixty miles, and returned in the same ten-hour day! We, and a few other desperate pioneers, took the first shock of outraged public opinion. Earls stood up in their belted barouches and cursed us. Gipsies, governess-carts, brewery waggons – all the world except the poor patient horses who would have been quite quiet if left alone joined in the commination service,[4] and *The Times* leaders on 'motor cars' were eolithic in outlook.

Then I bought me a steam-car called a 'Locomobile',[5] whose nature and attributes I faithfully drew in a tale called 'Steam Tactics'. She reduced us to the limits of fatigue and hysteria, all up and down Sussex. Next came the earliest Lanchester,[6] whose springing, even at that time, was perfect. But no designer, manufacturer, owner, nor chauffeur knew anything about anything. The heads of the Lanchester firm would, after furious telegrams, visit us as friends (we were all friends in those days) and sit round our hearth speculating Why What did That. Once, the proud designer – she was his newest baby – took me as far as Worthing, where she fainted opposite a vacant building-lot. This we paved completely with every other fitting that she possessed ere we got at her trouble. We then re-assembled her, a two hours' job. After which, she spat boiling water over our laps, but we stuffed a rug into the geyser and so spouted home.

But it was the heart-breaking Locomobile that brought us to the house called 'Bateman's'.[7] We had seen an advertisement of her, and we reached her down an enlarged rabbit-hole of a lane. At very first sight the Committee of Ways and Means said: 'That's her! The Only She! Make an honest woman of her – quick!' We entered and felt her Spirit – her Feng Shui – to be good. We went through every room and found no shadow of ancient regrets, stifled miseries, nor any menace, though the 'new' end of her was three hundred years old. To our woe the Owner said: 'I've just let it for twelve months.' We withdrew, each repeatedly telling the other that no sensible person would be found dead in the stuffy little valley where she stood. We lied thus while we pretended to look at other houses till, a year later, we saw her advertised again, and got her.

When all was signed and sealed, the seller said: 'Now I can ask you something. How are you going to manage about getting to and from the station? It's nearly four miles, and I've used up two pair of horses on the hill here.' 'I'm thinking of using this sort of contraption,' I replied from my seat in – Jane Cake-bread [8] Lanchester, I think, was her dishonourable name. 'Oh! *Those* things haven't come to stay!' he returned. Years after-wards I met him, and he confided that had he known what I had guessed, he would have asked twice the money. In three years from our purchase the railway-station had passed out of our lives. In seven, I heard my chauffeur say to an under-powered visiting sardine-tin: 'Hills? There ain't any hills on the London road.'

The House was not of a type to present to servants by lamp or candle-light. Hence electricity, which in 1902 was a serious affair. We chanced, at a week-end visit, to meet Sir William Willcocks, who had designed the Assouan Dam – a trifling affair on the Nile. Not to be over-crowed, we told him of our project for declutching the water-wheel from an ancient mill at the end of our garden, and using its microscopical mill-pond to run a turbine. That was enough! 'Dam?' said he. '*You* don't know anything about dams or turbines. *I'll* come and look.' That Monday morn he came with us, explored the brook and the mill-sluit, and foretold truly the exact amount of horse-power that we should get out of our turbine – 'Four and a half and no more.' But he called me Egyptian names for the state of my brook, which, till then, I had deemed picturesque. 'It's all messed up with trees and bushes. Cut 'em down and slope the banks to one in three.' 'Lend me a couple of Fellahîn [9] Battalions and I'll begin,' I said.

He said also: 'Don't run your light-cable on poles. Bury it.' So we got a deep-sea cable which had failed under test at twelve hundred volts – our voltage being one hundred and ten – and laid him in a trench from the Mill to the house, a full furlong, where he worked for a quarter of a century. At the end of that time he was a little fatigued, and the turbine had worn as much as one-sixteenth of an inch on her bearings. So we gave them both honourable demission – and never again got anything so faithful.

Of the little one-street village [10] up the hill we only knew that, according to the guide-books, they came of a smuggling, sheep-stealing stock, brought more or less into civilization within the past three generations. Those of them who worked for us, and who I presume would today be called 'Labour', struck for higher pay than they had agreed on as soon as we were committed to our first serious works. My foreman and general contractor, himself of their race, and soon to become our good friend, said: 'They think they've got ye. They think there's no harm in tryin' it.' There was not. I had sense enough to feel that most of them were artists and craftsmen, either in stone or timber, or wood-cutting, or drain-laying, or – which is a gift – the aesthetic disposition of dirt; persons of contrivance who could conjure with any sort of material. As our electric-light campaign developed, a London contractor came down to put a fifteen-inch eduction-pipe through the innocent-seeming mill-dam. His imported gang came across a solid core of ancient brickwork about as workable as obsidian. They left, after using very strong words. But every other man of '*our* folk' had known exactly where and what that core was, and when 'Lunnon' had sufficiently weakened it, they 'conjured' the pipe quietly through what remained.

The only thing that ever shook them was when we cut a little under the Mill foundations to fix the turbine; and found that she sat on a crib or raft of two-foot-square elm logs. What we took came out, to all appearance, as untouched as when it had been put under water. Yet, in an hour, the great baulk, exposed to air, became silver dust, and the men stood round marvelling. There was one among them,[11] close upon seventy when we first met, a poacher by heredity and instinct, a gentleman who, when his need to drink was on him, which was not too often, absented himself and had it out alone; and he was more 'one with Nature' than whole parlours full of poets. He became our special stay and counsellor. Once we wanted to shift a lime and a witch-elm into the garden proper. He said not a word till we talked of getting a tree-specialist from London. 'Have it *as* you're minded. *I* dunno as I should if I was you,' was his comment. By this we understood that he would take charge when the planets were favourable. Presently, he called up four of his own kin (also artists) and brushed us aside. The trees came away kindly. He placed them, with due regard for their growth for the next two or three generations; supported them, throat and bole, with stays and stiffenings, and bade us hold them thus for four years. All fell out as he had foretold. The trees are now close on forty foot high and have never flinched. Equally, a well-grown witch-elm that needed discipline, he climbed into and topped, and she carries to this day the graceful dome he gave her. In his later years – he lived to be close on eighty-five – he would, as I am doing now, review his past, which held incident enough for many unpublishable volumes. He spoke of old loves, fights, intrigues, anonymous denunciations 'by such folk as knew writing', and vindictive conspiracies carried out with Oriental thoroughness. Of poaching he talked in all its branches, from buying *Cocculus Indicus*[12] for poisoning fish in ponds, to the art of making silk-nets for trout-brooks – mine among them, and he left a specimen to me; and of pitched battles (guns barred) with heavy-handed keepers in the old days in Lord Ashburnham's woods[13] where a man might pick up a fallow deer. His sagas were lighted with pictures of Nature as he, indeed, knew her; night-pieces and dawn-breakings; stealthy returns and the thinking out of alibis, all naked by the fire, while his clothes dried; and of the face and temper of the next twilight under which he stole forth to follow his passion. His wife, after she had known us for ten years, would range through a past that accepted magic, witchcraft, and love-philtres, for which last there was a demand as late as the middle 'Sixties.

She described one midnight ritual at the local 'wise woman's' cottage, when a black cock was killed with curious rites and words, and '*all* de time dere was, like, *someone* trying to come *through* at ye from outside in de dark. Dunno as I believe so much in such things *now*, but when I was a maid I – I justabout *did*!' She died well over ninety, and to the last carried the tact, manner, and presence, for all she was so small, of an old-world Duchess.

There were interesting and helpful outsiders, too. One was a journeyman bricklayer, who, I remember, kept a store of gold sovereigns loose in his pocket, and kindly built us a wall; but so leisurely that he came to be almost part of the establishment.

When we wished to sink a well opposite some cottages, he said he had the gift of water-finding, and I testify that, when he held one fork of the hazel Y and I the other, the thing bowed itself against all the grip of my hand over an unfailing supply.

Then, out of the woods that know everything and tell nothing, came two dark and mysterious Primitives. They had heard. They would sink that well, for they had the 'gift'. Their tools were an enormous wooden trug, a portable windlass whose handles were curved, and smooth as ox-horns, and a short-handled hoe. They made a ring of brickwork on the bare ground and, with their hands at first, grubbed out the dirt beneath it. As the ring sank they heightened it, course by course, grubbing out with the hoe, till the shaft, true as a rifle-barrel, was deep enough to call for their Father of Trugs, which one brother down below would fill, and the other haul up on the magic windlass. When we stopped, at twenty-five feet, we had found a Jacobean tobacco-pipe, a worn Cromwellian latten spoon, and, at the bottom of all, the bronze cheek of a Roman horse-bit.

In cleaning out an old pond which might have been an ancient marl-pit or mine-head, we dredged two intact Elizabethan 'sealed quarts'[14] that Christopher Sly[15] affected, all pearly with the patina of centuries. Its deepest mud yielded us a perfectly polished Neolithic axe-head with but one chip on its still venomous edge.

These things are detailed that you may understand how, when my cousin, Ambrose Poynter,[16] said to me: 'Write a yarn about Roman times here,' I was interested. 'Write,' said he, 'about an old Centurion of the Occupation telling his experiences to his children.' 'What is his name?' I demanded, for I move easiest from a given point. 'Parnesius,'[17] said my cousin; and the name stuck in my head. I was then on Committee of Ways and Means (which had grown to include Public Works and Communications) but, in due season, the name came back – with seven other inchoate devils. I went off Committee, and began to 'hatch', in which state I was 'a brother to dragons and a companion to owls'.[18] Just beyond the west fringe of our land, in a little valley running from Nowhere to Nothing-at-all, stood the long, overgrown slag-heap of a most ancient forge, supposed to have been worked by the Phoenicians and Romans and, since then, uninterruptedly till the middle of the eighteenth century. The bracken and rush-patches still hid stray pigs of iron, and if one scratched a few inches through the rabbit-shaven turf, one came on the narrow mule-tracks of peacock-hued furnace-slag laid down in Elizabeth's day. The ghost of a road[19] climbed up out of this dead arena, and crossed our fields, where it was known as 'The Gunway', and popularly connected with Armada times. Every foot of that little corner was alive with ghosts and shadows. Then, it pleased our children[20] to act for us, in the open, what they remembered of *A Midsummer-Night's Dream*. Then a friend gave them a real birch-bark canoe, drawing at least three inches, in which they went adventuring on the brook. And in a near pasture of the water-meadows lay out an old and unshifting Fairy Ring.

You see how patiently the cards were stacked and dealt into my hands? The Old Things of our Valley glided into every aspect of our outdoor works. Earth, Air, Water, and People had been – I saw it at last – in full conspiracy to give me ten times as much as I could compass, even if I wrote a complete history of England, as that might have touched or reached our Valley.

I went off at score[21] – not on Parnesius, but a story told in a fog by a petty Baltic pirate, who had brought his galley to Pevensey and, off Beachy Head – where in the War we heard merchant ships being torpedoed – had passed the Roman fleet abandoning Britain to her doom. That tale may have served as a pipe-opener, but one could not see its wood for its trees, so I threw it away.

I carried the situation to the little house in Wiltshire, where my Father and Mother were installed; and smoked it over with the Father, who said – not for the first time: 'Most things in this world are accomplished by judicious leaving alone.' So we played cribbage (he had carved a perfect Lama and a little Kim for my two pegs), while the Mother worked beside us, or, each taking a book, lapsed into the silence of entire mutual com-prehension. One night, apropos of nothing at all, the Father said: 'And you'll have to look up your references rather more carefully, won't you?' That had *not* been my distinction on the little *Civil and Military*.

This led me on another false scent. I wrote a tale told by Daniel Defoe[22] in a brickyard (we had a real one of our own at that time where we burned bricks for barns and cottages to the exact tints we desired) of how he had been sent to stampede King James II,[23] then havering about Thames mouth, out of an England where no party had any use for him. It turned out a painstaken and meritorious piece of work, overloaded with verified references, with about as much feeling to it as a walking-stick. So it also was discarded, with a tale of Doctor Johnson telling the children how he had once thrown his spurs out of a boat in Scotland, to the amazement of one Boswell. Evidently my Daemon would not function in brickyards or schoolrooms. Therefore, like Alice in Wonderland,[24] I turned my back on the whole thing and walked the other way. Therefore, the whole thing set and linked itself. I fell first upon Normans and Saxons. Parnesius came later, directly out of a little wood above the Phoenician forge; and the rest of the tales in *Puck of Pook's Hill* followed in order. The Father came over to see us and, hearing 'Hal o' the Draft', closed in with fore-reaching pen, presently ousted me from my table, and inlaid the description of Hal's own drawing-knife. He liked that tale, and its companion piece 'The Wrong Thing' (*Rewards and Fairies*), which latter he embellished, notably in respect to an Italian fresco-worker, whose work never went 'deeper than the plaster'. He said that 'judicious leaving alone' did not apply between artists.

Of 'Dymchurch Flit', with which I was always unashamedly content, he asked: 'Where did you get that lighting from?' It had come of itself. *Qua* workmanship, that tale and two night-pieces in 'Cold Iron' (*Rewards and Fairies*) are the best in that kind I have ever made, but somehow 'The Treasure and the Law' (*Puck of Pook's Hill*) always struck me as too heavy for its frame.

Yet that tale brought me a prized petty triumph. I had put a well into the wall of Pevensey Castle *circa* AD 1100, because I needed it there. Archaeologically, it did not exist till this year (1935) when excavators brought such a well to light. But that I maintain was a reasonable gamble. Self-contained castles must have self-contained water-supplies. A longer chance that I took in my Roman tales was when I quartered the Seventh Cohort of the Thirtieth (Ulpia Victrix)[25] Legion on the Wall, and asserted that there Roman troops used arrows against the Picts. The first shot was based on honest 'research'; the second was legitimate inference. Years after the tale was told, a digging-party on the Wall sent me some heavy four-sided, Roman-made, 'killing' arrows found *in situ*[26] and – most marvellously – a rubbing of a memorial-tablet[27] to the Seventh Cohort of the Thirtieth Legion! Having been brought up in a suspicious school, I suspected a 'leg-pull' here, but was assured that the rubbing was perfectly genuine.

I embarked on *Rewards and Fairies* – the second book – in two minds. Stories a plenty I had to tell, but how many would be authentic and how many due to 'induction'? There was moreover the old Law: 'As soon as you find you can do anything, do something you can't.'

My doubt cleared itself with the first tale, 'Cold Iron', which gave me my underwood: 'What else could I have done?' – the plinth of all structures. Yet, since the tales had to be read by children, before people realized that they were meant for grown-ups; and since they had to be a sort of balance to, as well as a seal upon, some aspects of my 'Imperialistic' output in the past, I worked the material in three or four overlaid tints and textures, which might or might not reveal themselves according to the shifting light of sex, youth, and experience. It was like working lacquer and mother o' pearl, a natural combination, into the same scheme as niello[28] and grisaille,[29] and trying not to let the joins show.

So I loaded the book up with allegories and allusions, and verified references until my old Chief would have been almost pleased with me; put in three or four really good sets of verses; the bones of one entire historical novel for any to clothe who cared; and even slipped in a cryptogram,[30] whose key I regret I must have utterly forgotten. It was glorious fun; and I knew it must be very good or very bad because the series turned itself off just as *Kim* had done.

Among the verses in *Rewards* was one set called 'If –', which escaped from the book, and for a while ran about the world. They were drawn from Jameson's character,[31] and contained counsels of perfection most easy to give. Once started, the mechanization of the age made them snowball themselves in a way that startled me. Schools, and places where they teach, took them for the suffering Young – which did me no good with the Young when I met them later. ('Why did you write that stuff? I've had to write it out twice as an impot.') They were printed as cards to hang up in offices and bedrooms; illuminated text-wise and anthologized to weariness. Twenty-seven of the Nations of the Earth translated them into their seven-and-twenty tongues, and printed them on every sort of fabric.

Some years after the War a kind friend hinted that my two innocent little books might have helped towards begetting the 'Higher Cannibalism' in biography. By which I understood him to mean the exhumation of scarcely cold notorieties, defenceless females for choice, and tricking them out with sprightly inferences and 'sex'-deductions to suit the mood of the market. It was an awful charge, and anyway I felt that others had qualified as Chief Morticians to that trade.

For rest and refreshment and dearly-loved experiments and anxieties, during the six months or so of each year that we stayed in England, there was always the House and the land, and on occasion the Brook at the foot of our garden, which would flood devastatingly. As she supplied the water for our turbine, and as the little weir which turned her current into the little mill-race was of a frail antiquity, one had to attend to her often and at once, and always at the most inconvenient moment.

Undiscerning folks would ask: 'What do you find to *do* in the country?' Our answer was: 'Everything except time to do it.'

We began with tenants – two or three small farmers on our very few acres – from whom we learned that farming was a mixture of farce, fraud, and philanthropy that stole the heart out of the land. After many, and some comic, experiences, we

fell back on our own county's cattle – the big, red Sussex breed
who make beef and not milk. One got something at least for
one's money from the mere sight of them, and they did not tell
lies. Rider Haggard would visit us from time to time and give
of his ample land-wisdom.[32] I remember I planted some new
apple-trees in an old orchard then rented by an Irishman, who
at once put in an agile and hungry goat. Haggard met the
combination suddenly one morning. He had gifts of speech,
and said very clearly indeed that one might as well put Satan in
an orchard as a goat. I forget what – though I acted on it – he
said about tenants. His comings were always a joy to us and the
children, who followed him like hounds in the hope of 'more
South African stories'. Never was a better tale-teller or, to my
mind, a man with a more convincing imagination. We found by
accident that each could work at ease in the other's company.
So he would visit me, and I him, with work in hand; and
between us we could even hatch out tales together[33] – a most
exacting test of sympathy.

I was honoured till he died by the friendship of a Colonel
Wemyss Feilden,[34] who moved into the village to inherit a
beautiful little William and Mary[35] house on the same day as
we came to take over 'Bateman's'. He was in soul and spirit
Colonel Newcome;[36] in manner as diffident and retiring as an
old maid out of *Cranford*;[37] and up to his eighty-second year
could fairly walk me off my feet, and pull down pheasants
from high heaven. He had begun life in the Black Watch, with
whom, outside Delhi during the Mutiny, he heard one morning
as they were all shaving that a 'little fellow called Roberts' had
captured single-handed a rebel Standard and was coming
through the Camp. 'We all turned out. The boy was on horseback looking rather pleased with himself, and his mounted
Orderly carried the Colour behind him. We cheered him with
the lather on our faces.'

After the Mutiny he sold out, and having interests in Natal
went awhile to South Africa. Next, he ran the blockade of the
US Civil War, and wedded his Southern wife in Richmond
with a ring hammered out of an English sovereign 'because
there wasn't any gold in Richmond just then'. Mrs Feilden at

seventy-five was in herself fair explanation of all the steps he had taken – and forfeited.

He came to be one of Lee's aides-de-camp,[38] and told me how once on a stormy night, when he rode in with despatches, Lee[39] had ordered him to take off his dripping cloak and lie by the fire; and how when he waked from badly needed sleep, he saw the General on his knees before the flame drying the cloak. 'That was just before the surrender,'[40] said he. 'We had finished robbing the grave, and we'd begun on the cradle. For those last three months I was with fifteen thousand boys under seventeen, and I don't remember any one of them even smiling.'

Bit by bit I came to understand that he was a traveller and an Arctic explorer, in possession of the snow-white Polar ribbon; a botanist and naturalist of reputation; and himself above all.

When Rider Haggard heard these things, he rested not till he had made the Colonel's acquaintance. They cottoned to each other on sight and sound; South Africa in the early days being their bond. One evening, Haggard told us how his son[41] had been born on the edge of Zulu, I think, territory, the first white child in those parts. 'Yes,' said the Colonel, quietly out of his corner. 'I and' – he named two men – 'rode twenty-seven miles to look at him. We hadn't seen a white baby for some time.' Then Haggard remembered that visit of strangers.

And once there came to us with her married daughter the widow of a Confederate Cavalry leader;[42] both of them were what you might call 'unreconstructed' rebels. Somehow, the widow mentioned a road and a church beside a river in Georgia. 'It's still there, then?' said the Colonel, giving it its name. 'Why do you ask?' was the quick reply. 'Because, if you look in such-and-such a pew, you might find my initials. I cut them there the night —'s Cavalry stabled their horses there.' There was a pause. ''Fore God, then, *who* are you?' she gasped. He told her. 'You knew my husband?' 'I served under him. He was the only man in our corps who wore a white collar.' She pelted him with questions, and the names of the old dead. 'Come away,' whispered her daughter to me. 'They don't want *us*.' Nor did they for a long hour.

The Very-Own House

Sooner or later, all sorts of men cast up at our house. From India naturally; from the Cape increasingly after the Boer War and our half-yearly visits there; from Rhodesia when that province was in the making; from Australia, with schemes for emigration which one knew Organized Labour would never allow to pass its legislatures; from Canada, when 'Imperial Preference'[43] came to the fore, and Jameson, after one bitter experience, cursed 'that dam' dancing-master (Laurier)[44] who had bitched the whole show'; and from off main-line Islands and Colonies – men of all makes, each with his life-tale, grievance, idea, ideal, or warning.

There was an ex-Governor[45] of the Philippines, who had slaved his soul out for years to pull his charge into some sort of shape and – on a turn of the political wheel at Washington – had been dismissed at literally less notice than he would have dared to give a native orderly. I remembered not a few men whose work and hope had been snatched from under their noses, and my sympathy was very real. His account of Filipino political 'leaders', writing and shouting all day for 'independence' and running round to him after dark to be assured that there was no chance of the dread boon being granted – 'because then we shall most probably all be killed' – was cheeringly familiar.

The difficulty was to keep these interests separate in the head; but the grind of adjusting the mental eye to new perspectives was good for the faculties. Besides this *viva voce*, there was always heavy written work, three-fourths of which was valueless, but for the sake of the possibly worth-while residue all had to be gone through. This was specially the case during the three years before the War, when warnings came thick and fast, and the wise people to whom I conveyed them said: 'Oh, but you're *so-o* – extreme.'

Blasts of extravagant publicity alternated with my office-work. In the late summer of '06, for example, we took ship to Canada,[46] which I had not seen in any particularity for many years, and of which I had been told that it was coming out of its spiritual and material subjection to the United States. Our steamer was an Allan Liner with the earliest turbines and wireless. In the wireless-room, as we were feeling our way blind through the straits of Belle Isle,[47] a sister ship, sixty miles ahead, morsed that the fog with her was even thicker. Said a young engineer in the doorway: 'Who's yon talking, Jock? Ask him if he's done drying his socks.' And the old professional jest crackled out through the smother. It was my first experience of practical wireless.

At Quebec we met Sir William Van Horne,[48] head of the whole CPR system, but, on our wedding trip fifteen years before, a mere Divisional Superintendent who had lost a trunk of my wife's and had stood his Division on its head to find it. His deferred, but ample, revenge was to give us one whole Pullman car with coloured porter complete, to take and use and hitch on to and declutch from any train we chose, to anywhere we fancied, for as long as we liked. We took it, and did all those things to Vancouver and back again. When we wished to sleep in peace, it slid off into still, secret freight-yards till morning. When we would eat, chefs of the great mail trains, which it had honoured by its attachment, asked us what we would like. (It was the season of blueberries and wild duck.) If we even looked as though we wanted anything, that thing would be waiting for us a few score miles up the line. In this manner and in such state we progressed, and the procession and the progress was meat and drink to the soul of William the coloured porter, our Nurse, Valet, Seneschal, and Master of Ceremonies. (More by token, the wife understood coloured folk, and that put William all at ease.) Many people would come aboard to visit us at halting-places, and there were speeches of sorts to be prepared and delivered at the towns. In the first case: ''Nother depy-tation, Boss,' from William behind enormous flower-pieces; '*and* more bo-kays for de Lady.' In the second: 'Dere's a speech doo at —. You go right ahaid with what you're composin', Boss. Jest put your feets out an' I'll shine 'em meanwhile.' So, brushed up and properly shod, I was ushered into the public eye by the immortal William.

In some ways it was punishing 'all out' work, but in all ways worth it. I had been given an honorary Degree, my first, by the McGill University at Montreal. That University received me with interest, and after I had delivered a highly moral discourse, the students dumped me into a fragile horse-vehicle, which they hurtled through the streets. Said one nice child sitting in the hood of it: 'You gave us a dam' dull speech. Can't you say anything amusin' now?' I could but express my fears for the safety of the conveyance, which was disintegrating by instalments.

In '15 I met some of those boys digging trenches in France.

No words of mine can give any notion of the kindness and good-will lavished on us through every step of our road. I tried, and failed to do so in a written account of it. (*Letters to the Family.*[49]) And always the marvel – to which the Canadians seemed insensible – was that on one side of an imaginary line should be Safety, Law, Honour, and Obedience, and on the other frank, brutal decivilization; and that, despite this, Canada should be impressed by any aspect whatever of the United States. Some hint of this too I strove to give in my *Letters*.

Before we parted, William told us a tale of a friend of his who was consumed with desire to be a Pullman porter 'bekase he had watched me doin' it, an' thought he could do it – jest by watchin' me.' (This was the burden of his parable, like a deep-toned locomotive bell.) Overborne at last, William wangled for his friend the coveted post – 'next car ahaid to mine . . . I got *my* folks to baid early 'kase I guessed he'd be needin' me soon . . . But *he* thought he could do it. And den all *his* folk in *his* car, dey all wanted to go to baid at de same time – like dey allus do. An' he tried – Gawd knows he tried – to 'commodate 'em all de same time an' he couldn't. He jes' couldn't . . . He didn't know haow. He thought he did bekase he had,' etc. etc. 'An' den he quit . . . he jes' quit.' A long pause.

'Jumped out of window?' we demanded.

'No. Oh no. Dey wasn't no jump to him dat night. He went into de broom-closet – 'kase I found him dar – an' he cried, an' all his folks slammin' on de broom-house door an' cussin' him 'kase dey wanted to go to baid. An' he couldn't put 'em dar. He couldn't put 'em. He thought,' etc. etc. 'An' den? Why, o' course I jes' whirled in an' put 'em to baid for him, an' when I told 'em how t'wuz with dat sorerful cryin' nigger, dey laughed.

Dey laughed heaps an' heaps . . . But he thought he could do it by havin' watched me do it.'

A few weeks after we returned from the wonderful trip, I was notified that I had been awarded the Nobel Prize [50] of that year for Literature. It was a very great honour, in all ways unexpected.

It was necessary to go to Stockholm. Even while we were on the sea, the old King [51] of Sweden died. We reached the city, snow-white under sun, to find all the world in evening dress, the official mourning, which is curiously impressive. Next afternoon, the prize-winners were taken to be presented to the new King. [52] Winter darkness in those latitudes falls at three o'clock, and it was snowing. One half of the vast acreage of the Palace sat in darkness, for there lay the dead King's body. We were conveyed along interminable corridors looking out into black quadrangles, where snow whitened the cloaks of the sentries, the breeches of old-time cannon, and the shot-piles alongside of them. Presently, we reached a living world of more corridors and suites all lighted up, but wrapped in that Court hush which is like no other silence on earth. Then, in a great lit room, the weary-eyed, over-worked, new King, saying to each the words appropriate to the occasion. Next, the Queen, in marvellous Mary Queen of Scots mourning, a few words, and the return piloted by soft-footed Court officials through a stillness so deep that one heard the click of the decorations on their uniforms. They said that the last words of the old King had been: 'Don't let them shut the theatres for me.' So Stockholm that night went soberly about her pleasures, all dumbed down under the snow.

Morning did not come till ten o'clock; and one lay abed in thick dark, listening to the blunted grind of the trams speeding the people to their work-day's work. But the ordering of their lives was reasonable, thought out, and most comfortable for all classes in the matters of food, housing, the lesser but more desirable decencies, and the consideration given to the Arts. I had only known the Swede as a first-class immigrant in various parts of the earth. Looking at his native land I could guess whence he drew his strength and directness. Snow and frost are no bad nurses.

The Very-Own House

At that epoch staid women attached to the public wash-houses washed, in a glorious lather of soap, worked up with big bunches of finest pine-shavings (when you think of it, a sponge is almost as dirty a tool as the permanent tooth-brush of the European), men desirous of the most luxurious bath known to civilization. But foreigners did not always catch the idea. Hence this tale told to me at a winter resort in the deep, creamy contralto of the North by a Swedish lady who took, and pronounced, her English rather biblically. The introit you can imagine for yourself. Here is the finale: 'And then she – the old woman com-ed – came – in to wash that man. But he was angered – angry. He wented – he went dee-ep into the water and he say-ed – said – "Go a-way!" And she sayed, "But I comm to wash you, sare." And she made to do that. But he tur-ned over up-on his fa-ace, and wa-ved his legs in the airs and he sayed: "Go a-dam-way away!" So she went to the Direktor and she say-ed: "Comm he-ere. There are a mads in my bath, which will not let me wash of him." But the Direktor say-ed to her: "Oh, that are not a mads. That are an Englishman. He will himself – he will wash himself."'

Chapter 8

⟨ Working-Tools ⟩

Every man must be his own law in his own work, but it is a poor-spirited artist in any craft who does not know how the other man's work should be done or could be improved. I have heard as much criticism among hedgers and ditchers and woodmen of a companion's handling of spade, bill-hook, or axe, as would fill a Sunday paper. Carters and cattle-men are even more meticulous, since they must deal with temperaments and seasonal instabilities. We had once on the farms a pair of brothers between ten and twelve. The younger could deal so cunningly with an intractable cart-mare who rushed her gates, and for choice diagonally, that he was called in to take charge of her as a matter of course. The elder, at eleven, could do all that his strength allowed, and the much more that ancestral craft had added, with any edged tool or wood. Modern progress has turned them into meritorious menials.

One of my cattle-men had a son who at eight could appraise the merits and character of any beast in his father's care, and was on terms of terrifying familiarity with the herd-bull, whom he would slap on the nose to make him walk disposedly [1] before us when visitors came. At eighteen, he would have been worth two hundred a year to begin with on any ranch in the Dominions. But he was 'good at his books', and is now in a small grocery, but wears a black coat on the Sabbath. Which things are a portent.

I have told what my early surroundings were, and how richly they furnished me with material. Also, how rigorously newspaper spaces limited my canvases and, for the reader's sake, prescribed that within these limits must be some sort of beginning, middle, and end. My ordinary reporting, leader- and note-writing carried the same lesson, which took me an impatient while to learn. Added to this, I was almost nightly responsible for my output to visible and often brutally voluble critics at the Club. They were not concerned with my dreams. They wanted accuracy and interest, but first of all accuracy.

My young head was in a ferment of new things seen and realized at every turn and – that I might in any way keep abreast of the flood – it was necessary that every word should tell, carry, weigh, taste and, if need were, smell. Here the Father helped me incomparably by his 'judicious leaving alone'. 'Make your own experiments,' said he. 'It's the only road. If I helped, I'd hinder.' So I made my own experiments and, of course, the viler they were the more I admired them.

Mercifully, the mere act of writing was, and always has been, a physical pleasure to me. This made it easier to throw away anything that did not turn out well: and to practise, as it were, scales.

Verse, naturally, came first, and here the Mother was at hand, with now and then some shrivelling comment that infuriated me. But, as she said: 'There's no Mother in Poetry, my dear.' It was she, indeed, who had collected and privately printed verses[2] written at school up to my sixteenth year, which I faithfully sent out from the little House of the Dear Ladies. Later, when the notoriety came, 'in they broke, those people of importance',[3] and the innocent thing 'came on to the market', and Philadelphia lawyers, a breed by itself, wanted to know, because they had paid much money for an old copy, what I remembered about its genesis. They had been first written in a stiff, marble-backed MS book, the front page of which the Father had inset with a scandalous sepia-sketch of Tennyson and Browning in procession, and a spectacled schoolboy bringing up the rear. I gave it, when I left school, to a woman who returned it to me many years later – for which she will take an even higher place in Heaven than her natural goodness ensures – and I burnt it, lest it should fall into the hands of 'lesser breeds without the (Copyright) law'.[4]

I forget who started the notion of my writing a series of Anglo-Indian tales, but I remember our council over the naming of the series. They were originally much longer than when they appeared, but the shortening of them, first to my own fancy after rapturous re-readings, and next to the space available, taught me that a tale from which pieces have been raked out is like a fire that has been poked. One does not know that the operation has been performed, but everyone feels the effect. Note, though, that the excised stuff must have been honestly written for inclusion. I found that when, to save trouble, I 'wrote short' *ab initio* [5] much salt went out of the work. This supports the theory of the chimaera [6] which, having bombinated and been removed, *is* capable of producing secondary causes *in vacuo*. [7]

This leads me to the Higher Editing. Take of well-ground Indian ink as much as suffices and a camel-hair brush proportionate to the interspaces of your lines. In an auspicious hour, read your final draft and consider faithfully every paragraph, sentence and word, blacking out where requisite. Let it lie by to drain as long as possible. At the end of that time, re-read and you should find that it will bear a second shortening. Finally, read it aloud alone and at leisure. Maybe a shade more brushwork will then indicate or impose itself. If not, praise Allah and let it go, and 'when thou hast done, repent not'. [8] The shorter the tale, the longer the brushwork and, normally, the shorter the lie-by, and *vice versa*. The longer the tale, the less brush but the longer lie-by. I have had tales by me for three or five years which shortened themselves almost yearly. The magic lies in the Brush and the Ink. For the Pen, when it is writing, can only scratch; and bottled ink is not to compare with the ground Chinese stick. *Experto crede*. [9]

Let us now consider the Personal Daemon [10] of Aristotle and others, of whom it has been truthfully written, though not published:

This is the doom of the Makers – their Daemon lives in their pen.
If he be absent or sleeping, they are even as other men.
But if he be utterly present, and they swerve not from his behest,
The word that he gives shall continue, whether in earnest or jest.

Most men, and some most unlikely, keep him under an alias

which varies with their literary or scientific attainments. Mine came to me early when I sat bewildered among other notions, and said: 'Take this and no other.'[11] I obeyed, and was rewarded. It was a tale in the little Christmas magazine *Quartette* which we four wrote together, and it was called 'The Phantom Rickshaw'. Some of it was weak, much was bad and out of key; but it was my first serious attempt to think in another man's skin.

After that I learned to lean upon him and recognize the sign of his approach. If ever I held back, Ananias-fashion,[12] anything of myself (even though I had to throw it out afterwards) I paid for it by missing what I *then* knew the tale lacked. As an instance, many years later I wrote about a mediaeval artist, a monastery, and the premature discovery of the microscope. ('The Eye of Allah.'[13]) Again and again it went dead under my hand, and for the life of me I could not see why. I put it away and waited. Then said my Daemon – and I was meditating something else at the time – 'Treat it as an illuminated manuscript.' I had ridden off on hard black-and-white decoration, instead of pumicing the whole thing ivory-smooth, and loading it with thick colour and gilt. Again, in a South African, post-Boer War tale called 'The Captive',[14] which was built up round the phrase 'a first-class dress-parade for Armageddon', I could not get my lighting into key with the tone of the monologue. The background insisted too much. My Daemon said at last: 'Paint the background first once for all, as hard as a public-house sign, and leave it alone.' This done, the rest fell into place with the American accent and outlook of the teller.

My Daemon was with me in the *Jungle Books*, *Kim*, and both Puck books, and good care I took to walk delicately, lest he should withdraw. I know that he did not, because when those books were finished they said so themselves with, almost, the water-hammer click of a tap turned off. One of the clauses in our contract was that I should never follow up 'a success', for by this sin fell Napoleon[15] and a few others. *Note here*. When your Daemon is in charge, do not try to think consciously. Drift, wait, and obey.

I am afraid that I was not much impressed by reviews. But

my early days in London were unfortunate. As I got to know literary circles and their critical output, I was struck by the slenderness of some of the writers' equipment. I could not see how they got along with so casual a knowledge of French work and, apparently, of much English grounding that I had supposed indispensable. Their stuff seemed to be a day-to-day traffic in generalities, hedged by trade considerations. Here I expect I was wrong, but, making my own tests (the man who had asked me out to dinner to discover what I had read gave me the notion), I would ask simple questions, misquote or mis-attribute my quotations; or (once or twice) invent an author. The result did not increase my reverence. Had they been news-paper men in a hurry, I should have understood; but the gentle-men were presented to me as Priests and Pontiffs. And the generality of them seemed to have followed other trades – in banks or offices – before coming to the Ink; whereas I was free born. It was pure snobism on my part, but it served to keep me inside myself, which is what snobbery is for.

I would not today recommend any writer to concern himself overly with reviews. London is a parish, and the Provincial Press has been syndicated, standardized, and smarmed down out of individuality. But there remains still a little fun in that fair. In Manchester was a paper called the *Manchester Guardian*.[16] Outside the mule-lines I had never met anything that could kick or squeal so continuously, or so completely round the entire compass of things. It suspected me from the first, and when my 'Imperialistic' iniquities were established after the Boer War, it used each new book of mine for a shrill recount of my previous sins (exactly as C— used to do) and, I think, enjoyed itself. In return I collected and filed its more acid but uncommonly well-written leaders for my own purposes. After many years, I wrote a tale ('The Wish House'[17]) about a woman of what was called 'temperament' who loved a man and who also suffered from a cancer on her leg – the exact situation carefully specified. The review came to me with a gibe on the margin from a faithful friend: 'You threw up a catch *that* time!' The review[18] said that I had revived Chaucer's Wife of Bath even to the 'mormal on her

shinne'.[19] And it looked just like that too! There was no possible answer, so, breaking my rule not to have commerce with
any paper, I wrote to the *Manchester Guardian* and gave myself
'out – caught to leg'. The reply came from an evident human
being (I had thought red-hot linotypes composed their staff)
who was pleased with the tribute to his knowledge of Chaucer.

Per contra,[20] I have had miraculous escapes in technical
matters, which make me blush still. Luckily the men of the seas
and the engine-room do not write to the Press, and my worst
slip[21] is still underided.

The nearest shave that ever missed me was averted by my
Daemon. I was at the moment in Canada, where a young
Englishman gave me, as a personal experience, a story of a
body-snatching episode in deep snow, perpetrated in some
lonely prairie-town and culminating in purest horror. To get it
out of the system I wrote it detailedly, and it came away just a
shade too good; too well-balanced; too slick. I put it aside, not
that I was actively uneasy about it, but I wanted to make sure.
Months passed, and I started a tooth which I took to the dentist
in the little American town near 'Naulakha'. I had to wait a
while in his parlour, where I found a file of bound *Harper's
Magazines* – say six hundred pages to the volume – dating from
the 'Fifties. I picked up one, and read as undistractedly as the
tooth permitted. There I found my tale,[22] identical in every
mark – frozen ground, frozen corpse stiff in its fur robes in the
buggy – the inn-keeper offering it a drink – and so on to the
ghastly end. Had I published that tale, what could have saved
me from the charge of deliberate plagiarism? *Note here*. Always,
in our trade, look a gift horse at both ends and in the middle.
He may throw you.

But here is a curious case. In the late summer, I think, of
'13, I was invited to Manoeuvres round Frensham Ponds at
Aldershot. The troops were from the Eighth Division of the
coming year – Guardsmen, Black Watch, and the rest, down to
the horsed maxims – two per battalion. Many of the officers
had been juniors in the Boer War, known to Gwynne, one of
the guests, and some to me. When the sham fight was developing, the day turned blue-hazy, the sky lowered, and the

heat struck like the Karroo,[23] as one scuttled among the heaths, listening to the uncontrolled clang of the musketry fire. It came over me that anything might be afoot in such weather, pom-poms for instance, half heard on a flank, or the glint of a helio[24] through a cloud-drift. In short I conceived the whole pressure of our dead of the Boer War flickering and re-forming as the horizon flickered in the heat; the galloping feet of a single horse, and a voice once well-known that passed chanting ribaldry along the flank of a crack battalion. ('But Winnie is one of the lost – poor dear!'[25] was that song, if any remember it or its Singer in 1900–1901.) In an interval, while we lay on the grass, I told Gwynne what was in my head; and some officers also listened. The finale was to be manoeuvres aban-doned and a hurried calling-off of all arms by badly frightened Commandants – the men themselves sweating with terror though they knew not why.

Gwynne played with the notion, and added details of Boer fighting that I did not know; and I remember a young Duke of Northumberland,[26] since dead, who was interested. The notion so obsessed me that I wrote out the beginning at once. But in cold blood it seemed more and more fantastic and absurd, unnecessary and hysterical. Yet, three or four times I took it up and, as many, laid it down. After the War I threw the draft away. It would have done no good, and might have opened the door, and my mail,[27] to unprofitable discussion. For there is a type of mind that dives after what it calls 'psychical experi-ences'. And I am in no way 'psychic'. Dealing as I have done with large, superficial areas of incident and occasion, one is bound to make a few lucky hits or happy deductions. But there is no need to drag in the 'clairvoyance', or the rest of the modern jargon. I have seen too much evil and sorrow and wreck of good minds[28] on the road to Endor[29] to take one step along that perilous track. Once only was I sure that I had 'passed beyond the bounds of ordinance'. I dreamt that I stood, in my best clothes, which I do not wear as a rule, one in a line of similarly habited men, in some vast hall, floored with rough-jointed stone slabs. Opposite me, the width of the hall, was another line of persons and the impression of a crowd behind them. On my left some ceremony was taking place that I wanted to see, but could not unless I stepped out of my line because the fat stomach of my neighbour on my left barred my vision. At the ceremony's close, both lines of spectators broke up and moved forward and met, and the great space filled with people. Then a man came up behind me, slipped his hand beneath my arm, and said: 'I want a word with you.' I forget the rest: but it had been a perfectly clear dream, and it stuck in my memory. Six weeks or more later, I attended in my capacity of a Member of the War Graves Commission a ceremony[30] at Westminster Abbey, where the Prince of Wales dedicated a plaque to 'The Million Dead' of the Great War. We Commissioners lined up facing, across the width of the Abbey Nave, more members of the Ministry and a big body of the public behind them, all in black clothes. I could see nothing of the ceremony because the stomach of the man on my left barred my vision. Then, my eye was caught by the cracks of the stone flooring, and I said to myself: 'But here is where I have been!' We broke up, both lines flowed forward and met, and the Nave filled with a crowd, through which a man came up and slipped his hand upon my arm saying: 'I want a word with you, please.' It was about some utterly trivial matter that I have forgotten.

But how, and why, had I been shown an unreleased roll of my life-film? For the sake of the 'weaker brethren' – and sisters – I made no use of the experience.

In respect to verifying one's references, which is a matter in which one can help one's Daemon, it is curious how loath a man is to take his own medicine. Once, on a Boxing Day, with hard frost coming greasily out of the ground, my friend, Sir John Bland-Sutton,[31] the head of the College of Surgeons, came down to 'Bateman's' very full of a lecture which he was to deliver on 'gizzards'. We were settled before the fire after lunch, when he volunteered that So-and-so had said that if you hold a hen to your ear, you can hear the click in its gizzard of the little pebbles that help its digestion. 'Interesting,' said I. 'He's an authority.' 'Oh yes, but' – a long pause – 'have you any hens about here, Kipling?' I owned that I had, two hundred yards down a lane, but why not accept So-and-so? 'I can't,' said

John simply, 'till I've tried it.' Remorselessly, he worried me into taking him to the hens, who lived in an open shed in front of the gardener's cottage. As we skated over the glairy ground, I saw an eye at the corner of the drawn-down Boxing-Day blind, and knew that my character for sobriety would be blasted all over the farms before night-fall. We caught an outraged pullet. John soothed her for a while (he said her pulse was a hundred and twenty-six), and held her to his ear. 'She clicks all right,' he announced. 'Listen.' I did, and there was click enough for a lecture. '*Now* we can go back to the house,' I pleaded. 'Wait a bit. Let's catch that cock. He'll click better.' We caught him after a loud and long chase, and he clicked like a solitaire-board. I went home, my ears alive with parasites, so wrapped up in my own indignation that the fun of it escaped me. It had not been *my* verification, you see.

But John was right. Take nothing for granted if you can check it. Even though that seem waste-work, and has nothing to do with the essentials of things, it encourages the Daemon. There are always men who by trade or calling know the fact or the inference that you put forth. If you are wrong by a hair in this, they argue: 'False in one thing, false in all.' Having sinned, I know. Likewise, never play down to your public – not because some of them do not deserve it, but because it is bad for your hand. All your material is drawn from the lives of men. Re-member, then, what David did with the water brought to him in the heat of battle.[32]

And, if it be in your power, bear serenely with imitators. My *Jungle Books* begat Zoos of them. But the genius of all the genii was one who wrote a series called *Tarzan of the Apes*.[33] I read it, but regret I never saw it on the films, where it rages most successfully. He had 'jazzed' the motif of the *Jungle Books* and, I imagine, had thoroughly enjoyed himself. He was reported to have said that he wanted to find out how bad a book he could write and 'get away with', which is a legitimate ambition.

Another case was verses of the sort that are recited. An Edinburgh taxi-driver in the War told me that they were much in vogue among the shelters and was honoured to meet me, their author. Afterwards, I found that they were running neck-

and-neck with 'Gunga Din' in the military go-as-you-pleases and on the Lower Deck, and were always ascribed to my graceful hand. They were called 'The Green Eye of the Little Yellow God'.[34] They described an English Colonel and his daughter at Khatmandhu in Nepal where there was a military Mess; and her lover of the name of 'mad Carew' which rhymed comfortably. The refrain was more or less 'And the green-eyed yellow Idol looking down'. It was luscious and rampant, with a touch, I thought, of the suburban Toilet-Club school favoured by the late Mr Oscar Wilde.[35] Yet, and this to me was the Devil of it, it carried for one reader an awesome suggestion of 'but for the Grace of God there goes Richard Baxter'.[36] (Refer again to the hairdresser's model which so moved Mr Dent Pitman.) Whether the author had done it out of his own head, or as an inspired parody of the possibilities latent in a fellow-craftsman, I do not know. But I admired him.

Occasionally one could test a plagiarist. I had to invent a tree, with name to match, for a man who at that time was rather riding in my pocket. In about eighteen months – the time it takes for a 'test' diamond, thrown over the wires into a field of 'blue' rock, to turn up on the Kimberley sorting-tables – my tree appeared in his 'nature-studies' – name as spelt by me and virtues attributed. Since in our trade we be all felons, more or less, I repented when I had caught him, but not too much.

And I would charge you for the sake of your daily correspondence, never to launch a glittering generality, which an older generation used to call 'Tupperism'.[37] Long ago I stated that 'East was East and West was West and never the twain should meet.'[38] It seemed right, for I had checked it by the card, but I was careful to point out circumstances under which cardinal points ceased to exist. Forty years rolled on, and for a fair half of them the excellent and uplifted of all lands would write me, apropos of each new piece of broad-minded folly in India, Egypt, or Ceylon, that East and West *had* met – as, in their muddled minds, I suppose they had. Being a political Calvinist,[39] I could not argue with these condemned ones. But their letters had to be opened and filed.

Again. I wrote a song called 'Mandalay'[40] which, tacked

to a tune with a swing, made one of the waltzes of that distant age. A private soldier reviews his loves and, in the chorus, his experiences in the Burma campaign.[41] One of his ladies lives at Moulmein,[42] which is not on the road to anywhere, and he describes the amour with some minuteness, but always in his chorus deals with 'the road to Mandalay', his golden path to romance. The inhabitants of the United States, to whom I owed most of the bother, 'Panamaed' that song (this was before copyright), set it to their own tunes, and sang it in their own national voices. Not content with this, they took to pleasure cruising, and discovered that Moulmein did not command any view of any sun rising across the Bay of Bengal. They must have interfered, too, with the navigation of the Irrawaddy Flotilla steamers,[43] for one of the Captains SOS-ed me to give him 'something to tell these somethinged tourists about it'. I forget what word I sent, but I hoped it might help.

Had I opened the chorus of the song with 'Oh' instead of 'On the road', etc., it might have shown that the song was a sort of general mix-up of the singer's Far-Eastern memories against a background of the Bay of Bengal as seen at dawn from a troopship taking him there. But 'On' in this case was more singable than 'Oh'. That simple explanation may stand as a warning.

Lastly – and this got under my skin because it touched something that mattered – when, after the Boer War, there seemed an off-chance of introducing conscription into England, I wrote verses called 'The Islanders'[44] which, after a few days' newspaper correspondence, were dismissed as violent, untimely, and untrue. In them I had suggested that it was unwise to 'grudge a year of service to the lordliest life on earth'. In the immediate next lines I described the life to which the year of service was grudged as:

Ancient, effortless, ordered – cycle on cycle set –
Life so long untroubled that ye who inherit forget
It was not made with the mountains; it is not one with the deep.
Men, not Gods, devised it. Men, not Gods, must keep.

In a very little while it was put about that I had said that 'a year of compulsory service' would be 'effortless, ordered', etc. etc. – with the rider that I didn't know much about it. This perversion was perversified by a man who ought to have known better; and I suppose I should have known that it was part of the 'effortless, ordered' drift towards Armageddon. You ask: 'Why inflict on us legends of your Middle Ages?' Because in life as in literature, its sole enduring record, is no age. Men and Things come round again, eternal as the seasons.

But, attacking or attacked, so long as you have breath, on no provocation explain. What you have said may be justified by things or some man, but never take a hand in a 'dog-fight' that opens: 'My attention has been drawn to,' etc.

I came near to breaking this Law with *Punch*, an institution I always respected for its continuity and its utter Englishdom, and from whose files I drew my modern working history. I had written during the Boer War a set of verses based on unofficial criticisms of many serious junior officers. (Incidentally they contained one jewel of a line that opened 'And which it may subsequently transpire' – a galaxy of words I had long panted to place in the literary firmament.) Nobody loved them, and indeed they were not conciliatory; but *Punch* took them rather hard.[45] This was a pity because *Punch* would have been useful at that juncture. I knew none of its staff, but I asked questions and learned that *Punch* on this particular issue was – non-Aryan 'and German at that'. It is true that the Children of Israel are 'people of the Book', and in the second Surah of the Koran Allah is made to say: 'High above mankind have I raised you.'[46] Yet, later, in the fifth Surah, it is written: 'Oft as they kindle a beacon-fire for war, shall God quench it. And their aim will be to abet disorder on the earth: but God loveth not the abettors of disorder.'[47] More important still, my bearer in Lahore never announced our good little Jew Tyler but he spat loudly and openly in the verandah. I swallowed my spittle at once. Israel is a race to leave alone. It abets disorder.

Many years later, during the War, *The Times*, with which I had had no dealings for a dozen years or so, was 'landed' with what purported to be some verses by me, headed 'The Old

Volunteer'.⁴⁸ They had been sent in by a Sunday mail with some sort of faked postmark and without any covering letter. They were stamped with a rubber-stamp from the village office, they were written on an absolutely straight margin, which is beyond my powers, and in an un-European fist. (I had never since typewriters began sent out press-work unless it was typed.) From my point of view the contribution should not have deceived a messenger-boy. Ninthly and lastly, they were wholly unintelligible.

Human nature being what it is, *The Times* was much more annoyed with me than anyone else, though goodness knows – this, remember, was in '17 – I did not worry them about it, beyond hinting that the usual week-end English slackness, when no one is in charge, had made the mess. They took the matter up with the pomp of the Public Institution which they were, and submitted the MS to experts, who proved that it must be the work of a man who had all but 'spoofed' *The Times* about some fragments of Keats. He happened to be an old friend of mine, and when I told him of his magnified 'characteristic' letters, and the betraying slopes at which they lay – *his*, as I pointed out, 'very C's and U's and T's', he was wrath and, being a poet, swore a good deal that if he could not have done a better parody of my 'stuff' with his left hand he would retire from business. This I believed, for, on the heels of my modest disclaimer which appeared, none too conspicuously, in *The Times*, I had had a letter in a chaffing vein about 'The Old Volunteer' from a non-Aryan who never much appreciated me; and the handwriting of it, coupled with the subtlety of choosing a week-end (as the Hun had chosen August Bank Holiday of '14) for the work, *plus* the Oriental detachedness and insensitiveness of playing that sort of game in the heart of a life-and-death struggle, made me suspect him more than a little. He is now in Abraham's bosom, so I shall never know. But *The Times* seemed very happy with its enlarged letters, and measurements of the alphabet, and – there really *was* a war on which filled my days and nights. Then *The Times* sent down a detective to my home. I didn't see the drift of this, but naturally was interested. And It was a Detective out of a book, down to the very creaks of Its boots. (On the human side at lunch It knew a lot about second-hand furniture.) Officially, It behaved like all the detectives in the literature of that period. Finally, It settled Itself, back to the light, facing me at my work-table, and told me a long yarn about a man who worried the Police with complaints of anonymous letters addressed to him from unknown sources, all of which, through the perspicacity of the Police, turned out to have been written by himself to himself for the purpose of attracting notoriety. As in the case of the young man on the Canadian train, that tale felt as though it had come out of a magazine of the 'Sixties; and I was so interested in its laborious evolution that I missed its implication till quite the end. Then I got to thinking of the psychology of the detective, and what a gay life of plots It must tramp through; and of the psychology of *The Times*-in-a-hole, which is where no one shows to advantage; and of how Moberly Bell,[49] whose bows I had crossed in the old days, would have tackled the matter; what Buckle,[50] whom I loved for his sincerity and gentlehood, would have thought of it all. Thus I forgot to defend my 'injured honour'. The thing had passed out of reason into the Higher Hysterics. What could I do but offer It some more sherry and thank It for a pleasant interview?

I have told this at length because Institutions of idealistic tendencies sometimes wait till a man is dead, and then furnish their own evidence. Should this happen, try to believe that in the deepest trough of the War I did not step aside to play with *The Times*, Printing House Square, London, E.C.

In the come-and-go of family talk there was often discussion as to whether I could write a 'real novel'. The Father thought that the setting of my work and life would be against it, and Time justified him.

Now here is a curious thing. At the Paris Exhibition of 1878 I saw, and never forgot, a picture of the death of Manon Lescaut,[51] and asked my Father many questions. I read that amazing 'one book' of the Abbé Prévost, in alternate slabs with Scarron's *Roman Comique*,[52] when I was about eighteen, and it brought up the picture. My theory is that a germ lay dormant till my change of life to London (though that is not Paris) woke it up, and that *The Light that Failed* was a sort of inverted, metagrobolized phantasmagoria based on *Manon*. I was confirmed in my belief when the French took to that *conte*[53] with relish, and I always fancied that it walked better in translation than in the original. But it was only a *conte* – not a built book.

Kim, of course, was nakedly picaresque and plotless – a thing imposed from without.

Yet I dreamed for many years of building a veritable three-decker[54] out of chosen and long-stored timber – teak, green-heart, and ten-year-old oak knees – each curve melting deliciously into the next that the sea might nowhere meet resistance or weakness; the whole suggesting motion even when, her great sails for the moment furled, she lay in some needed haven – a vessel ballasted on ingots of pure research and knowledge, roomy, fitted with delicate cabinet-work below-decks, painted, carved, gilt and wreathed the length of her, from her blazing stern-galleries outlined by bronzy palm-trunks, to her rampant figure-head – an East Indiaman worthy to lie alongside *The Cloister and the Hearth.*[55]

Not being able to do this, I dismissed the ambition as 'beneath the thinking mind'. So does a half-blind man dismiss shooting and golf.

Nor did I live to see the day when the new three-deckers should hoist themselves over the horizon, quivering to their own power, overloaded with bars, ball-rooms, and insistent chromium plumbing; hellishly noisy from the sports' deck to the barber's shop; but serving their generation as the old craft served theirs. The young men were already laying down the lines of them, fondly believing that the old laws of design and construction were for them abrogated.

And with what tools did I work in my own mould-loft? I had always been choice, not to say coquettish, in this respect. In Lahore for my *Plain Tales* I used a slim, octagonal-sided, agate penholder with a Waverley nib. It was a gift, and when in an evil hour it snapped I was much disturbed. Then followed a procession of impersonal hirelings each with a Waverley, and next a silver penholder with a quill-like curve, which promised well but did not perform. In Villiers Street I got me an outsize office pewter ink-pot, on which I would gouge the names of the tales and books I wrote out of it. But the housemaids of married life polished those titles away till they grew as faded as a palimpsest.

I then abandoned hand-dipped Waverleys – a nib I never changed – and for years wallowed in the pin-pointed 'stylo' and its successor the 'fountain' which for me meant geyser-pens. In later years I clung to a slim, smooth, black treasure (Jael [56] was her office name) which I picked up in Jerusalem. [57] I tried pump-pens with glass insides, but they were of 'intolerable entrails'.

For my ink I demanded the blackest, and had I been in my Father's house, as once I was, would have kept an ink-boy to grind me Indian ink. All 'blue-blacks' were an abomination to my Daemon, and I never found a bottled vermilion fit to rubricate initials when one hung in the wind waiting.

My writing-blocks were built for me to an unchanged pattern of large, off-white, blue sheets, of which I was most wasteful. All this old-maiderie did not prevent me when abroad from buying and using blocks, and tackle, in any country.

With a lead pencil I ceased to express – probably because I had to use a pencil in reporting. I took very few notes except of names, dates, and addresses. If a thing didn't stay in my memory, I argued, it was hardly worth writing out. But each man has his own method. I rudely drew what I wanted to remember.

Like most men who ply one trade in one place for any while, I always kept certain gadgets on my work-table, which was ten feet long from North to South and badly congested. One was a long, lacquer, canoe-shaped pen-tray full of brushes and dead 'fountains'; a wooden box held clips and bands; another, a tin one, pins; yet another, a bottle-slider, kept all manner of unneeded essentials from emery-paper to small screw-drivers; a paper-weight, said to have been Warren Hastings'; [58] a tiny, weighted fur-seal and a leather crocodile sat on some of the papers; an inky foot-rule and a Father of Penwipers which a much-loved housemaid of ours presented yearly, made up the main-guard of these little fetishes.

My treatment of books, which I looked upon as tools of my trade, was popularly regarded as barbarian. Yet I economized on my multitudinous pen-knives, and it did no harm to my fore-finger. There were books which I respected, because they were put in locked cases. The others, all the house over, took their chances.

Left and right of the table were two big globes, on one of which a great airman [59] had once outlined in white paint those air-routes to the East and Australia which were well in use before my death. [60]

Explanatory Notes

In compiling these notes, I have consulted the following works: Lord Birkenhead, *Rudyard Kipling* (Weidenfeld & Nicolson, 1978); Charles Carrington, *Rudyard Kipling: His Life and Work* (Macmillan, 1978); Charles Carrington (ed.), *Kipling's Horace* (Methuen, 1978); L. C. Dunsterville, *The Adventures of Dunsterforce* (Edwin Arnold, 1920); L. C. Dunsterville, *Stalky's Reminiscences* (Cape, 1928); John Gross (ed.), *Rudyard Kipling: The Man, his Work, and the World* (Weidenfeld & Nicolson, 1972); Roger Lancelyn Green, *Kipling and the Children* (Elek Books, 1965); Roger Lancelyn Green, *Kipling: The Critical Heritage* (Routledge & Kegan Paul, 1971); Norman Page, *A Kipling Companion* (Macmillan, 1984); and Thomas Pinney (ed.), *Kipling's India: Uncollected Sketches 1884–88* (Macmillan, 1986). I am particularly indebted to two publications from The Kipling Society: *The Kipling Journal* and R. E. Harbord's *The Reader's Guide to Rudyard Kipling* (8 vols., privately printed, 1961–72), volume 7 of which has notes on *Something of Myself* by Roger Lancelyn Green. I am also grateful to the following for advice and information: Janet Arnold, Peter Barry, Pamela Bickley, Jacqueline Bratton, Peter Caracciolo, Maria Couto, Martin Dzelzainis, Angus Easson, Warwick Gould, Barbara Rosenbaum and Hans van Marle.

Notes

Chapter 1: A Very Young Person

1. *Give me . . . the rest*: Kipling adapts a statement generally ascribed to the Jesuits: 'Give me the first seven years of a child's life, and he is mine for life.' The source is untraced, and the statement is probably a Protestant invention. The chapter that follows includes both the first and second 'six years' of Kipling's life. Some of the implications of the epigraph are, perhaps, suggested by the concluding words of 'Baa Baa, Black Sheep', Kipling's fictional account of his years at Southsea: 'when young lips have drunk deep of the bitter waters of Hate, Suspicion, and Despair, all the Love in the world will not wholly take away that knowledge.'

2. *Looking back*: Kipling was born on 30 December 1865. He started work on his autobiography on 1 August 1935.

3. ayah: From the Portuguese '*aia*' ('governess'), the word exists in most Indian languages to mean either a lady's maid or, as here, a children's nurse or nanny.

4. *my sister*: Alice ('Trix') Kipling, 1868–1948.

5. *Meeta*: He is described, in 'Baa Baa, Black Sheep', as 'the big *Surti* boy, with the red and gold turban'.

6. *the Mahim Woods*: The Mahim Woods were seven or eight miles from the Kipling house – too far for the walk described here. Kipling is perhaps thinking of the Maidan, which had coconut palms around it, or of the Esplanade.

7. *Parsees*: These are the descendants of Zoroastrian Persians who fled to India in the seventh and eighth centuries. They settled in Bombay in the seventeenth century.

8. *Lord Mayo*: Lord Mayo (1822–72) was Governor-General and Viceroy of India from 1869 to 1872. On 8 February 1872, he was assassinated by Ameer Khan, a Wahabi convict, while visiting the penal settlement at Port Blair on the Andaman Islands. Kipling's memory is faulty here since, by this time, he was at Southsea.

9. *my Father's School of Art*: John Lockwood Kipling (1837–1911) was 'Professor of Architectural Sculpture' in the School of Art in

Bombay from 1865 until he left in 1874. The School was founded in March 1857 by a wealthy Parsee, Sir Jamsetjee Jeejeebhoy.

10. *Mr 'Terry Sahib'*: Mr Wilkins Terry was the original Director of the Sir Jamsetjee Jeejeebhoy School of Art. He recruited Lockwood Kipling (and other teachers) on a visit to England in 1863.

11. *a time in a ship*: Kipling confuses two separate journeys to England. The first was in February 1868, when Kipling's mother returned to England for the birth of 'Trix', taking him with her. They travelled overland across the Isthmus of Suez, since the Suez Canal was not opened until 1869. On 15 April 1871, all four members of the Kipling family left Bombay for England, and, on this second journey, travelled via the Suez Canal.

12. *a halt in it*: This occurred during the first journey (1868). The 'halt' was at Zagazig. Kipling describes it in 'Egypt of the Magicians' (1913), collected in *Letters of Travel* (1920).

13. *a new small house*: 'Lorne Lodge', 4 Campbell Road, Southsea.

14. *a woman who took in children*: Sarah Holloway. Her husband, P. A. Holloway (1810–74), was not an 'old Navy Captain'. He ended his career, on retiring from the Merchant Navy, as Chief Officer of the Coastguard at Southsea. The couple appear as 'Auntie Rosa' and 'Uncle Harry' in 'Baa Baa, Black Sheep', and Mrs Holloway reappears as Mrs Jennett in the first chapter of *The Light That Failed*.

15. *at Navarino*: The Battle of Navarino was fought on 20 October 1827 in Navarino Bay (on the south-west coast of Greece). Admiral Codrington's forces defeated the combined Turkish and Egyptian fleets. Holloway was a midshipman on HMS *Brisk* from November 1825 to June 1829. In 'Baa Baa, Black Sheep', 'Uncle Harry' has a model of the *Brisk*, and he tells Punch 'the story of the battle of Navarino'. According to 'Uncle Harry's' song, 'the little *Brisk* was sore exposed/That day at Navarino.'

16. *By Celia's Arbour*: Written by Walter Besant and James Rice, and published in 1878, this novel is set in Portsmouth during the 1850s. One of its secondary characters, referred to as 'the Captain', fought on board the *Asia* at the Battle of Navarino and, like 'Uncle Harry', has a model of the ship on which he fought.

17. Alert (or Discovery): Both ships were on the Arctic Expedition of 1875–6, which returned to Portsmouth, but Holloway died in 1874.

18. *an only son*: Henry Thomas Holloway.

19. Aunt Judy's Magazine: This was edited by Margaret Gatty (1809–73). Kipling's 'bound copy' was volume X, January to October, 1872.

20. Six to Sixteen: Published as a book in 1875, this tells of two young girls sent from India to be brought up in England. Mrs Ewing (1841–85) was Margaret Gatty's daughter.

21. Tales at Tea-Time: E. H. Knatchbull-Hugessen (1829–93) was the author of thirteen volumes of stories. *Tales at Tea-Time*, a volume of invented fairy-stories, was published in 1872. He also served as a Lord of the Treasury (1859–66), Under-Secretary for the Home Office (1868–71), and Under-Secretary for the Colonies (1871–3).

22. The Old Shikarri: 'The Old Shekarry' was the pseudonym of Major H. A. Leveson (1828–75), author of *The Hunting Grounds of the Old World* (1860), *Sport in Many Lands* (1877), etc.

23. '*I climbed ... mighty Helvellyn*': Sir Walter Scott's 'Helvellyn' (1805).

24. '*A. Tennyson*': He found these in the early volume of *Sharpe's Magazine* in which he discovered the picture of the Griffin and the poem which he describes in 'Baa Baa, Black Sheep'.

25. The Hope of the Katzekopfs: first published in 1844 as by William Churne; subsequently reprinted with the author's real name, F. E. Paget (1806–82).

26. '*Farewell Rewards and Fairies*': 'The Fairies' Farewell' by Richard Corbet (1582–1635) was first published in *Poetica Stromata* (1648). Two stanzas are quoted in the Introduction to *The Hope of the Katzekopfs*: these include the injunction to 'pray for the "noddle" of William Churne' but not the first stanza and the words 'Farewell Rewards and Fairies', which Kipling probably found in Percy's *Reliques*. Kipling's *Rewards and Fairies* (1910) was the sequel to *Puck of Pook's Hill*.

27. a lion-hunter: The story is *King Lion*, which was serialized anonymously in the *Boy's Own Magazine* in 1864. When it was reprinted in 1891, it was accredited to James Greenwood (1832–1929).

28. blue and fat: This was *Poems written for a Child* (1868) by Menella Bute Smedley (1820–77) and her sister, Elizabeth Anna Hart (c. 1822–90). The 'nine white wolves' appear in 'A North Pole Story', pp. 1–8; the 'name of England' appears in 'Heroes', but Kipling significantly mis-remembers. In fact, the 'black men' think 'the name of England/Is something that will burn'.

29. *brown and fat*: This was *Child Nature* (1869) by Elizabeth Anna Hart. The 'water-rat' is from 'The Water Rat', pp. 80–8; the 'Urchin' is from 'Miss Pip', pp. 164–77; the 'Darling' is from 'Sweeping the Skies', pp. 6–12. (See Roger Lancelyn Green, *Kipling and the Children*, pp. 39–42, 117–18.)

30. *'And thrice ... Cumnor Hall.'*: From the ballad 'Cumnor Hall' (1784) by W. J. Mickle (1735–88). A stanza from 'Cumnor Hall' (including these two lines) is quoted in the final chapter of Sir Walter Scott's novel, *Kenilworth*.

31. *the Provost of Oriel*: Edward Hawkins (1789–1882) was Provost of Oriel from 1828 to 1874, when he retired to the precincts at Rochester. Newman speaks appreciatively of Hawkins in his *Apologia pro Vita sua* (1864).

32. *an old gentleman*: Holloway's brother, General Sir Thomas Holloway, of West Lodge, Havant. Carrington suggests that his death in July 1875 – and the non-fulfilment of expectations – perhaps led to Henry Holloway's leaving school for the bank.

33. *Exempli gratia*: (Latin) 'For example'.

34. *the Collect*: The prayer appointed to be used for a particular day or season (in the Church of England).

35. *Aunt Georgie*: Georgiana Macdonald (1840–1920) was one of eleven children. Of the five daughters, four were married: Alice · Macdonald (1837–1910) married Lockwood Kipling in 1865; Georgiana Macdonald married Edward Burne-Jones (1833–98), the Pre-Raphaelite painter, in 1860; Agnes (1843–1906) married another artist, Edward Poynter (1836–1919); and Louisa (1845–1925) married Alfred Baldwin MP (1841–1908).

36. *my two cousins*: Philip Burne-Jones (1861–1926) and Margaret Burne-Jones (1866–1953).

37. *William Morris*: William Morris (1834–96) had launched the firm of 'fine art workmen' (which later became 'Morris and Co.') in 1861. The firm produced furniture, wallpapers and hangings, glass and tiles, and tapestry. Morris was also the author of a number of books of poetry and prose including *The Defence of Guenevere* (1858), *The Earthly Paradise* (1868–70), *News from Nowhere* (1891), and translations of the *Aeneid* (1875), the *Odyssey* (1887) and Icelandic sagas. (See note 42.)

38. The Pirate: Sir Walter Scott's novel *The Pirate* (1821) includes 'Norna of the Fitful Head' among its characters. In chapter 21, Euphane Fea, the housekeeper, installs herself in the recess of a large window 'studiously darkened' with drapery 'to listen to the

rhythmical inquiries which should be made to her, and return an extemporaneous answer'. This game turns to earnest when Euphane Fea is replaced by Norna with her supernatural powers.

39. The Arabian Nights: *The Arabian Nights' Entertainments* or *The Thousand and One Nights* was first translated into English at the start of the eighteenth century. It was many times reprinted and re-translated, and it was immensely popular in the nineteenth century.

40. '*Mummy Brown*': also known as 'Asphaltum Brown', a natural pigment made from mummy by the Camden Town firm, Roberson & Company.

41. *Mizraim and Memphis*: Mizraim is a biblical name for Egypt (Genesis, 10:6); Memphis was the ancient capital of Egypt; the reference is probably to Hosea 9:6: 'Egypt shall gather them up, Memphis shall bury them.'

42. *Burnt Njal*: J. M. S. Tompkins has pointed out that the dream of the cow's tail does not occur in *The Saga of Burnt Njal* but in the *Eyrbyggja Saga*, which was published as the second volume in Morris's *Saga Library* in 1892.

43. *Brother Lippo Lippi*: Fra Filippo Lippi (*c.* 1406–69) was one of the most important early Renaissance Florentine painters. He was the subject of one of Vasari's *Lives* and of the poem by Robert Browning from which Kipling quotes, 'Fra Lippo Lippi' (*Men and Women*, 1855).

44. *day-school*: 'Hope House', Somerset Place, Green Street, Southsea. Carrington suggests that Kipling was here for 1875 and 1876 (*The Kipling Journal*, June 1972).

45. *auto-da-fé*: Literally, 'act of faith' (Portuguese), this signifies the execution of a sentence of the Inquisition – especially the public burning of a heretic.

46. '*Liar*': Kipling's sister also mentions this in her memoirs, but Carrington suggests that this incident was borrowed from *David Copperfield* for 'Baa Baa, Black Sheep' and subsequently converted into a memory.

47. '*Who having known . . . with glass?*': Kipling is misquoting the Koran.

48. *a man came down*: In 'Baa Baa, Black Sheep', the visitor announces himself as 'Inverarity Sahib'. J. D. Inverarity was the Kiplings' doctor in Bombay at the time of Rudyard Kipling's birth.

49. *the Mother returned*: In March 1877.

50. *Epping Forest*: After a round of visits to relations, they spent May to November of 1877 at 'Goldings Hill', near Loughton, on the edge of Epping Forest.

51. *Prime Minister*: Stanley Baldwin (1867–1947), son of Alfred and Louisa Baldwin (see note 35, above), was Prime Minister for 1923–4, 1924–9, 1935–7.

52. *Brompton Road*: At 227 Brompton Road.

53. *one of Dickens' novels*: The Forster Collection, which contains the manuscripts of eleven of Dickens's novels (and part of the manuscript of *Oliver Twist*), was bequeathed to the South Kensington Museum (now the Victoria and Albert Museum) in 1876.

54. Sidonia the Sorceress: *Sidonia von Bork, die Klosterhexe* (1847), by the German novelist Johann Wilhelm Meinhold (1797–1851), was translated into English (via the French) by Lady Wilde. William Morris reprinted it at the Kelmscott Press in 1893.

55. *Emerson's poems*: Ralph Waldo Emerson (1803–82), American poet and essayist.

56. *Bret Harte's stories*: Francis Bret Harte (1836–1902), American humorist, short-story writer and poet. He wrote the story 'The Luck of Roaring Camp' (1868) and the humorous poem 'The Heathen Chinee'. (See p. 53.)

Chapter 2: The School before its Time
1835

1. *Cornell Price*: Price (1853–1910) was a school-fellow of Edward Burne-Jones and Henry Macdonald at the King Edward's School, Birmingham, and subsequently a member of the William Morris set at Oxford. From 1863 to 1874, he taught at Haileybury, one of the new 'Public Schools' founded in imitation of Thomas Arnold's Rugby. In 1874 he became the headmaster of the newly-founded United Services College.

2. *three dear ladies*: Mary Craik, Georgiana Craik and their friend, Miss Winnard, lived at 26 Warwick Gardens, South Kensington. Georgiana Craik was the author of a number of novels including *The Cousin from India* (1871) and *Theresa* (1875). She and her sister were the daughters of Carlyle's friend, George Lillie Craik.

3. Carlyle: Thomas Carlyle (1795–1881), historian and essayist, author of *Chartism* (1839), *The French Revolution* (1837), *Past and Present* (1843), *Latter-day Pamphlets* (1850), etc.

4. *Mr and Miss de Morgan*: William de Morgan (1839–1917) was

closely associated with Morris and Burne-Jones. In the 1860s he experimented with stained glass and tiles; in later life he began writing novels. Mary Augusta de Morgan (1850–1907) was a celebrated writer of original fairy-stories: *On a Pincushion* (1877), *The Necklace of Princess Fiorimode* (1880), *The Wind Fairies* (1900). From 1871 to 1882, the de Morgan family lived in Cheyne Row, Chelsea.

5. *Jean Ingelow*: (1820–97), Poet and writer of children's stories, notably *Mopsa the Fairy* (1869) and *The Little Wonder Box* (1872).

6. *Christina Rossetti*: (1830–94), Poet, author of *Goblin market* (1862), *The prince's progress* (1866), *Sing-Song* (1872).

7. Firmilian: A 'Spasmodic Tragedy', written in 1854 by W. E. Aytoun (1813–65) as a parody of the 'Spasmodic' school of poets (e.g. Sydney Dobell and 'Festus' Bailey).

8. The Moonstone *and* The Woman in White: Both by the novelist William Wilkie Collins (1824–89).

9. *Wellington's Indian Despatches*: Arthur Wellesley, First Duke of Wellington, served in India from 1796 to 1805. *The Despatches of . . . the Duke of Wellington . . . during his various campaigns . . . from 1799 to 1818* was published, in thirteen volumes, between 1834 and 1839. *Supplementary Despatches* for India (1797–1805) was published, in fifteen volumes, between 1858 and 1872. *A selection from the despatches . . .* came out as a single volume from the Clarendon Press in 1880.

10. *Army Exams*: Gladstone made competitive examination the rule in the home Civil Service in 1870. (The Indian Civil Service had been recruited by examination since 1855.) In 1871 he abolished the purchase of officers' commissions in the army and introduced the Army Entrance Examination instead. The rise of the new 'Public Schools' was closely connected with the introduction of competitive examinations as the sole means of qualifying for the public services.

11. *'all smiles stopped together'*: From Robert Browning's 'My Last Duchess', *Bells and Pomegranates*, No. III, 1842.

12. *Jules Verne*: (1828–1905), Author of *Twenty-Thousand Leagues under the Sea* (1869), *From the Earth to the Moon* (1865), *Round the World in Eighty Days* (1873), etc.

13. *I hold . . . in Paradise*: Kipling's own verse, modelled on the opening stanza of Tennyson's *In Memoriam*.

14. *Stalky, M'Turk and Beetle*: I.e. L. C. Dunsterville (1865–1946), G. C. Beresford (1864–1938) and Kipling himself.

15. *We had been oppressed*: This incident was described in the first Stalky story, 'Slaves of the Lamp', when it first appeared in the magazine *Cosmopolis* (April 1897) but it was omitted when the story was collected in *Stalky & Co.* in 1899. See also G. C. Beresford, 'The Battle of One Against Three', *The Kipling Journal*, 42 (June 1937), pp. 40–3.

16. *Ruskin*: John Ruskin (1819–1900), author of *The Seven Lamps of Architecture* (1849), *The Stones of Venice* (1851–3) and *Modern Painters* (1834–60). In the 1870s he turned to social reform: *Fors Clavigera* was published as a series of 'Letters to the Workmen and Labourers of Great Britain' (1871–84). L. C. Dunsterville specifies *Fors Clavigera* as a work the trio read (*Stalky's Reminiscences*, p. 44).

17. *'socialization of educational opportunities'*: See 'The Impressionists' in *Stalky & Co.*: '"The work is combined in that study," said the chaplain. "Stalky does the mathematics, M'Turk the Latin, and Beetle attends to their English and French."'

18. *Little Hartopp*: I.e. H. A. Evans.

19. *'brute beasts'*: In 'The Impressionists' Hartopp observes that 'Beetle is as the brutes that perish about sines and cosines.'

20. *'I know a maiden fair to see'*: 'Beware!', adapted from the German by Henry Wadsworth Longfellow (1807–82), the American poet, Professor of Modern Languages at Harvard.

21. *Adventures of Dunsterforce*: In January 1918, Dunsterville was sent into the Southern Caucasus to prevent German and Turkish penetration into the area. In *The Adventures of Dunsterforce* (London, Edwin Arnold, 1920), he describes how 'by a kind of moral camouflage, the original first party of twelve officers and forty-one men filled the gap left in North Persia by the evacuating Russians on 300 miles of road' (p. 3).

22. *my House-master*: M. H. Pugh (the original of 'Prout' in *Stalky & Co.*) succeeded the Rev. J. C. Campbell as Kipling's House-master early in 1879.

23. ripostes: (French) Originally a fencing term, now in general use to signify a quick counter-thrust.

24. *Sandhurst or Woolwich Preliminary:* Entrance examinations for the Royal Military College, Sandhurst, and the Royal Military Academy, Woolwich.

25. *'pi-jaw'*: (Slang) Moral advice, admonishment.

26. *one exception*: This was F. W. Haslam, who taught Kipling Latin in his first two years at USC. He left in 1879 to become Professor

at a college in Christchurch, New Zealand, where Kipling met him in October 1891. (See p. 91 ff.)

27. C—: William Crofts (1846–1912).

28. *Theocritus*: The Greek poet of pastoral Idylls, who lived *c.* 270 BC.

29. *'Regulus'*: According to Kipling, this was written as early as 1908, although it was not published until April 1917 (in *Nash's Magazine*). It was collected in *A Diversity of Creatures* (1917). In the first part, King takes a class through the Fifth Ode in Horace's Third Book. Regulus, who is celebrated in the Ode, was a defeated Roman general, who went willingly to his death at the hands of the Carthaginians.

30. *the 27th of the Third Book*: This Ode has no reference to Cleopatra. It is addressed to Galatea, a young woman going overseas to be married, and tells the myth of Europa, taken from her father by Jupiter in the form of a bull. Perhaps Kipling meant the thirty-seventh Ode of the First Book.

31. *Horace*: Quintus Horatius Flaccus (65–8 BC), one of the most important Roman poets.

32. The City of Dreadful Night: A connected series of poems by James Thomson (1834–82), serialized in *The National Reformer* (1874) and published in book form in 1880.

33. Parables from Nature: These were published in five series between 1855 and 1871 with illustrations by a variety of artists (including Millais, Holman Hunt and Burne-Jones). (See also note 19, chapter 1.)

34. Hiawatha: A narrative poem by Longfellow (see note 20, above) first published in 1855. Longfellow derived the metre from the Finnish epic *The Kalevala*.

35. *Dante*: Dante Alighieri (1265–1321), Florentine poet, author of the *Divina Commedia*. The *Inferno* section describes a journey through the nine circles of hell.

36. *'as rare things will'*: From Robert Browning's 'One Word More', *Men and Women*, 1855. The words refer to a lost volume of sonnets by Raphael.

37. Aurora Leigh: A narrative poem by Elizabeth Barrett Browning (1806–61) published in 1857.

38. Atalanta in Calydon: A poetic drama by A. C. Swinburne (1837–1909), published in 1865. In *Stalky & Co.*, when Beetle is given the run of the Head's study, the list of its treasures ends with '*The Earthly Paradise*; *Atalanta in Calydon*; and Rossetti'.

39. The Pink 'Un: The popular name for *The Sporting Times*, which was published weekly, printed on pink paper.

40. *the School Paper*: *The United Services College Chronicle*. Kipling edited numbers four to ten (30 June 1881–24 July 1882).

41. *the men of Crom's youth*: This would have included most of the Pre-Raphaelites. In 'An English School', *The Youth's Companion* (19 October 1893), Kipling wrote: 'And the Head would sometimes tell him . . . about his own early days at college when Morris and Swinburne and Rossetti . . . were all young.'

42. *Vevey*: A cigar made from tobacco grown at Vevey (Indiana, USA).

43. *'The Battle of Assaye'*: This was fought in the course of the Second Anglo–Maratha War (1803–1805). The English army, led by Wellington, defeated the combined armies of Daulat Rao Sindhia and the Rajah of Berar (23 September 1803). Kipling's poem was published in *The United Services College Chronicle* (2 July 1886).

44. *Joaquin Miller*: The pseudonym of the American poet Cincinnatus Hiner Miller (1839–1913). His best-known volume of verse was *Songs of the Sierras* (1871).

45. Competition Wallah: Sir George Otto Trevelyan (1838–1928) paid a long visit to India in 1863 as private secretary to his father, Sir Charles Trevelyan, Governor of Madras. *The Competition Wallah* (1864) was in the form of a series of letters from a young member of the Indian Civil Service describing his experience of India.

46. *'The bodies . . . and of Birth.'*: from the second Choric Ode in *Atalanta in Calydon*. The lines should read:

> And bodies of things to be
> In the houses of death and of birth.

On 25 September 1897, the Kiplings moved into 'The Elms', but after 1899 'The Elms' was painfully associated with memories of their dead daughter, Josephine, and they began to look for another house. (See pp. 137–9.)

Chapter 3: Seven Years' Hard

1. *Seven Years' Hard*: E. Kay Robinson in 'Kipling in India', *McClure's Magazine* (July 1896), supplies an explanation for this chapter-title: 'I strongly urged him to go to England . . . To all

such suggestions he always returned the answer that when he *knew* he could do good work, it would be time for him to strive for a place in the English world of letters, and that, in any case, the proprietors of the *Civil and Military Gazette* had taken him on trust . . . and he would serve them loyally, like Jacob in the Bible, for his full seven years.' (See Genesis 29: 13–21.)

2. *at Bombay*: Kipling sailed from Tilbury on 20 September 1882 and reached Bombay on 18 October.

3. *School of Art*: Lockwood Kipling was Principal of the Mayo School of Art and Curator of the Lahore Museum from 1875 until his retirement in 1893. The Museum is described in the opening chapter of *Kim*.

4. *the one daily paper*: The *Civil and Military Gazette* had been founded ten years earlier by James Walker and William Rattigan. Kipling became assistant editor in November 1882, and worked under Stephen Wheeler ('My Chief') until 1887, when Wheeler was promoted to the *Pioneer*.

5. *per diem*: (Latin) 'Per day, every day'.

6. *an outbreak*: September 1884.

7. *Fort Lahore*: Enlarged and repaired by Akbar (1542–1605), the third Mughul Emperor; added to by Shah Jahan (1592–1666), Aurangzeb (1618–1707) and Runjit Singh. It is the scene of 'With the Main Guard' in *Soldiers Three*.

8. *Runjit Singh's wives*: Runjit Singh (1780–1839) created a compact Sikh kingdom extending from Peshawar to the Sutlej and from Kashmir to Sind, with Lahore as his capital. Near his ashes are those of his four wives and seven concubines who died, according to *suttee* rites, at his funeral.

9. *D.T.*: *Delirium tremens*, a species of delirium resulting from alcohol abuse. (See also p. 68.)

10. *openings of big bridges*: E.g., 'The Sutlej Bridge', *Civil and Military Gazette*, 2 March 1887 (Thomas Pinney, *Kipling's India*, pp. 206–14), and 'The Chak-Nizam Bridge', *CMG*, 18 May 1887 (Pinney, pp. 215–23).

11. *floods on railways*: E.g., 'A Break on the Line', *CMG*, 6 August 1887 (Pinney, pp. 249–54).

12. *communal riots*: E.g., 'The City of Two Creeds', *C M G*, 19 and 22 October 1885, and 'The City of the Two Creeds', *CMG*, 1 October 1887 (Pinney, pp. 265–9). Both describe the Mohurrum festival in Lahore. The 1887 article identifies the 'troops' as the 14th Bengal Lancers.

13. *the Mosque of Wazir Khan*: According to Lockwood Kipling's article in *The Journal of Indian Art* (vol. II, pp. 17–18), the Mosque was built in 1634 by Hakim Ali ud din, who is better known by his title ('Wazir Khan'). Hakim Ali ud din ruled Lahore under the Emperor Jahangir and his successor, Shah Jahan, from 1628 to 1657.

14. *visits of Viceroys*: E.g., 'The Viceroy at Patiala', *CMG*, 22 March 1884 (Pinney, pp. 26–31), on the visit of Lord Ripon to the Maharajah of Patiala.

15. *to move against Russia:* After General Komaroff had driven the Afghans from Panjdeh in March 1885, the British expected a Russian invasion of India.

16. *an Afghan Potentate*: Abdur Rahman, Emir of Afghanistan from 1880 to 1901. In March 1885, Kipling was sent to Rawalpindi for the meeting between Lord Dufferin, the Viceroy, and Emir Abdur Rahman. See 'To Meet the Ameer', *CMG*, 24 March–14 April 1885 (Pinney, pp. 77–104).

17. *rapparee*: A bandit or robber (derived from the term for Irish irregular soldiers, of the kind prominent in the war of 1688–92).

18. *an inquiry*: Pinney was unable to find an article on this topic. He offers instead 'Typhoid at Home' (*CMG*, 14 February 1885), an exploration of unhygienic conditions of milk-production.

19. *Squeers' method*: Wackford Squeers, the schoolmaster of Dotheboys Hall in Dickens's novel, *Nicholas Nickleby*, was an exponent of 'the practical mode of teaching'.

20. *first bribe*: Birkenhead quotes a letter from Kipling to Edith Macdonald (February 1884), which tells a totally different story as his first experience of attempted bribery (pp. 65–68).

21. *the Decalogue*: The Ten Commandments given to Moses (Exodus 20:3–17).

22. more Asiatico: (Latin) 'According to the custom of Asia'.

23. *Kay Robinson*: Edward Kay Robinson (1857–1928) came from London to be assistant editor of the *Pioneer* in 1885. He was editor of the *Civil and Military Gazette* from 1887 to 1895.

24. *'Timeo . . . et dona ferentes'*: (Latin) 'I fear the Greeks even when they bring gifts'; from Virgil's *Aeneid* (Book II, line 49), where it refers to the wooden horse left at Troy by the Greeks.

25. *Eurasian*: 'Of mixed European and Asian descent'.

26. *Novoie Vremya*: (Russian) 'New Time'.

27. sax-aul: This is not 'sage-brush' but 'Haloxylon ammodendron', a small tree that is limited to Central Asia.

28. *Ten or twelve years later*: Kipling took ill on 20 February 1899 and

did not recover until 17 April. He dictated an account of this delirium, which is reproduced in Birkenhead's *Rudyard Kipling* (pp. 370–6). Kipling's daughter, Josephine, died while he was ill.

29. *a Liberal Government*: Gladstone's second ministry (April 1880 to June 1885).

30. *a matter of principle*: The Ilbert Bill proposed to remove the European privilege of trial by European judges (one of the provisions of the Criminal Procedure Code of 1873). As a result of the European 'revolt' to which Kipling refers, the Government altered the Bill to allow Europeans the right of trial by jury (one half of the jury to be European).

31. *the then Viceroy*: Lord Ripon (1827–1909) was Viceroy of India from 1880 to 1884.

32. *C. P. Ilbert*: He came out to India in 1882 as Law Member of the Viceroy's Executive Council. He returned to England in 1886 to become assistant parliamentary counsel to the Treasury. From 1902 to 1921 he was Clerk of the House of Commons.

33. *the Indian White Paper*: A government White Paper of 1933 set out a first draft of the proposals that were finally embodied in the Government of India Act of 1935. The most important developments were, (1) the bringing of the princely states into federation with the rest of India; (2) the conferring of autonomy on previously subordinate provinces; (3) the expansion of the electorate for the provincial assemblies. This marked a major step towards the goal of Dominion status.

34. *when one is twenty*: Kipling was, in fact, only seventeen when the Ilbert Bill was introduced.

35. *received the decoration*: Carrington points out that none of the three proprietors was knighted till some years later.

36. *Simla*: A hill-station, situated in the east Punjab on the southern slopes of the Himalyas. From 1864 to 1947 it was the summer headquarters (May to October) of the British Administration in India. (See Pat Barr and Ray Desmond, *Simla: A Hill Station in British India*, Scolar Press, London, 1982.)

37. *India Bill*: The Government of India Act, which received Royal Assent on 4 August 1935 – three days after Kipling began writing *Something of Myself*. (See note 33, above.)

38. *made a Freemason*: On 5 April 1886.

39. *the Arya and Brahmo Samaj*: The Brahmo movement was started in 1828 by Raja Ram Mohan Roy (1772–1833), based on a monotheistic interpretation of the Hindu scriptures (the Upa-

nishads). The Brahmo Samaj also advocated social reforms such as female education, the abolition of caste restrictions and widow-remarriage. The Arya Samaj was founded by Swami Dayananda Saraswati (1824–83) in 1875. It was inspired by the Brahmo Samaj but was localized to Uttar Pradesh, the Punjab, Rajputana and Gujarat. It was more evangelical and its concern for religious and social reform was more orientated towards Hindu nationalism. Of the twenty-six members of Kipling's Lodge, at least six were Indian including Mohammed Hayat Khan (Muslim), Sirdar Bikrama Singh (Sikh) and Protul Chander Chatterjee, Gopal Das and Dr Brij Lal Ghose (of Hindu origin).

40. *Tyler*: In Freemasonry, the title given to the man who has the job of standing at the door of the chamber.

41. *up to the Hills*: I.e. to hill-stations such as Simla (see note 36, above) and Dalhousie (p. 67).

42. *one took . . . and walked*, A biblical echo (John 5:9).

43. *the Club*: The Punjab Club, then at Nedou's Hotel.

44. *Mian Mir Cantonments*: Five miles beyond the walled city of Lahore was the Mian Mir Cantonments, where there was permanently stationed a British infantry battalion and a battery of artillery. It is the 'Fort Amara' of *Soldiers Three*.

45. *the fourth dimension*: An allusion, perhaps, to *The Time Machine* by H. G. Wells.

46. *'The wages . . . is death'*: Romans 6:23.

47. *Lock Hospitals*: Hospitals for the treatment of venereal diseases.

48. *Lord Roberts*: Lord Roberts (1832–1914) was Commander-in-Chief from 1885 to 1893. Kipling's ride with him up Simla Mall took place in the period 22 June to 15 July 1888.

49. *one or two stories about soldiers*: *Plain Tales from the Hills* began to appear serially in the *Civil and Military Gazette* from 2 November 1886 and was published in book form in January 1888. Nine stories in the book deal with army life. *Soldiers Three* was also published in 1888 as the first volume of the 'Railway Library'. (See note 80, below.)

50. *the Correspondent*: Howard Hensman, writer on social, military, naval, Indian and South African topics.

51. *Madame Blavatsky*: Helena Petrovna Blavatsky (1831–91) founded the Theosophical Society in 1875 with Colonel H. S. Olcott. She came to India in 1879 and set up the Society's headquarters at Adyar near Madras. Theosophy 'as taught by Madame Blavatsky' emphasized mystical experience, esoteric doctrine and

occult phenomena. All the major religions of the world were seen as different expressions of the same fundamental truth. This led, in turn, to the idea of the 'Secret Doctrine', which Madame Blavatsky claimed to have received from certain adepts, the 'Mahatmas', with whom she was in psychical communication. Manifestations of 'occult phenomena', which she claimed were the outcome of her connection with the 'Mahatmas', were produced in a house in Simla.

52. *whose Editor*: A. P. Sinnett (1840–1921) was the author of a number of works on Theosophy and the occult.

53. *one of my Simla leaves*: May 1885. The party included Stanley de Brath (from the Public Works Department) and his wife.

54. *'all might . . . henceforth and forever'*: Unidentified.

55. All in a Garden Fair: This was published in 1883 and read by Kipling in 1886. It tells of three men, who are rivals for the love of a young woman whom they have all known since their childhood together in Epping Forest. One of the men is a poet who becomes a journalist.

56. *our paper changed*: There was a major overhaul of the paper in August 1887 that brought in new type and a rearranged lay-out. See 'Our Change: By "Us"', *CMG*, 1 August 1887 (Pinney, pp. 243–6).

57. *the little pink* Globe: This was a London evening newspaper published from 1 January 1803 to 31 December 1922. It was printed on pink paper and had the special feature of a short, middle-page article that occupied the right-hand column and 'turned over' to finish on the following page. Kay Robinson had worked for the *Globe* in London.

58. *All the queer outside world*: See the opening of 'The Man who would be King' in *The Phantom Rickshaw* (1888).

59. *an old schoolmate*: This was F. H. G. Cunliffe, who was at the United Services College from January 1876 to December 1879. He enlisted in the 9th Lancers in 1883 and commanded the Nigeria Regiment during 1914–18.

60. Quartette: This was issued by the *Civil and Military Gazette*. It included 'The Phantom Rickshaw' and 'The Strange Ride of Morrowbie Jukes'.

61. *a series of tales*: The first 'Plain Tale' to appear under this heading in the *Gazette* was 'The Other Man', on 13 November 1886. Three earlier stories were included in the 1888 volume: 'The Gate of the Hundred Sorrows' (26 September 1884); 'In the House of Suddhoo' (30 April 1886); 'Mohammed Din' (8 September 1886).

62. Indigo Planters' Gazette: This title is not listed in the *British Union Catalogue of Periodicals*. Perhaps Kipling means the *Indian Planters' Gazette*, which was published in Calcutta from about 1881 to November 1924.

63. *Elia-like*: Charles Lamb (1775–1834) published a series of essays under the pseudonym 'Elia' in the *London Magazine* during the 1820s. These were collected as *Essays of Elia* (1823) and *The Last Essays of Elia* (1833).

64. *Browning*: This review has not been discovered. Kipling reviewed Morris's *The Day is Coming* in the *Civil and Military Gazette* (7 November 1883).

65. *qua*: (Latin) 'In the capacity of'.

66. *Harvest Festival*: A service to celebrate the gathering of the harvest, for which the church is usually decorated with fruit, in English Protestant churches.

67. *Club*: Kipling lived at the Allahabad Club during the cold weather of 1887–8. In June 1888, he moved in with Professor Aleck Hill and his wife, 'Ted'.

68. *a most holy river*: The Ganges.

69. *its chief proprietor*: George Allen.

70. *a weekly edition*: *The Week's News*.

71. *'sight . . . to do ill deeds'*: Unidentified.

72. *'ask . . . for more's ready,'*: from Browning's 'Fra Lippo Lippi'. (See note 43, chapter 1.)

73. *my Daemon*: see 'Introduction' (pp. 12–13) and note 10, chapter 8.

74. *'Gyp'*: the pseudonym of the French novelist Sibylla Gabrielle Riquetti de Mirabeau (1849–1932).

75. *Autour du Mariage*: Published in 1883, this novel set in Paris society was one of Gyp's best-known works.

76. The Story of the Gadsbys: This appeared in *The Week's News* from April to August 1888 and was published in book form in the autumn of the same year. It was published in England in 1890.

77. *'A Wayside Comedy'*: This appeared in *The Week's News* on 21 January 1888; it was later included in *Under the Deodars* (1888).

78. *a Frenchman*: Unidentified.

79. clou: Literally, 'nail' (French), this term is used to refer to the central idea of a work of art.

80. *railway bookstalls*: The firm of A. H. Wheeler & Co. held the contract for Indian railway bookstalls. The 'man' referred to here was E. E. Moreau (1866–1937), senior partner in the firm, who had the idea of issuing cheap reprints for railway reading. The

first six volumes of his 'Indian Railway Library' were Kipling's *Soldiers Three, Wee Willie Winkie, Under the Deodars, The Story of the Gadsbys, In Black and White* and *The Phantom Rickshaw*.

81. *I left India*: He left Lahore on 3 March 1889 and sailed, with the Hills, from Calcutta to Rangoon, as the first stage of a leisurely journey to San Francisco. The journey is described in *From Sea to Sea*.

82. *Try as he will ... our hearts will be!*: The first two stanzas of Kipling's poem 'The Virginity', published in *Nash's Magazine* (June 1914) and collected in *The Years Between*.

Chapter 4: The Interregnum

1. *The youth ... Must travel ...*: From Wordsworth's 'Ode: Intimations of Immortality from Recollections of Early Childhood'.

2. *the autumn of '89*: Kipling arrived at Liverpool from New York on 5 October 1889.

3. *Mary Kingsley*: Mary Kingsley (1862–1900) was a traveller, author, ethnologist and naturalist. She made her first journey to West Africa in 1893, her second in 1894–5. *Travels in West Africa* was published in 1897, *West African Studies* in 1899. See Kipling's essay, 'Mary Kingsley', *Uncollected Prose*, vol. 2 (Sussex Edition).

4. Mowbray Morris: Morris (1847–1911) had been art editor of the *Pioneer*. He was editor of *Macmillan's Magazine* from 1885 to 1907.

5. *... and some verses*: 'The Ballad of the King's Mercy' was published in the issue for November 1889. 'The Ballad of East and West' appeared with 'The Incarnation of Krishna Mulvaney' in the December 1889 issue.

6. *'Lord ... none of I'*: These are the last two lines of an anonymous nursery song, which begins –

> There was a little woman
> As I have heard tell
> She went to market
> Her eggs for to sell.

7. *the editor*: This was Sidney Low (1857–1932). Kipling was introduced to him by Stephen Wheeler, who was now working for the *St James's Gazette*. D. Chapman-Huston's *Sidney Low: The Lost*

Historian (1935) includes Low's account of his first meeting with Kipling.

8. *the* St James's Gazette: This was a London evening paper, which ran from May 1880 to March 1905 (when it was incorporated into the *Evening Standard*).

9. *a weekly paper*: This was probably either the *World* (1874–1922) or *Truth* (1877–1957). The interview with the *World* took place in April 1890.

10. *'feeling my oats'*: (Slang) 'Becoming conceited'.

11. *quarters in Villiers Street*: In Embankment Chambers, which was only a few doors away from the London office of the *Pioneer*. (These are the rooms in which Dick Heldar lives in *The Light that Failed*.)

12. *Lion and Mammoth Comiques*: 'Lions Comiques' were comic singers who specialized in 'swell songs' – part idealization, part parody of the fashionable 'man-about-town'. See Peter Bailey, 'Champagne Charlie: Performance and Ideology in the Music Hall Swell Song' in J. S. Bratton (ed.), *Music Hall: Performance and Style* (Open University Press, 1986, pp. 49–69), and note 41, below.

13. *Bessies and Bellas*: Serio-comic female music-hall performers.

14. viva-voce: Literally, 'by the living voice' (Latin), this usually refers to examinations conducted orally rather than in writing. (See p. 92.)

15. *'Mary, pity Women'*: In *The Seven Seas* (1896).

16. *Henley*: W. E. Henley (1849–1903), poet, critic and editor. He edited the *Scots Observer* (which changed its name to the *National Observer* in November 1890) from its first issue in November 1888 until 1894 (when Frank Harris took over) and then the *New Review* from 1895 to 1898. 'Danny Deever', the first of the *Barrack-Room Ballads*, appeared in the *Scots Observer* on 22 February 1890.

17. *happy company*: Henley's 'young men' or 'the Henley Regatta' (as Max Beerbohm called them). W. B. Yeats, in *Autobiographies* (1926), records Sunday-night meetings of this group which included Henley's assistant Charles Whibley, Kenneth Grahame, R. A. M. Stevenson, George Wyndham and Kipling 'sometimes' (p. 156).

18. *Essays and Reviews*: Henley's essay, 'Arabian Nights Entertainments', appeared originally in *London* in 1878 and was reprinted in his book, *Views and Reviews* (1890).

19. *free verse*: E.g., his 'In Hospital' verses, which were written in the 1870s and collected in *A Book of Verses* (1888).

20. *Mr Gladstone*: William Ewart Gladstone (1809–98) was an MP from 1832 to 1894 and was four times Prime Minister. He was Leader of the Opposition in 1890 and supported Home Rule for Ireland.

21. *Commission of Enquiry*: In 1887 *The Times* had published a series of articles entitled 'Parnellism and Crime', in which Charles Parnell, the Irish nationalist MP, and many of his parliamentary colleagues were charged with conniving at crimes during the days of the Land League. The last article in the series (18 April 1887) included a letter, which purported to be from Parnell, extenuating the assassination of Lord Frederick Cavendish, Chief Secretary for Ireland, and Thomas Henry Burke, Under-Secretary of Ireland, in Phoenix Park, Dublin, in May 1882. After a libel action against *The Times* in July 1888, a Government Commission was set up. On 23 February 1889, Richard Pigott, who had sold the incriminating letters to *The Times*, confessed that they were forgeries. On 13 February 1890 the Commission's report was laid on the table of the House of Commons: it fully acquitted Parnell.

22. *Irish Land Leaguers*: The National Land League was founded by Michael Davitt in 1879. It was launched with the slogan, 'The land of Ireland for the people of Ireland.'

23. *'Cleared!'*: published in the *Scots Observer* on 8 March 1890 and collected in *Barrack-Room Ballads* (1892).

24. *Frank Harris*: Frank Harris (1856–1931) was editor of the *Fortnightly Review* from 1886 until 1894. He was the author of a number of books including novels, short stories, a biography of Oscar Wilde and *The Man Shakespeare* (1909). His most significant contribution to literature was his period as editor of the *Saturday Review* (1894–8), but he is probably best-known now for his autobiography, *My Life and Loves* (1922–7).

25. *the Savile*: The Savile Club was founded in 1868. It moved from Savile Row to 107 Piccadilly in 1882. Kipling was taken there by Andrew Lang in October 1889 after only a few days in London, but he was not elected a full member until 30 January 1891.

26. *the Authors' Society*: The Society of Authors was founded in 1884 'with the object of representing, assisting and protecting authors'. Walter Besant (1836–1901) was chairman of the Society from its foundation until 1892.

27. *Gosse*: Sir Edmund Gosse (1849–1928) was an influential figure in English literary circles around the turn of the century. He wrote numerous volumes of poetry, criticism, and biography, but he is

now best-known for *Father and Son* (1907), his account of his childhood.

28. *Andrew Lang*: Andrew Lang (1844–1912), classical scholar, poet, novelist, folklorist and historian, was perhaps the most influential figure in English literary circles at the time.

29. *Eustace Balfour*: Colonel Eustace Balfour (1854–1911), architect and soldier, was the youngest brother of A. J. Balfour (see note 45, chapter 6).

30. *Herbert Stephen*: Herbert Stephen (1857–1932), writer on Law, and Clerk of Assize for the Northern Circuit (1889–1927).

31. *Rider Haggard*: Sir Henry Rider Haggard (1856–1925), author of adventure stories and romances including *King Solomon's Mines* (1886) and *She* (1887). (See also note 83, below.)

32. *Saintsbury*: George Saintsbury (1845–1933), journalist, literary critic, literary historian, Professor of English at Edinburgh University from 1895 to 1915.

33. *the* Saturday Review: A weekly paper founded in 1855. Lang was its literary critic and Saintsbury a frequent contributor until it was taken over by Frank Harris in 1894. (See note 24, above.)

34. *the Albany*: Built in 1770–4 for Viscount Melbourne, this building, situated just off Piccadilly, was converted into sixty-nine sets of chambers for gentlemen in 1802.

35. '*Proofs of Holy Writ*': Written in 1932–3 and published in the *Strand Magazine* in April 1934.

36. *the Cellar-book*: Saintsbury contributed 'The Cellar' to *The Book of the Queen's Dolls' House* (1924), which was edited by A. C. Benson and Sir Lawrence Weaver.

37. *Tokay*: A sweetish, heavy wine produced in Hungary, described by Saintsbury as 'a prince of liqueurs' in his *Notes on a Cellarbook* (1920).

38. *that ambulance*: The ambulance and the police of E Division appear in 'Brugglesmith', first published in *Black and White* (10 October 1891) and collected in *Many Inventions* (1893).

39. *St Clement Danes*: A church in the Strand.

40. *the pious British householder*: Cf. 'In Partibus', first published in the *Civil and Military Gazette* (23 December 1889) and collected in *Abaft the Funnel* (1909):

> And, when I take my nightly prowl,
> 'Tis passing good to meet
> The pious Briton lugging home
> His wife and daughter sweet,

Through four packed miles of seething vice
Thrust out upon the street.

41. *Lion Comique*: This was probably James Fawn. Kipling refers to him by name in 'The Army of a Dream', *Traffics and Discoveries* (1904). J. S. Bratton, in *Kipling's Magic Art* (The British Academy, 1978), notes that Fawn appeared at Gatti's from 11 November to 23 December 1889 and that Kipling supplied a sketch of the London music hall in 'My Great and Only', *Civil and Military Gazette* (January 1890), *Uncollected Prose*, volume 1 (Sussex Edition), pp. 259–67.

42. *knockin' 'em*: (Slang) 'To capture and hold an audience'. Hence George Robey appeared in 'Mr Punch's Reformed House of Lords' (*Punch*, 1910) as 'Lord Knockham of Tivoli'.

43. *a . . .' kick-up*: (Slang) 'A dance'.

44. *'nothing since Dickens'*: In an anonymous article' The New Writer' in the *Scots Observer* (3 May 1890), Henley wrote 'here is such a promise as has not been perceived in English letters since young Mr Dickens broke in suddenly upon the precincts of immortality.' (See *The Critical Heritage*, pp. 55–8.)

45. *my portrait*: By John Collier (1850–1934), shown at the Royal Academy in 1891.

46. *a flying visit*: They returned in May 1890, but (according to Carrington) it was far from 'a flying visit' since they stayed for about a year.

47. *my Mother, all Celt*: The Kiplings were a Yorkshire family; the Macdonalds were Highlanders who had migrated to Fermanagh after the 'Forty-Five Rebellion and then come to England in 1795.

48. *'The English Flag'*: Collected in *Barrack-Room Ballads*.

49. *'Unto them . . . among the reeds'*: From Elizabeth Barrett Browning's poem 'The Romance of the Swan's Nest' (*Poems*, 1844) – 'Unto him I will discover/That swan's nest among the reeds.'

50. *Army and Navy Stores List*: The Army and Navy Stores in Victoria Street, London, was founded in 1871 to supply the needs of members of the Forces. Its annual catalogue ran to over a thousand pages. (See also p. 129.)

51. *arriding per se*: 'Scorning, or laughing at, by itself'.

52. *J.K.S*: J. K. Stephen (1859–92), barrister and Fellow of Trinity College, Cambridge, published the 'stanzas' in the *Cambridge Review* (February 1891). They are reprinted in *The Critical Heritage*, pp. 76–7. (For Herbert Stephen, see note 30, above.)

53. *to Italy*: On 2 October 1890.

54. *Lord Dufferin*: First Marquis of Dufferin and Ava (1826–1902), Viceroy of India (1884–8).

55. *'The Song of the Women'*: Published in the *Pioneer* (17 April 1888) and collected in the fourth edition of *Departmental Ditties* (1890). As a result of representations from Dr Elizabeth Bielby, the Kiplings' physician at Lahore, concerning the need for medical help for Indian women, the Lady Dufferin Fund was established for a chain of hospitals throughout India.

56. *the great J. M. himself*: J. M. Cook was the 'Son' of 'Thomas Cook & Son'. Thomas Cook (1808–92) began the firm in 1841 with the first special 'excursion train'. By 1870, it had become a world-wide organization.

57. *to Mecca*: The *'Hajj'*, the annual pilgrimage to Mecca, the birth-place of Mohammed and the great holy city of Islam, takes place during the last month of the Arab year. Every Moslem is expected to perform the *'Hajj'* at least once in his lifetime. (See the Koran, Surah 3, 97–8.)

58. *to Cape Town*: Kipling's memories of this journey are unreliable. He had booked to sail on the SS *Moor* on 8 August 1891, but he postponed his departure and left London on 22 August on the SS *Mexican*. He arrived at Cape Town on 10 September.

59. *a Navy Captain*: E. H. Bayly (1849–1904). (See P. W. Brock, 'My friend Captain Bagley', *The Kipling Journal* [September 1963].)

60. *stoeps*: (Dutch) 'A raised platform or verandah along the front – and sometimes also round the side – of a house.'

61. *hubshees*: From the Arabic 'habashi' or the Persian 'habshi', this means literally 'Abyssinians' but it is applied in India to Africans generally.

62. *'rags'*: (Slang) 'Displays of noisy, disorderly conduct; high-spirited practical jokes.'

63. *Lieutenant-Commander*: Lieutenant S. de Horsey, who then commanded HMS *Griper*. (He was the model for Judson in 'Judson and the Empire', *Many Inventions*.)

64. *Adderley Street*: The principal street of Cape Town.

65. *Cecil Rhodes*: Cecil Rhodes (1852–1902) went to southern Africa in 1870 and made a fortune in the Kimberley diamond fields. In 1880 he established the De Beers Mining Company; in 1888 he acquired interests in the gold-mining corporation which became Consolidated Goldfields; in 1889 he founded the British South

Africa Company, which took control of the territory which was named 'Rhodesia' after him. He was Prime Minister of the Cape from 1890 to 1896.

66. *to Melbourne*: The SS *Doric* left Cape Town on 25 September 1891 and arrived at Wellington, New Zealand on 18 October. Kipling went to Australia *after* he had visited New Zealand. (He arrived at Melbourne on 12 November.) 'McAndrews' Hymn' refers to this voyage, 'Fra' Cape Town east to Wellington'.

67. *the Melbourne Cup*: An Australian horse-race.

68. *Sir George Grey*: The meeting took place at Auckland not Hobart. Sir George Grey (1812–98) was Governor of Cape Colony from 1853 to 1861. During the Indian Mutiny (1857–8), also known as the First War of Indian Independence, Grey had made a name for himself by the promptitude with which he sent off horses, stores and artillery in response to a despatch from Lord Elphinstone in Bombay.

69. '*Pelorus Jack*': This dolphin in fact haunted Cook Strait in the French Pass (not Wellington Harbour).

70. '*income . . . of an Ambassador*': Not located.

71. *a rising river*: The Esk. Kipling travelled by train from Wellington to Napier, by buggy from Napier to Cambridge, and from Cambridge to Auckland by train. The 'great plains' were the Kaingaroa Plains. (See Margaret Newsom, 'Kipling in New Zealand', *The Kipling Journal* [19 April 1972], pp. 8–12.)

72. *a kiwi*: A. O. F. Caddick has suggested that this is unlikely, since the kiwi was partially protected from 1864, and proposed the weka, which is also flightless, as an alternative. (See *The Kipling Journal* [March 1973].)

73. *Stevenson at Samoa*: Robert Louis Stevenson (1850–94) lived at Vailima, Samoa, from 1890 until his death. His works include *Treasure Island* (1883) and *Dr Jekyll and Mr Hyde* (1886).

74. The Wrong Box: This novel was written by Stevenson in collaboration with his stepson, Samuel Lloyd Osbourne, and published in 1889. The language of this passage – 'Eminent Past Master' and 'the Test Volume of that Degree' – is derived from Freemasonry.

75. *Boston in '89*: 16 September 1889.

76. '*Mrs Bathurst*': First published in *Windsor Magazine* and *Metropolitan Magazine* (March 1904), and collected in *Traffics and Discoveries* (1904).

77. *General Booth*: William Booth (1829–1912) founded the Christian

Mission in Whitechapel in 1865. In 1878 the 'Mission' was re-organized on a quasi-military basis and by June 1880 the title 'Salvation Army' had been adopted.

78. *my P. & O.*: The Peninsular and Oriental Steam Navigation Company was founded in 1834, running to Egypt, India, Ceylon (Sri Lanka), Singapore, Australia and New Zealand. Kipling travelled by the SS *Valetta* to Colombo.

79. *'if by any ... save some'*: Cf. I Corinthians 9:22 ('I am made all things to all men, that I might by all means save some').

80. *in gaol*: See T. H. Huxley's attack on Booth's financial arrangements in the course of a series of letters to *The Times* (1 December 1890 to 22 January 1891).

81. *Isaiah and ... the Prophet*: Isaiah, the Hebrew prophet, and Mohammed, the prophet of Islam.

82. *at Oxford*: In 1907 Booth was awarded a DCL; Kipling was awarded a D.Litt.

83. *had worked with him*: When Haggard was preparing his *Report on the Salvation Army Colonies in the United States* (1905), reprinted as *The Poor and the Land*, and his book *Regeneration: Being an account of the Social Work of the Salvation Army in Great Britain* (1910).

84. *in the belly*: Cf. Matthew 12:40 ('Jonas was three days and three nights in the whale's belly').

Chapter 5: The Committee of Ways and Means

1. *The Committee of Ways and Means*: In Britain, this is a committee of the whole House of Commons, which sits to receive the annual financial statement from the Chancellor of the Exchequer and to consider means of procuring the necessary annual supply. In America, this is a standing committee of the House of Representatives, to which are referred bills dealing with revenue, etc.

2. *to be married*: Kipling received a cable from Caroline Balestier while he was at Lahore, calling him back to England because of the death of her brother, Wolcott Balestier, on 6 December 1891. Kipling arrived in London on 10 January, and the wedding took place, by special licence, on 18 January 1892.

3. *Manchuria*: A generalized term for China.

4. *the church*: All Soul's Church, Langham Place, at the north end of Regent Street.

5. *all the congregation present*: In addition to Gosse, James and

Poynter, there were also Gosse's wife and son and William Heinemann, the publisher, who had been Wolcott Balestier's partner.

6. *a wedding breakfast:* At Brown's Hotel, Albemarle Street.

7. *our magic carpet*: They left Liverpool for New York on 3 February 1892 on the SS *Teutonic*. After a visit to New England their journey continued, via Chicago, St Paul and Winnipeg, to Vancouver. For the 'magic carpet', see the story 'Prince Ahmad and the Fairy Peri-Banu' in *The Arabian Nights*.

8. *to Vancouver*: On 3 April 1892.

9. *to Yokohama*: They arrived on 20 April. Mr and Mrs Hunt acted as their hosts.

10. *an earthquake*: There were two earthquakes: one on 11 May and a more severe one on 3 June.

11. *suspended payment*: Kipling had nearly £2,000 in the New Oriental Banking Company when it suspended payment on 9 June 1892. His immediate resources were a return ticket to Vancouver and $100 in a New York bank.

12. *a child to be born*: Josephine Kipling. (See note 21, below.)

13. *a little New England town*: Brattleboro, Vermont. Joseph Balestier (d. 1888) had settled at 'Beechwood', Brattleboro in 1868. The Kiplings arrived back in Brattleboro on 9 August 1892.

14. *my Adjutant of Volunteers*: See p. 63.

15. *Leuconoë agreeing with Horace*: Kipling is referring to the Eleventh Ode in Horace's First Book. His own version ('To Lucy') runs:

> Lucy, do not look ahead: We shall be a long time dead.
> Take whatever you can see: And, incidentally, take me.

He presumably means that his wife agreed that they should take the insurance policy.

16. *a tale*: 'In the Rukh', first published in *Many Inventions* (1893).

17. *the Masonic Lions*: See note 27, chapter 1.

18. Nada the Lily: This Zulu romance, in which Umslopogaas is presented as running with a pack of wolves, was published in May 1892 after serialization in the *Illustrated London News* (2 January to 7 May 1892).

19. *to write stories*: Kipling finished 'Toomai of the Elephants' on 16 November and 'Mowgli's Brothers' on 29 November 1892.

20. *my Daemon*: see 'Introduction' (pp. 12–13) and note 10, chapter 8.

21. *My first child*: Josephine Kipling (died 6 March 1899). She appears as Taffimai in the *Just So Stories*.

22. *'Naulakha'*: This is a Hindi word meaning 'nine lakhs' (one lakh

= 100,000). This was the name of the jewel which Nick Tarvin fails to bring back with him in *The Naulahka* (sic), the novel which Kipling wrote in collaboration with Wolcott Balestier. 'Naulakha' was also the name of a famous necklace belonging to Nana Sahib and the name of the pavilion built by Shah Jahan in Lahore. In each case, the name refers to either the value or the cost (900,000 rupees).

23. *the Vendôme Column*: This column in the Place Vendôme was pulled down on 16 May 1871 by order of the Paris Commune because it celebrated militarism and Napoleonic imperialism. It was rebuilt, after the fall of the Commune. (Kipling was in Paris in 1878.)

24. *Marcus Aurelius*: After the Roman Emperor and Stoic philosopher (AD 121–180).

25. *'A Walking Delegate'*: Written during August and September of 1894, published in the *Century Magazine* in December of 1894 and collected in *The Day's Work* (1898).

26. *Morgans*: A celebrated American strain of horses, which originated in Vermont and was named after Justin Morgan, their first breeder.

27. *a 'Dry' State*: I.e., a state in which alcohol was prohibited.

28. *John Hay*: John Hay (1838–1905) became Assistant Secretary of State in 1878, after making his name as a poet, journalist and diplomat. He was Ambassador to Britain 1897–8.

29. *a visit to him*: The Kiplings spent six weeks in Washington in spring 1895, when Hay was at the State Department.

30. *Theodore Roosevelt*: (1858–1919) Assistant Secretary of the US Navy (1896–8) and President (1901–1908). (The Secretary of the US Navy was the easy-going John D. Long.)

31. *conforming-Dopper*: A Calvinist sect found among the Boers of the Transvaal. The name is derived from the Dutch word 'doper' – 'to baptise'.

32. *'Verdomder Hollanders'*: (Dutch) 'Damned Dutch'. The correct form would be 'verdomde'.

33. *Hannibal Chollops*: An American character in Dickens's novel, *Martin Chuzzlewit* (1843). He is described in chapter 33: 'He always introduced himself to strangers as a worshipper of Freedom; and was the consistent advocate of Lynch law, and slavery.'

34. *'twisting the Lion's tail'*: England was represented as a lion in political cartoons of the period.

35. *New York Police Court Judge*: On 26 July 1935, there was an anti-Nazi demonstration in New York against the SS *Bremen*, during which the ship's Nazi flag was pulled down and seven men were arrested. On 6 September Mr Louis Brodsky, the police magistrate, acquitted five of the men and handed down a written opinion in which he characterized the Nazi regime as a 'throwback to pre-medieval if not barbaric social and political conditions', and described the *Bremen*'s flag as 'the black flag of piracy'. On 8 September, there were complaints from Berlin about 'a Jew' acting as judge and acquitting 'desecrators of the German flag'. On 15 September the American Secretary of State, Cordell Hull, apologized for the judge's critical remarks on a power with which the American Government maintained friendly relations.

36. *Professor Langley*: S. P. Langley (1834–1906) was a pioneer in research into solar radiation and heavier-than-air flying-machines. He was Secretary of the Smithsonian Institute from 1887 until his death. Kipling met him in 1895. In 1896 two of Langley's models made the first sustained free flights of power-propelled heavier-than-air machines, covering 3,000 feet and 4,200 feet respectively, before landing on the Potomac River.

37. *the Smithsonian*: The Smithsonian Institute in Washington, DC, was founded in 1846 after a bequest from James Smithson (1765–1829). It consists of an art gallery, a zoo, an observatory and a museum (relating mainly to zoology, biology and anthropology). The zoo and observatory were established by Professor Langley.

38. *the Philippines*: America acquired these islands in December 1898 by the treaty that concluded the Spanish-American War. Kipling's poem 'The White Man's Burden' was written in response to this war.

39. *his subject was Egypt*: Kipling's chronology in this paragraph is confused. Roosevelt's speech on Egypt was given in the Guildhall, London, on 31 May 1910, and was published in Roosevelt's *African and European Addresses* (1910).

40. *Panama*: Until November 1903 Panama was part of the Republic of Colombia. In June 1902 the American Congress had approved the Panama route for the new canal, but Colombia subsequently rejected the Hay–Herran Treaty. Representatives of the New Panama Canal Company then stirred up a secessionist movement in Panama. American warships prevented Colombian troops from landing to suppress the revolt and, when Panama seceded from Colombia on 3 November, the new country received prompt re-

cognition from America. Within a month Panama had negotiated in its own name the treaty that Colombia had rejected.

41. *a brother-President*: José Marroquin was President of Colombia from 1900 to 1904.

42. *'Pithecanthropoid'*: from 'Pithecanthropos' (Greek, meaning 'ape-man'), Haeckel's name for a hypothetical link between apes and man.

43. *two of his delightful sons*: Roosevelt had four sons: Theodore, Kermit, Archibald and Quentin. All four were at the front in the 1914–18 war. Theodore (1887–1944) was among the first American troops to fight in France when America joined the war in 1917. Kermit (1889–1943), who had an honorary commission in the British forces, met Kipling in 1917.

44. *Sam McClure*: He was founder and editor of *McClure's Magazine* (1893–1928), to which Kipling contributed many stories. He went into partnership with Frank Doubleday to form the publishing company, Doubleday & McClure Co. (See note 46, below.)

45. *Ecclesiasticus:* Ecclesiasticus (or 'The Book of Jesus, son of Sirach') is one of the apocryphal books of the Old Testament. It belongs to the Hokmah or 'Wisdom Literature' of Judaism and is included in the Talmud.

46. *Doubleday, Doran & Co.*: Doubleday & McClure Co. became Doubleday, Page & Co. in 1901, and this became Doubleday, Doran & Co. in 1928.

47. *American Copyright law*: America was not a signatory of the Berne Convention (1887), and non-American authors had no copyright protection in America until the Chace Act (1891). This Act accepted the principle of international copyright, but it required simultaneous publication in America and the country of origin. It further required that the book published in America be 'manu-factured' (i.e., printed and bound) in America. It was only with the US Copyright Act (1909) that these requirements were removed.

48. *the bootleggers*: Dealers in alcohol during Prohibition.

49. *the Copyright League*: The American Publishers' Copyright League was formed in 1887. It worked with the Authors' Copyright League in a copyright campaign which led to the Chace Act. Kipling, however, seems to be referring to a pirate publisher.

50. *Charles Eliot Norton*: Norton (1827–1908) was Professor of the History of Art, Harvard University (1875–98), the author of a number of books on architecture and a translator of Dante.

51. *Brahmins*: Brahmins are the highest caste in Hinduism. Here the term is figuratively used to denote 'people of the highest culture'.

52. *Montaigne ... Mon-tes-ki-ew*: Montaigne (1533–92) was famous for his *Essays*. Montesquieu (1689–1755) was the author of *The Persian Letters* (1721) and *The Spirit of Laws* (1748), a work of political theory.

53. *Emerson ... Holmes ... Longfellow ... the Alcotts*: Ralph Waldo Emerson, see note 55, chapter 1; Oliver Wendell Holmes (1809–94), doctor, poet, essayist, Professor of Anatomy at Harvard; Henry Wadsworth Longfellow see note 20, chapter 2; Amos Bronson Alcott (1799–1888), philosopher and educationalist, and his daughter, Louisa May Alcott (1832–88), author of *Little Women* (1868), *Good Wives* (1869), etc.

54. *Abraham Lincoln*: Lincoln (1809–65) was President of the United States from 1861 until his death. The idea expressed here is put into the mouth of Mrs Burton in 'The Edge of the Evening', *A Diversity of Creatures* (1917).

55. *one million*: The official figure is under 650,000.

56. *two flying visits*: The visits occupied April to August 1894 and July to August 1895. The Lockwood Kiplings had retired in 1893 and settled at 'The Gables', Tisbury, Wiltshire.

57. *William Dent Pitman*: In *The Wrong Box* (1889), William Dent Pitman 'stared long and earnestly at the proud, high-born waxen lady in evening dress' in the hairdresser's window, and acknowledged 'a haughty, indefinable something about that figure'. (See note 74, chapter 4.)

58. *once or twice*: Three times, in fact.

59. *Pocahontas coal*: Pocahontas (1595–1617) was the daughter of Powhatan, the head of the Indian confederacy in Virginia. She married John Rolfe in 1613 and died in England. Pocahontas coal is, presumably, American coal.

60. *off the Banks*: The Grand Banks, an important fishing ground, is a submarine plateau stretching 400 to 500 miles south-east from the south coast of Newfoundland towards mid-Atlantic at a depth of 300 to 600 feet.

61. *a railway magnate*: F. N. Finney. Kipling wrote to him for information on 2 March 1896.

62. *a Super-film Magnate*: The film was in preparation in 1935 and was first shown in 1937. It was made by MGM, directed by Victor Fleming, and the cast included Spencer Tracy, Lionel

Barrymore and Mickey Rooney. The 'Magnate' has not been positively identified.

63. *hostile*: This is the closest Kipling comes to referring to his quarrel with his brother-in-law, Beatty Balestier. On 7 May 1896, Kipling laid information against his brother-in-law for threatening to murder him. After court appearances on 9 May and 12 May, which received considerable press attention, the case was postponed until September. Kipling left America before the case re-opened. (See Carrington, chapter 9; Birkenhead, chapter 11.) At the same time, Kipling had also been affected by the Venezuela crisis. In July 1895 the dispute between Britain and America about the frontier between Venezuela and British Guiana had flared up. On 17 December President Cleveland denounced Britain and asserted America's right to defend Venezuela from British aggression. For the next six months, war between America and Britain seemed likely, and, as early as January 1896, Kipling seems to have felt that the American phase of his life was drawing to a close.

64. *another small daughter*: Elsie Kipling, born 2 February 1896.

65. *Wilt thou . . . wrote the bill*: from 'Solution', *May Day, and Other Pieces* (1867).

66. *in Torquay*: They took up residence at 'Rock House', Maidencombe, Torquay, on 9 September 1896. Kipling used it for the story 'The House Surgeon', *Actions and Reactions* (1909).

67. *and fled*: On 11 May 1897 they moved to London, where they stayed in a hotel for the rest of the month. (See note 69, below.)

68. *at the time*: Price visited the Kiplings from 28 to 30 December 1896. According to Birkenhead, Kipling began the first story on 13 December 1896. According to other sources, 'Slaves of the Lamp' was the first story to be written, and it was started on 14 January 1897. Price visited the Kiplings again in October 1897, by which time the stories were well under way.

69. *at Rottingdean*: The Kiplings moved into 'North End House' on 2 June 1897 and transferred to 'The Elms' in September.

70. *. . . the Ridsdales*: Stanley Baldwin married Lucy Ridsdale on 12 September 1892.

71. *my son John*: John Kipling was born on 17 August 1897. He was killed at the Battle of Loos, 27 September 1915.

72. *'Sussex'*: First published in *The Five Nations* (1903).

73. *Mr Micawber*: In Dickens's novel, *David Copperfield*, at the end of chapter 36, Mr Micawber 'placed his IOU in the hands of Traddles', and David Copperfield observes 'I am persuaded that

this was quite the same to Mr Micawber as paying the money.'

74. *Alfred Morrison*: Alfred Morrison (1821–97) was a collector of Persian carpets, Chinese porcelain, Greek gems and gold work. He had a small collection of paintings, an extensive collection of engravings and an unrivalled collection of autographs and letters.

75. *the Wyndhams*: The Hon. Percy Scawen Wyndham (1835–1911) of 'Clouds', East Knowle, Salisbury, Wilts.

76. *'Backward . . . in your flight'*: the first line of the song, 'Rock me to sleep, mother', by Elizabeth Akers Allen (1832–1911).

77. *the brass bottle*: This refers to 'The Story of the Fisherman' in *The Arabian Nights*.

78. *Cervantes*: Miguel de Cervantes Saavedra (1547–1616) Spanish novelist, dramatist and poet; the author of *Don Quixote* (1605).

79. *the India Office:* In 1801, the East India Company established a library to house its collection of Oriental books and manuscripts. A Record Office had already been formed, in 1771, for part of the Company's archives. In 1858 the Library and Record Office were transferred to the newly created India Office.

80. *Charles Reade*: Charles Reade (1814–84), novelist, best-known for *The Cloister and the Hearth* (1861).

81. *the Grand Trunk Road*: This is the main road from Calcutta to the Khyber Pass. Kipling refers to a passage, in chapter 4, which begins, 'By this time the sun was driving broad golden spokes through the lower branches of the mango trees.'

82. *the Jatakas*: This is a collection of stories, recounting the Buddha's exploits in previous existences. It includes fables and folktales and is said to be the source of many of the fables of Aesop and La Fontaine. (See Peter Caracciolo, 'Buddhist Teaching Stories and their influence on Conrad, Wells and Kipling', *The Conradian*, 11:1 (May 1986), pp. 24–34.)

83. *my old Classics master*: W. C. Crofts. (See note 27, chapter 2.)

84. *an illustrated edition of my works*: *Kim* was published in book form in England and America in 1901. The New York edition contained ten illustrations by Lockwood Kipling. In 1902 *Kim* was added to the 'Outward Bound' edition (begun in 1897) with the same illustrations.

85. *'If you get . . . God invents'*: From Browning's 'Fra Lippo Lippi'.

86. *the Higher Cannibalism*: See p. 146.

87. *elected to the Athenaeum*: On 2 April 1897.

88. *an old General*: R. L. Green suggests that this was probably Sir Evelyn Wood (1838–1919). Wood entered the Royal Navy as a

midshipman in 1852; he served in the *Queen* during the Crimean War; and he was promoted to General in 1895. However, the Athenaeum is not listed among his clubs in *Who's Who*.

89. *Parsons*: Sir Charles Parsons (1854–1931) was the inventor of the Parsons Steam Turbine and Chairman of the Parsons Marine Steam Turbine Company.

90. au gratin: (French) 'Dressed with bread-crumbs or grated cheese and either baked in the oven or grilled.'

91. *Hercules Read*: Sir Hercules Read (1857–1929), Keeper of British and Medieval Antiquities and Ethnography at the British Museum (1896–1921), President of the Royal Anthropological Institute.

92. *Carlton, and Beefsteak*: The Carlton, a Conservative club, was established in 1832, and situated (in Kipling's time) in Pall Mall; the Beefsteak was established in 1876 as a social club in the West End of London.

93. *'rag'*: (Slang) 'Banter, abuse'.

94. *'skittles'*: (Slang) 'Nonsense'.

95. *Addison's time*: Joseph Addison (1672–1719), essayist and founder of the original *Spectator*.

96. *Doctor Johnson*: Samuel Johnson (1709–84), critic and lexicographer; James Boswell (1740–95), his friend and biographer. Boswell's *The Life of Samuel Johnson* was published in 1791.

Chapter 6: South Africa

1. *the Jameson Raid*: In 1895, at a time of tension between the Boers and the 'Outlanders' (a mainly British majority, disenfranchised by the policies of President Kruger), Dr L. S. Jameson (1853–1917) led a force of around 500 police into the Transvaal to promote an armed rising against Kruger. They crossed the border on 29 December, but were forced to surrender on 2 January 1896.

2. *'a sound . . . the mulberry trees'*: from II Samuel 5:24 ('And let it be, when thou hearest the sound of a going in the tops of the mulberry trees, that then thou shalt bestir thyself').

3. *Diamond Jubilee*: 1897 was the sixtieth anniversary of Queen Victoria's accession to the throne.

4. *'Recessional'*: Kipling began the poem on 21 June, and it was published in *The Times* on 17 July.

5. *Captain E. H. Bayly*: Kipling had met Bayly on board SS *Mexican* on his first trip to South Africa in 1891. (See p. 89 and notes 58

and 59, chapter 4.) In 1897 and 1898 Kipling accepted Bayly's earlier invitation and joined him for a cruise on HMS *Pelorus*. (See *A Fleet in Being*, 1898.]

6. *Joseph Chamberlain, Rhodes, Lord Milner*: Chamberlain (1836–1914) was Secretary of State for the Colonies in Lord Salisbury's Third Cabinet (1895–1902); Sir Alfred Milner (1854–1925) was High Commissioner for South Africa (1897–1905); for Rhodes, see note 65, chapter 4.

7. *the winter of '97*: Kipling left Southampton on 8 January 1898 and arrived in South Africa on 25 January. He was back in England by the end of April.

8. *Wynberg*: A suburb of Cape Town.

9. *Dutch Ministry*: Kipling is perhaps referring to the Fruit Export Board, which was set up in 1925 (after Hertzog's election victory) with wide powers to regulate all fruit exports from South Africa.

10. *the South African War*: Britain declared war on 11 October 1899, and peace was signed on 1 June 1902. Kipling arrived in Cape Town on 5 February 1900 and was on active service outside Cape Town from 19 March to 3 April 1900.

11. *'The Absent-minded Beggar'*: published in the *Daily Mail* on 31 October 1899.

12. *Sir Arthur Sullivan*: Sir Arthur Sullivan (1842–1900), a composer best-known for his comic operas, written in collaboration with W. S. Gilbert.

13. *RE sergeants*: Sergeants from the Royal Engineers.

14. persona gratissima: Kipling is playing on the Latin phrase *persona (non) grata* – i.e., 'a person who is (not) wanted'. *Gratissima* is the superlative, 'most wanted'.

15. *Wynberg Hospitals*: See Kipling's 'Surgical and Medical', which appeared serially in the *Daily Mail* during April and May of 1900, for an account of visits to the base hospital in Wynberg.

16. *Bloemfontein*: A town in the centre of the Orange River Colony, taken by Lord Roberts on 1 March 1900.

17. *Kadir Baksh*: Kipling's servant in India. He is mentioned in several stories, including 'Garm – a Hostage', 'Collar-Wallah and the Poison Stick', and 'My Own True Ghost Story'.

18. *on Lord Roberts' order*: On 13 March Lord Roberts arranged for the establishment of an army newspaper in Bloemfontein. The Boer paper, the *Express*, was suppressed, and the English-run paper, the *Friend of the Free State*, was commandeered. Four war-correspondents, H. A. Gwynne, Perceval Landon, Julian Ralph

and F. W. Buxton (of the Johannesburg *Star*) were sent for to staff the paper. On 17 March Roberts wired to Kipling asking him to join the staff of the paper as well. Kipling arrived at Bloemfontein on 21 March. (Most of Kipling's contributions to the *Friend* are reprinted in Julian Ralph's *War's Brighter Side* [1901].)

19. *H. A. Gwynne*: Gwynne (1865–1950), a war-correspondent and journalist, organized Reuters' South African war service. He was subsequently editor of the *Standard* (1902–11) and of the *Morning Post* (1911– 37).

20. *Perceval Landon*: Landon (1869–1927) was Special Correspondent to *The Times* for the South African War. In 1904 he became Special Correspondent to the *Daily Telegraph*.

21. *stereos*: I.e., stereotype plates, solid metal plates used for printing.

22. *Julian Ralph*: Ralph (1853–1903) was an American war-correspondent working in Africa for the London *Daily Mail*. His son, Lester Ralph (1876–1927), was a magazine illustrator, covering the South African War as a war-artist.

23. *wearing a fringe*: Presumably the fringe was not her own hair, and she would have used alcohol to clean it.

24. *the death-rate*: 4,000 Boers were killed and 5,774 on the British side, but 16,000 people died of disease.

25. *'dead to the wide'*: (Slang) 'Utterly exhausted'.

26. *Mauser-wound*: The Mauser was a repeating rifle, which the Boers used. It was named after its inventor.

27. *Paardeberg*: This was the decisive battle of the war. After relieving Kimberley, Lord Roberts engaged General Cronje at Paardeberg. More than 1,500 British soldiers were killed or wounded, before Cronje and his 4,000 men surrendered on 27 February 1900.

28. *Philip Sidney's name*: Sir Philip Sidney (1554–86) was a soldier, statesman, and poet. In his *Life of Sir Philip Sidney* (1652), Sir Fulke Greville records the incident to which Kipling alludes. After receiving a mortal injury at the Battle of Zutphen, 'being thirstie with excess of bleeding, he called for drink, which was presently brought him; but as he was putting the bottle to his mouth, he saw a poor Souldier carried along, who had eaten his last at the same Feast, gastly casting up his eyes at the bottle. Which Sir Philip perceiving, took it from his head, before he drank, and delivered it to the poor man, with these words, *Thy necessity is yet greater than mine.*'

29. *the 'solitary horseman' of the novels*: Reference unidentified.

30. *'Sanna's Post'*: On 31 March 1900, the Boer General, de Wet, ambushed a column of the 10th Hussars under General Broadwood: about thirty officers and 500 men were killed, wounded or missing. (See Arthur Conan Doyle, *The Great Boer War* [1900], pp. 374–81, for a full account of this incident.)

31. *a donga*: An African word for a gully or ravine.

32. *the Battle of Kari Siding*: The battle took place on 28 March 1900. Roberts attempted to encircle a Boer force, but his cavalry did not move fast enough and the Boers slipped away before the trap could close.

33. *a well-known war-correspondent*: Bennet Burleigh of the *Daily Telegraph*. (See the *Daily Telegraph*, 13 April 1900.)

34. secundum artem: (Latin) 'In accordance with the rules of the art'.

35. *Krupp*: Alfred Krupp (1812–87), German metallurgist, engaged in the production of artillery from 1847. The family firm underwent enormous expansion under him and his son, Friedrich Alfred Krupp (1854–1902).

36. *Le Gallais*: Colonel Le Gallais was in command of the Mounted Infantry.

37. vice: (Latin) 'In place of'.

38. Maffeesh: (Arabic) 'Dead, defunct, useless'.

39. *French*: J. D. P. French (1852–1925) was the General in command at Karee Siding. In World War I, he was Commander-in-Chief of Allied Forces in France until 1916.

40. *Tantie Sannie*: Presumably 'Aunt Sanna'. Boer women were usually addressed as 'Tante' (Dutch for 'aunt') as a form of respect.

41. *Miss Hobhouse*: Emily Hobhouse (1860–1926) was involved in the South African Conciliation Committee at the outbreak of the war in 1899. In 1900, she formed the 'South African Women and Children Distress Fund'. In December 1901, she went to South Africa and produced her *Report of a Visit to the Camps of Women and Children in the Cape and Orange River Colonies*.

42. *'Woolsack'*: 'The Woolsack' was built for the Kiplings by Rhodes on his 'Groote Schuur' estate. They spent the winters there from 1901 to 1908.

43. *De Wet*: Christian Rudolph de Wet (1854–1922), a Boer general and the commander-in-chief of the Free State Forces from 1900, was a specialist in guerrilla tactics.

44. *Smuts*: Jan Christiaan Smuts (1870–1950), a Boer general, had studied law at Cambridge (1891–4) and was an Honorary Fellow (1895). In 1916, he was a lieutenant-general in the British Army

(in command of Imperial Forces in East Africa). He was sent to London in 1917 to represent the Union of South Africa at the Imperial Conference, and he remained as a member of the British War Cabinet (1917–18). He was twice the Prime Minister of South Africa (1919–24 and 1939–48).

45. *Mr Balfour*: Arthur James Balfour (1848–1930), Prime Minister (1902–1906), became First Earl of Balfour in 1922.

46. *for the pot*: (Slang) 'for food'.

47. *Armageddon*: This is the name of a valley near Jerusalem, where, according to Revelation 16:6, the battle which precedes the end of the world will take place. Here it is used figuratively of the major European war that was already anticipated. (See Kipling's story 'The Captive' and p. 157.)

48. *Magersfontein*: Magersfontein is 100 miles west of Bloemfontein. At the battle fought there on 11 December 1899, Lord Methuen's forces were repulsed by General Cronje's.

49. *Lord Dundonald*. He was in command of the Natal Field Force in 1899, and headed the relief of Ladysmith (28 February 1900).

50. *'handy-pandy'*: A children's game in which an object is concealed in one hand by one of the players and the other player is required to guess which hand contains it ('handy dandy, prickly prandy, which hand will you have?').

51. *the Matabele Wars*: In 1817 Mosilikatze and a large division of the Zulu Army had settled in territories north of the Vaal. In 1837, driven out of the Transvaal by the Boers, they crossed the Limpopo and occupied the territory subsequently known as Matabeleland. In the First Matabele War (1893–4), Jameson (see note 1, above) defeated the Matabele and put 'Rhodesia' under the administration of the Chartered Company. The Second Matabele War (1896) sprang from Matabele grievances about their treatment after the First Matabele War. It ended after an *indaba* between Rhodes and the Matabele leaders in September 1896.

52. *from one of these*: This was probably Brigadier-General T. E. Hickman (1859–1930). He served in Sudan from 1897 to 1900 and in South Africa from 1900 to 1908.

53. *one of the criminal classes*: Jameson was sentenced to 15 months' imprisonment in July 1896 for the Jameson Raid (see note 1, above), but he was released from Holloway Prison in December 1896 on the grounds of ill health.

54. *near the Line*: I.e., near the equator.

55. *the Strubens at 'Strubenheim'*: Henry William Struben (1840–1915)

was one of the developers of the Rand goldfields before he settled in Cape Town. He built 'Strubenheim' in 1890 at Rosebank on Table Mountain, and lived there with his wife and their six children.

56. *Kaffirs*: From 'kafir' (Arabic for 'infidel'), this word was used in the nineteenth century by Europeans to refer to the Bantus. It was later used to refer disparagingly to any black African.

57. *baby lion*: See Kipling's 'My Personal Experiences with a Lion' in the *Ladies Home Journal* of January 1902; it was reprinted as 'How to bring up a lion' in *The Kipling Reader* (1912).

58. *the Scholarships*: Scholarships to Oxford University for young men from the United States, the Dominions and Germany. Kipling became, until his resignation in June 1925, one of the Rhodes Trustees involved in the administration of the money.

59. *heart*: Rhodes had had heart problems since 1874 when his doctor gave him 'not six months to live'. He had his first heart attack in 1877, and he died on 26 March 1902.

60. *a man*: Unidentified.

61. *a young officer*: According to Webb-Johnson, this was Winston Churchill (1874–1965), but Rhodes, Kipling and Churchill do not seem to have been in Cape Town at the same time.

Chapter 7: The Very-Own House

1. The Fires: By Kipling, first published in *Collected Verse* (1907).

2. *Mr Harmsworth*: Alfred Charles Harmsworth (1865–1922), created Viscount Northcliffe in 1917, had founded the *Daily Mail* in 1896. In 1903 he took over the *Daily Mirror*, and he became chief proprietor of *The Times* in 1908. He visited Kipling by motor-car in October 1899, and Kipling hired the 'Embryo' in December.

3. *victoria-hooded*: With a collapsible hood like a 'victoria' – a light, low, four-wheeled carriage (usually a two-seater), named after Queen Victoria.

4. *the commination service*: A recital of divine threatenings against sinners. In the Anglican Church, this forms part of an office to be read after the Litany on Ash Wednesday.

5. *a 'Locomobile'*: Bought in 1900 and used for two years.

6. *the earliest Lanchester*: Kipling bought his first Lanchester on 5 June 1902. F. W. Lanchester (1868–1946) founded the Lanchester Engine Co. in 1899, and this became the Lanchester Motor Co. in

1905. P. W. Kingsford's biography of Lanchester reveals that Lanchester used to lend Kipling experimental cars to test-drive.

7. *'Bateman's'*: 'Bateman's', at Burwash in Sussex, is now a Kipling museum. The Kiplings' first visit took place on 14 August 1900, but they did not move in until September 1902.

8. *Jane Cakebread*: Jane Cakebread was a woman who was reported to have appeared in court more than ninety times on charges of 'disorderly conduct'. The name reflects the 'disorderly' behaviour of what seems to have been Kipling's second Lanchester.

9. *Fellahîn*: The plural of '*fellâh*', which is Arabic for a husbandman or peasant, but was used in English as a general term for Egyptian workmen.

10. *one-street village*: I.e., Burwash.

11. *one among them*: His name was Isted, but he appears in the *Puck* stories (and in the poem 'The Land') as Hobden.

12. Cocculus Indicus: The dried berry of *Anamista Cocculus*, a climbing plant found in Malabar and Ceylon.

13. *Lord Ashburnham's woods*: Bertram Ashburnham (1840–1913), Fourth Earl of Ashburnham, of Ashburnham Place, Battle, Sussex.

14. *'sealed quarts'*: Quart pots with a seal impressed upon them to indicate that their capacity had been tested by the appropriate authority.

15. *Christopher Sly*: The drunken tinker who appears in the 'Induction' to Shakespeare's *The Taming of the Shrew*. Kipling refers to scene II, lines 87–90.

16. *Ambrose Poynter*: The artist, Sir Ambrose Poynter (1867–1923), was the son of Agnes Macdonald. (See note 35, chapter 1.)

17. *Parnesius*: This would mean 'the Parnesian' – i.e., a man from Mount Parnes, near Athens – but why Poynter suggested the name has not been explained.

18. *'a brother . . . a companion to owls'*: A misquotation from Isaiah 34:13 – 'an habitation of dragons, and a court for owls'.

19. *ghost of a road*: Cf. Kipling's poem 'The Way through the Woods' in *Rewards and Fairies*.

20. *our children*: John and Elsie Kipling performed this play in October 1904 in the quarry across the road from 'Bateman's'.

21. *at score*: (Of a horse) 'To make a sudden dash at full speed'.

22. *Daniel Defoe*: (1660–1731) Journalist, novelist, pamphleteer; the author of *Robinson Crusoe* (1720).

23. *King James II*: The last Stuart monarch of the direct male line,

James II (1633–1701) was King from 1685 until his forced 'abdication' in 1689 after the 'Glorious Revolution' of 1688.

24. *Alice in Wonderland*: Kipling is referring to chapter 2 of *Alice through the Looking Glass*.

25. *Ulpia Victrix*: (Latin) 'The Ulpian conqueror'. 'Ulpius' was the name of a Roman family, and the reference here is to a member of that family, Marcus Ulpius Trajanus, Roman emperor (reigned 98–117) and conqueror of the Dacians. The implication is that the legion was raised by Trajan for his Dacian wars.

26. in situ: (Latin) 'In its (original) place'.

27. *a memorial-tablet*: The stone was found at Corbridge in 1912, six years after the publication of *Puck of Pook's Hill*. The inscription reads 'Leg XXX VV' (i.e., 'Legio Tricesima Ulpia Victrix') but the first X is written in a different style. The original inscription would have read 'Leg XX VV' (i.e., 'Legio Vicesima Valeria Victrix'), and there is other evidence that the Twentieth Legion were engaged in building Hadrian's Wall, whereas there is no evidence that the Thirtieth Legion were in Britain. The additional 'X' seems to have been added by student-members of the digging-party as a hoax.

28. *niello*: (Italian) A black, metallic composition, consisting of alloys of silver, lead, copper and sulphur, used to fill in designs engraved on silver.

29. *grisaille*: (French) A method of painting in grey monochrome to represent objects in relief.

30. *a cryptogram*: Not conclusively identified.

31. *Jameson's character*: Jameson visited 'Bateman's' in October 1909, and the verses were written some time during the next six months.

32. *land-wisdom*: In addition to his adventure stories and romances, Haggard also wrote books on agriculture: *A Farmer's Year* (1899) and *Rural England* (1902).

33. *together*: According to R. L. Green, manuscripts exist for Haggard's *The Ghost Kings* (1908) and *Allan and the Ice Gods* (1927), in which outline plots have alternate paragraphs written by the two men. He also draws attention to a page of notes and drawings for *Red Eve* (1911).

34. *Feilden*: Colonel Feilden (1838–1922) of 'Rampyndene', Burwash, had served in India and in China; in the Confederate Army (1862–5) during the American Civil War; and in both Boer Wars (1881 and 1900–1901). He was Naturalist to the British Polar Expedition (1875–6), for which he was awarded the 'Polar ribbon'.

35. *William and Mary*: I.e., dating from the period 1689–1702, the reign of William of Orange (William III) and his wife, Mary, the daughter of James II (see note 23, above).

36. *Colonel Newcome*: A character in Thackeray's novel *The Newcomes* (1853).

37. Cranford: A novel by Elizabeth Gaskell about a small town whose society largely consists of single women.

38. aides-de-camp: (French) Officers in attendance on a general.

39. *Lee*: Robert E. Lee (1807–70). Commander of the Army of Northern Virginia from 1861 and General-in-Chief of the Confederate armies from 1862 to 1865.

40. *the surrender*: Lee surrendered to General Grant at Appomattox on 9 April 1865.

41. *his son*: Arthur John Rider Haggard (1881–91) was born on 23 May 1881 at 'Hilldrop', Newcastle, Natal.

42. *a Confederate Cavalry leader*: This was probably Joseph Eggleston Johnston (1807–91), the General under whom Feilden served. He retreated from Georgia in 1864.

43. *'Imperial Preference'*: In 1897 Canada gave Britain a preferential tariff (amounting to one third of duty), which led to increased imports into Canada from Britain, but in 1907 the Liberals won the election on a 'free trade' mandate, which doomed this special · concession.

44. *Laurier*: Sir Wilfrid Laurier (1841–1919) was Premier of Canada from 1896 to 1911.

45. *an ex-Governor*: R. L. Green suggests that this was probably Henry C. Ide (1844–1921). Ide served on the Philippine Commission from March 1900; in 1901 he became Secretary of Finance and Justice for the Philippines; he was appointed Vice-Governor in February 1904, Acting-Governor in November 1905 and Governor-General in April 1906. He resigned in September 1906.

46. *to Canada*: In fact, this was in the autumn of 1907. They arrived in Quebec on 26 September 1907, and Kipling received an honorary degree from McGill University on 23 October.

47. *the straits of Belle Isle*: Between Newfoundland and Labrador.

48. *Van Horne*: Sir William Van Horne (1843–1915) was General Manager of the Canadian Pacific Railway in 1881, Vice-President in 1884, President in 1888 and Chairman of the Board of Directors from 1899 to 1910.

49. Letters to the Family: These essays appeared in the *Morning Post* (London), *Collier's Weekly* (New York) and *Vancouver World* in

March, April and May of 1908. They were published as a volume (Toronto, 1908) and in *Letters of Travel* (1919).

50. *the Nobel Prize*: It was awarded to Kipling in 1909. Endowed by the Swedish engineer Alfred Nobel (1833–96), the prize had been awarded annually since 1901.

51. *the old King*: King Oskar II, who reigned from 1872 to 1907.

52. *the new King*: King Gustav V, who reigned from 1907 to 1950.

Chapter 8: Working-Tools

1. *walk disposedly*: R. L. Green noted the submerged quotation of the description of Mary Queen of Scots from Sir James Melville's *Memoirs* (1683). Kipling drew on the same passage in 'The Last Term' in *Stalky & Co.*, when he described Beetle 'walking high and disposedly round the wreck of the Armada galleon'.

2. *verses*: *Schoolboy Lyrics* (Lahore, 1881).

3. *'in they broke . . . people of importance'*: from Robert Browning's poem 'One Word More'.

4. *'lesser breeds . . . the (Copyright) law'*: Kipling adapts a line from his poem 'Recessional' to refer to American publishers who continued to publish those of his works which had appeared before 1892 (which were thus not protected by American Copyright Law). (See note 47, chapter 5.)

5. ab initio: (Latin) 'From the beginning'.

6. *the chimaera*: The fire-breathing monster of Greek legend. Kipling is alluding to *Gargantua and Pantagruel* (II:7) by François Rabelais. Among the books found in the library of St Victor by Pantagruel was a treatise on the question *'utrum Chimaera, in vacuo bombinans, possit comedere secundas intentiones'* ('whether the Chimaera, bombinating in the Void, can be nourished on secondary intentions').

7. in vacuo: (Latin) 'In a vacuum'.

8. *'when thou . . . repent not'*: Unidentified.

9. Experto crede: (Latin) 'I have done it; believe me.'

10. *the Personal Daemon*: In an early stage of Greek religion, *Daimones* were powers or spirits which were thought to inhabit trees, springs, rivers etc. Later, the word *daimōn* was used for the spirit that guides a person's life. *To daimonon* was the term used by Socrates for his genius, or the spirit within him. (It was Socrates rather than Aristotle who referred to his 'Personal Daemon'.) For

account of Kipling's conception of the 'Daemon', see the Introduction (pp. 12–13).

11. *'Take this ... and no other'*: Perhaps an echo of Genesis 12:19 ('behold thy wife, take her, and go thy way').

12. *Ananias-fashion*: Ananias, having sold a possession, kept back half the price and pretended that he gave the whole price to the apostles (Acts 5:1–15).

13. *'The Eye of Allah'*: Begun in July 1924; published in *McCall's Magazine* and *Strand Magazine* in September 1925; collected in *Debits and Credits* (1926).

14. *'The Captive'*: Published in *Collier's Weekly*, 6 December 1902; collected in *Traffics and Discoveries* (1904).

15. *Napoleon*: Napoleon Bonaparte (1769–1821) was Emperor of the French from 1804 to 1814. Kipling perhaps has in mind his dethroning of the Spanish Bourbons in 1808 which marked the climax of a series of successes, starting with the Battle of Austerlitz in August 1805. It led, however, to a popular rising (May to June 1808), which marred Napoleon's plans to overthrow the British and Turkish empires, and was the start of the decisive turn in his fortunes.

16. the Manchester Guardian: A daily paper of Liberal tendencies, it has been called simply the *Guardian* since 1959. It began printing in London in 1961.

17. *'The Wish House'*: Written in January and February of 1924, it was first published in *Maclean's Magazine* on 15 October 1924, and collected in *Debits and Credits* (1926).

18. *review*: Manchester Guardian, 15 September 1926, by H. B. Charlton.

19. the *'mormal on her shinne'*: In fact, it was the Cook, not the Wife of Bath, who was thus afflicted. In the General Prologue to *The Canterbury Tales*, Chaucer informs us that 'on his shyne a mormal hadde he' (line 386). A 'mormal' was a species of dry-scabbed ulcer.

20. per contra: (Latin) 'On the other hand'.

21. *my worst slip:* Not positively identified.

22. *my tale*: The original has not been identified.

23. *the Karroo*: The Great Karroo is a desert north-east of Cape Town.

24. *a helio*: I.e., a heliograph, an instrument for signalling by means of flashes of sunlight.

25. *'But Winnie ... poor dear!'*: Unidentified.

26. *a young Duke of Northumberland*: Alan Ian Percy (1880–1930),

Eighth Duke of Northumberland, served in South Africa (1901–1902) and in France (1914–16) with the Grenadier Guards. Two short stories by him were published posthumously: *The Shadow on the Moor* (1930) and *La Salamandre* (1934).

27. *my mail*: During the war Kipling received many letters from 'psychics' offering to get in touch with his son, John.

28. *wreck of good minds*: Kipling is perhaps thinking of his sister, Trix. She had taken up crystal-gazing and automatic writing as a young woman and, from 1903 to 1910, she made numerous contributions to the proceedings of the British Society for Psychical Research (under the name 'Mrs Holland'). In 1910, she suffered a major breakdown.

29. *the road to Endor*: After the death of Samuel, Saul went to the woman of En-dor to consult his spirit (I Samuel 28). See Kipling's story 'They', *Scribner's Magazine* (August 1904), later revised for *Traffics and Discoveries*. See also Kipling's poem, 'En-dor', written in April 1918 and collected in *The Years Between* (1919), which warns of the dangers of spiritualism:

> And those who have passed to the farther shore
> May be hailed – at a price – on the road to Endor.

30. *a ceremony*: On 19 July 1922.

31. *Sir John Bland-Sutton*: Sir John gives his own slightly different account of this episode in his book, *The Story of a Surgeon* (1930).

32. *the heat of battle*: He 'would not drink thereof, but poured it out unto the Lord' since he held it to be 'the blood of the men that went in jeopardy of their lives' (II Samuel 23:16–17).

33. Tarzan of the Apes: This was the first of twenty-five 'Tarzan' books by Edgar Rice Burroughs (1875–1950).

34. '*The Green Eye of the Little Yellow God*': a song written by James Milton Hayes (1884–1940) to music by Cuthbert Clarke.

35. *Mr Oscar Wilde*: Oscar Wilde (1854–1900), wit and dramatist, author of *Lady Windermere's Fan* (1893), *A Woman of No Importance* (1894), *An Ideal Husband* (1895), *The Importance of Being Earnest* (1899) and other works.

36. '*But for the grace . . . Richard Baxter*': The sentence should end 'there goes John Bradford'. Bradford (1510–55) was a Fellow of Pembroke Hall, Cambridge; he became Chaplain to Bishop Ridley and was one of the Protestant Martyrs burned at Smithfield. He made this observation on seeing prisoners being led to execution. Baxter (1615–91) was a Presbyterian pastor and writer.

37. '*Tupperism*': After Martin Tupper (1810–89), author of *Proverbial Philosophy* (1838), a collection of commonplace observations set out in a verse-like form, which was enormously popular, especially in America.

38. '*East was East . . . should meet*': In 'The Ballad of East and West'; published in the *Pioneer* on 2 December 1889; collected in *Barrack-Room Ballads*.

39. *a political Calvinist*: Kipling is referring to the Calvinist doctrine of predestination. In his political application of the doctrine, 'election' or 'damnation' is predetermined and cannot be affected by argument.

40. '*Mandalay*': First published in the *Scots Observer* on 21 June 1890; collected in *Barrack-Room Ballads*; set to music by many composers – the first, G. F. Cobb in 1892, is probably referred to here.

41. *the Burma campaign*: The Third Burmese War, 1885–6.

42. *at Moulmein*: In his visit to Burma in March 1889, Kipling put in briefly at Rangoon and Moulmein. He clearly drew on his memories of this visit when writing 'Mandalay'. In *From Sea to Sea*, Kipling's third letter describes Moulmein and tells how he fell 'deeply and irrevocably in love with a Burmese girl' on the steps of the pagoda.

43. *the Irrawaddy Flotilla steamers*: The Irrawaddy River provides a highway from Rangoon to Mandalay. The first Irrawaddy Flotilla was organized by Lord Dalhousie in 1852 for the Second Burmese War. In 1885 steamers belonging to the Irrawaddy Flotilla Company (founded 1868) were requisitioned to convey troops and stores for the advance on Mandalay in the Third Burmese War.

44. '*The Islanders*': First published in *The Times*, 4 January 1902; collected in *The Five Nations* (1903). It contained a contemptuous reference to 'flannelled fools at the wicket' and 'muddied oafs at the goal'.

45. *rather hard*: 'The Return' (first published in *The Five Nations*) contains the line 'Things 'ave transpired', but *Punch* makes no reference to it. 'The Islanders' and 'The Lesson' were ridiculed in a sketch called 'The Islanders' in *Punch*, CXXII (15 January 1902).

46. '*High above . . . I raised you*': Surah 2, verse 42.

47. '*Oft as they . . . the abettors of disorder*': Surah 5, verse 65.

48. '*The Old Volunteer*': Published in *The Times*, 27 May 1918.

49. *Moberly Bell*: C. F. M. Bell (1847–1911) was correspondent for *The Times* in Egypt (1865–90), Assistant Manager (1890–1908) and Managing Director from 1908.

50. *Buckle*: G. E. Buckle (1854–1935) was Assistant Editor of *The Times* from 1880 to 1884 and Editor from 1884 to 1912.

51. *Manon Lescaut*: The eponymous heroine of a novel by Abbé Prévost (1697–1763). The painting was by Pascal Dagnan-Bouveret. It shows Des Grieux kneeling before the dead body of Manon, and it was exhibited at the Paris Salon, 1878.

52. *Scarron's* Roman Comique: Paul Scarron (1610–60), French novelist, poet and playwright, published *Le Roman Comique* between 1651 and 1657. Margaret Newsom has drawn attention to the inserted story, 'Histoire De La Capricieuse Amante', in which an elusive woman is pursued by an adventurous young man (who suffers a head wound), as a source for *The Light That Failed*.

53. *conte*: (French) 'A short story'.

54. *three-decker*: Kipling plays on two current meanings of this word: (1) a three-volume novel (2) a ship with three decks.

55. *The Cloister and the Hearth*: a novel by Charles Reade (see note 80, chapter 5) published in 1861.

56. *Jael*: Jael, the wife of Heber the Kenite, drove a tent-peg through the head of the sleeping Sisera (Judges 4:8–22 and 5:24–27).

57. *Jerusalem*: Kipling visited Jerusalem on 21 March 1929.

58. *Warren Hastings*: Hastings (1732–1818) was Governor-General of India from 1773–84. He was impeached on his return to England in 1785 on charges of 'high crimes', but in 1795 was acquitted of all charges.

59. *a great airman*: Sir William Geoffrey Hanson Salmond (1878–1933), one of the pioneers of the Flying Corps and the Royal Air Force.

60. *before my death*: These words were written around 20 December 1935. Kipling died on 18 January 1936.

Index

Index

Index

Index

Discover more about our forthcoming books through Penguin's FREE newspaper...

Penguin
Quarterly

It's packed with:

- exciting features
- author interviews
- previews & reviews
- books from your favourite films & TV series
- exclusive competitions & much, much more...

Write off for your free copy today to:
Dept JC
Penguin Books Ltd
FREEPOST
West Drayton
Middlesex
UB7 0BR
NO STAMP REQUIRED

READ MORE IN PENGUIN

In every corner of the world, on every subject under the sun, Penguin represents quality and variety – the very best in publishing today.

For complete information about books available from Penguin – including Puffins, Penguin Classics and Arkana – and how to order them, write to us at the appropriate address below. Please note that for copyright reasons the selection of books varies from country to country.

In the United Kingdom: Please write to *Dept. JC, Penguin Books Ltd, FREEPOST, West Drayton, Middlesex UB7 OBR.*

If you have any difficulty in obtaining a title, please send your order with the correct money, plus ten per cent for postage and packaging, to *PO Box No. 11, West Drayton, Middlesex UB7 OBR*

In the United States: Please write to *Consumer Sales, Penguin USA, P.O. Box 999, Dept. 17109, Bergenfield, New Jersey 07621-0120.* VISA and MasterCard holders call 1-800-253-6476 to order all Penguin titles

In Canada: Please write to *Penguin Books Canada Ltd, 10 Alcorn Avenue, Suite 300, Toronto, Ontario M4V 3B2*

In Australia: Please write to *Penguin Books Australia Ltd, P.O. Box 257, Ringwood, Victoria 3134*

In New Zealand: Please write to *Penguin Books (NZ) Ltd, Private Bag 102902, North Shore Mail Centre, Auckland 10*

In India: Please write to *Penguin Books India Pvt Ltd, 706 Eros Apartments, 56 Nehru Place, New Delhi 110 019*

In the Netherlands: Please write to *Penguin Books Netherlands bv, Postbus 3507, NL-1001 AH Amsterdam*

In Germany: Please write to *Penguin Books Deutschland GmbH, Metzlerstrasse 26, 60594 Frankfurt am Main*

In Spain: Please write to *Penguin Books S. A., Bravo Murillo 19, 1° B, 28015 Madrid*

In Italy: Please write to *Penguin Italia s.r.l., Via Felice Casati 20, I–20124 Milano*

In France: Please write to *Penguin France S. A., 17 rue Lejeune, F–31000 Toulouse*

In Japan: Please write to *Penguin Books Japan, Ishikiribashi Building, 2–5–4, Suido, Bunkyo-ku, Tokyo 112*

In Greece: Please write to *Penguin Hellas Ltd, Dimocritou 3, GR–106 71 Athens*

In South Africa: Please write to *Longman Penguin Southern Africa (Pty) Ltd, Private Bag X08, Bertsham 2013*

READ MORE IN PENGUIN

RUDYARD KIPLING

'The most complete man of genius I have ever known' – Henry James

The Light That Failed
A Diversity of Creatures
The Day's Work
Debits and Credits
Wee Willie Winkie
Just So Stories
Traffics and Discoveries
Short Stories
  Volumes I and II
Selected Stories
Kim

The Jungle Books
Life's Handicap
Limits and Renewals
Something of Myself
Plain Tales from the Hills
Puck of Pook's Hill
Rewards and Fairies
Selected Poems
Soldiers Three *and* In Black
  and White

'For my own part I worshipped Kipling at thirteen, loathed him at seventeen, enjoyed him at twenty, despised him at twenty-five, and now again rather admire him. The one thing that was never possible, if one had read him at all, was to forget him' – George Orwell